CURRENT PUBLICATIONS
BY
MEMBER SOCIETIES

Tenth Edition

Compiled by

Elizabeth Hampson

FEDERATION OF FAMILY HISTORY SOCIETIES

Published by
The Federation of Family History Societies (Publications) Ltd
2-4 Killer Street, Ramsbottom
Bury, Lancs BL0 9BZ

Tenth edition published 1999

Copyright © FFHS (Publications) Ltd

ISBN 1 86006 085 4

Printed and bound at The Alden Press
Oxford and Northampton

Federation of Family History Societies

Publications in Book Form

READ THESE NOTES BEFORE ORDERING PLEASE

All enquiries, applications for price lists, quotations etc., must be accompanied by return postage, preferably a stamped addresses envelope (U.K.) or 2 international reply paid coupons.

U.K. Societies

Only sterling prices are given as many societies will not accept cheques in foreign currencies. Most U.K. banks now make a handling charge of £3.00 or more per cheque: thus, those made out for small amounts are rendered valueless. Payment in currencies other than sterling must be negotiated in advance with individual societies.

Postage and packing is included in most prices quoted. Where the price does NOT include postage this is stated. Where one price only is quoted this is the U.K. price. Where more than one price is given columns have been labelled as follows (unless the particular Society requested an alternative format, which will be stated).

(a) U.K. & Europe (EEC)
(b) Overseas Surface Mail (World-wide)
(c) Overseas Airmail (General)
(d) Airmail U.S.A. & Canada
(e) Airmail Australia & New Zealand

Postal charges are those current in May 1999. Please make any necessary additions to prices to allow for subsequent increases in postal rates. We cannot guarantee postal prices to be accurate for a stated length of time.

The name and address given for each Society is that of the Publications Sales Officer or person dealing with despatch of goods on behalf of the Society. It should not be assumed this is the Secretary of the Society, whose name and address may be found on the back cover of the Federations publication *Family History, News and Digest*.

Cheques, money orders, postal orders etc. should be made payable to the Society, not to the individual unless specifically requested.

Non U.K. Societies

Societies from Australia, New Zealand, U.S.A., Canada and the Netherlands have contributed to this edition. Prices quoted are in LOCAL currency. Please check with the Society for rates for overseas postage and methods of payment.

This 10th edition of *Current Publications by Member Societies* has been compiled over a period of months during 1998/1999. A slight delay occurred due to John Perkins not being able to finish the publication, I have contacted many of the societies for updates on prices and also I have accessed their Web Sites as a further means of updating prices.

The order of this book has been changed, it now follows the order of the List of Member Societies given on the cover of the Federation of Family History Societies *Family History News and Digest*.

I would like to thank John Perkins for initially showing me the way, and handing over the partly completed work and a very big thank-you goes to my husband Rodney for the hours he spent with me checking material and generally making time for me to fulfil this task.

Elizabeth Hampson

Federation of Family History Societies

Web Site: http://www.ffhs.org.uk/
FFHS Publications, 2-4 Killer Street, Ramsbottom, Bury, Lancs BL0 9BZ
(Please include payment with order, made out to FFHS Publications)

	UK	O/S Surface	O/S Air
Basic Sources for Family History (3rd ed.)	£4.65	£5.05	£6.30
Beginning Your Family History (7th ed.)	£4.75	£5.10	£6.40
Book of Trades Part 1, Part 2, Part 3. (price each)	£3.60	£3.90	£4.75
Company & Business Records	£4.65	£4.85	£5.85
The Complete Parish Officer	£4.65	£5.00	£6.10
Computer Genealogy Update	£3.20	£3.30	£3.80
Computer Programmes (for Amstrad PCW Computers)	£5.70	£6.05	£7.10
Current Publications by Member Societies (10th ed.)			
Current Publications by Member Societies on Microfiche (4th ed)	£5.65	£6.00	£7.25
Dating Old Photographs (2nd ed)	£5.65	£6.00	£7.15
Looking at Old Photographs	£6.60	£6.90	£7.75
Photography for Family Historians	£5.60	£5.90	£6.75
Understanding Old Photographs	£5.65	£6.00	£7.25
Exploring Scottish History	£7.90	£8.50	£10.65
Family Historians Enquire Within (5th ed.) Reprint with amendments	£11.05	£11.80	£14.75
Family History Record Sheets	£1.75	£1.95	£2.60
First Name Variants	£5.65	£6.00	£7.20
Forming a One-Name Group (4th ed.)	£2.05	£2.25	£2.90
Gedcom Data Transfer (moving your family tree) (3rd ed.)	£4.00	£4.20	£4.85
Glossary of Household, Farming & Trade Terms (3rd ed.)	£4.60	£4.85	£5.75
How to Record Your Family Tree	£2.05	£2.25	£2.90
IGI on Computer	£2.90	£3.00	£3.40
In and Around Record Repositories in Great Britain & Ireland	£6.60	£6.90	£7.75
Introduction to Irish Research (Revised edition)	£5.60	£5.85	£6.70
Latin Glossary for Family Historians (Reprint)	£3.05	£3.25	£3.60
Let's Start Family History	£0.75	£0.90	£1.10
Local History: A Handbook	£11.10	£11.95	£14.55
Manorial Records (How to Locate and Use)	£2.55	£2.75	£3.35
Mediaeval Records	£5.20	£5.55	£6.80
Monumental Inscriptions (4th ed.)	£1.55	£1.80	£2.90
New to Kew ?	£7.10	£7.80	£9.65
Nonconformity (Understanding the History & Records of)	£2.35	£2.55	£3.20
Nuts and Bolts: Family History Problem Solving	£3.60	£3.80	£4.45
Oral History	£4.55	£4.85	£5.50
Parish Law (Handy Book of)	£4.70	£5.05	£6.15
Practice Makes Perfect (A Genealogical Workbook)	£6.00	£6.50	£8.70
Records of the RAF	£4.55	£4.85	£5.65

Federation of Family History Societies (continued)

Register of One-Name Studies (13th ed.)	£4.10	£4.35	£5.70
Researching Family History in Wales	£6.25	£6.50	£7.80
Spreadsheet Family Trees	£3.55	£3.75	£4.70
Surnames of Wales for Family Historians and Others	£11.10	£11.95	£14.55
Tracing your Irish Ancestry	£12.55	£13.10	£15.85
Web Publishing for Genealogy (2nd ed.)	£4.60	£4.80	£5.60
Welsh Family History: A Guide to Research (2nd ed.)	£11.40	£12.15	£14.70
Was Your Grandfather a Railwayman? (3rd ed.) Reprint with amendments	£6.15	£6.40	£7.30
Second Stages in Researching Welsh Ancestry	£16.45	£17.15	£19.70
World War I Army Ancestry (3rd ed.)	£6.30	£6.50	£7.60
World War I More Sources (3rd ed.)	£6.10	£6.40	£7.25
Location of British Army Records (4th ed.)	£6.80	£7.00	£8.10
Writing and Publishing Your Family History	£5.65	£6.00	£7.20

Genealogical Bibliography Series

British Genealogical Microfiche	£9.25	£9.50	£10.40
British Genealogical Books in Print	£9.80	£10.10	£11.20
English Genealogy (3rd ed.)	£4.90	£5.15	£6.20
Occupational Sources (2nd ed.)	£5.65	£5.95	£7.00
Genealogical Bibliography: Buckinghamshire	£5.60	£5.85	£6.75
Genealogical Bibliography: Cheshire Vol.1- Sources	£10.20	£10.55	£11.65
Genealogical Bibliography: Cheshire Vol.2- Family Histories	£7.55	£7.75	£8.30
Genealogical Bibliography: Dorset	£6.70	£7.05	£8.30
Genealogical Bibliography: Essex Vol 1 Genealogical Sources	£7.60	£7.75	£8.45
Genealogical Bibliography: Essex Vol 2 Family History and Pedigrees	£6.10	£6.30	£7.00
Genealogical Bibliography: Hampshire	£9.10	£9.45	£10.60
Genealogical Bibliography: Kent Vol.1	£8.15	£8.45	£9.50
Genealogical Bibliography: Kent Vol.2	£6.60	£6.75	£7.60
Genealogical Bibliography: Kent Vol.3	£5.60	£5.85	£6.75
Genealogical Bibliography: Lancashire Vol.1	£7.00	£7.30	£8.30
Genealogical Bibliography: Lancashire Vol.2	£5.60	£5.90	£6.80
Genealogical Bibliography: Lancashire Vol.3	£5.60	£5.90	£6.80
Genealogical Bibliography: Lincolnshire	£8.20	£8.60	£9.80
Genealogical Bibliography: London/Middlesex Vol.1 (2nd ed)	£9.00	£9.60	£11.50
Genealogical Bibliography: London/Middlesex Vol.2 (2nd ed)	£5.60	£5.85	£6.75
Genealogical Bibliography: Norfolk	£6.70	£7.05	£8.30
Genealogical Bibliography: Oxfordshire	£5.60	£5.85	£6.75
South West Family Histories	£8.55	£9.15	£11.00

Federation of Family History Societies (continued)

Poll Books

Norfolk, 1768	£18.10	£19.35	£20.70
Norfolk, 1806	£17.75	£18.15	£19.35
Norfolk, 1817	£18.25	£18.65	£19.85
Suffolk, 1710	£14.40	£14.75	£15.75
Suffolk, 1790	£14.75	£15.15	£16.35
London, 1768	£14.90	£15.25	£16.20
Westminster, 1774	£19.55	£20.10	£21.25
Westminster, 1818	£23.50	£24.20	£25.65
Westminster, 1841	£19.25	£19.70	£20.65
Yorkshire (West Riding), 1835	£25.10	£26.00	£28.15

Electoral Registers

Somerset, Eastern Division, 1832	£19.35	£19.85	£21.20
Somerset, Western Division, 1832	£19.35	£19.85	£21.20

Basic Facts Series

About Archives
About Contacting Relatives
About Family History Research in Ireland (2nd ed)
About Wills after 1858 and First Avenue House
An Approach to Keeping your Family Records
An Approach to Latin for Family Historians
English Nonconformity for Family Historians
Family History Research in Glamorgan
Family History in Lancashire
Family History Research in Yorkshire
Heraldry for Family Historians
Nonconformity in England
Sources for Family History in the Home
Tracing Catholic Ancestry in England
Using Baptism Records
Using Death and Burial Records
Using the Family Records Centre
Using Marriage Records
Using Merchant Ship Records
Using Record Offices

All one price (each) £1.95   £2.25   £2.85

An Introduction to ... Series

British Army Traditions & Records (Reprint)	£3.65	£3.75	£4.40
Census Returns of England & Wales (Special Offer)	£1.30	£1.84	£1.91
Poor Law before 1834	£2.50	£2.70	£3.35
Reading Old Title Deeds (2nd ed.)	£3.00	£3.20	£3.85
Church Registers	£3.05	£3.25	£3.90
Civil Registration	£3.10	£3.30	£3.95

Fedration of Family History Societies *(continued)*

Occupations	£3.10	£3.25	£3.90
Using Newspapers & Periodicals	£2.50	£2.70	£3.35
Using Computers in Genealogy (2nd ed.)	£3.65	£3.75	£4.40
Wills, Probate & Death Duty Records (Reprint)	£3.65	£3.75	£4.40
Planning Research: Short Cuts in Family History	£3.60	£3.90	£4.55
Tracing Your German Ancestors	£3.85	£4.15	£5.00

Gibson Guides for Genealogists

Poor Law Union Records			
1. South East & East Anglia (2nd ed.)	£4.60	£4.95	£6.20
2. The Midlands & Northern England (2nd ed.)	£4.60	£4.95	£6.20
3. South West England, The Marches & Wales	£4.60	£4.95	£6.20
4. Gazetteer of England & Wales	£5.15	£5.50	£6.75
Protestation Returns	£4.60	£4.95	£6.20
Probate Jurisdictions (4th ed.) reprint	£4.20	£4.55	£5.55
Hearth Tax Returns & Other Later Stuart Tax Lists (2nd ed.)	£5.20	£5.55	£6.60
Bishops' Transcripts & Marriage Licences (4th ed.)	£4.00	£4.25	£4.60
Census Returns on Microfilm (6th ed.) Reprint	£4.10	£4.30	£5.10
Coroners' Records (2nd ed.)	£3.45	£3.65	£4.35
Land and Window Tax Assessments (2nd ed.)	£4.55	£4.75	£5.40
Lists of Londoners (2nd ed.)	£3.05	£3.25	£3.90
Local Census Listings (3rd ed.)	£3.55	£3.70	£4.55
Marriage & Census Indexes (7th ed., retitled)	£4.10	£4.30	£5.10
Militia Lists & Musters (1757-1876) (3rd ed.)	£3.10	£3.40	£4.05
Poll Books c.1695-1872 (3rd ed.)	£3.10	£3.40	£4.05
Quarter Session Records (4th ed.)	£3.10	£3.40	£4.05
Record Offices: How to find them (8th ed.)	£4.10	£4.30	£5.10
Specialist Indexes	£4.10	£4.30	£5.10
Tudor & Stuart Muster Rolls	£3.10	£3.40	£4.05
Victuallers' Licences (2nd ed.)	£4.20	£4.55	£5.55

Other Publications

Ancestor Trail in Ireland	£2.90	£3.10	£3.75
Army Records for the Family Historian at the PRO (2nd ed)	£9.15	£9.80	£11.50
Army Service Records of the First World War (2nd ed.)	£8.15	£8.50	£9.50
Computer-Aided Genealogy (2nd ed.)	£6.45	£6.60	£7.65
Computers in Family History (4th ed.)	£4.10	£4.40	£5.45
Family Tree Detective (3rd ed.)	£12.10	£12.80	£14.55
Genealogical Computer Packages	£3.85	£4.00	£4.55
Genealogy on the Macintosh	£4.00	£4.20	£4.70
Hatred Pursued Beyond the Grave	£11.00	£11.65	£13.85
Internet for Genealogy (2nd ed.)	£2.15	£2.35	£2.85
Local History, A Handbook for Beginners	£11.10	£11.95	14.55
Making Use of the Census (3rd ed.)	£6.75	£7.10	£8.10
Marriage Laws, Records, Rites and Customs	£6.25	£6.70	£8.15
Never Been Here Before (A Guide to the PRO)			
(Revised edition)	£8.05	£8.55	£9.90

Federation of Family History Societies (continued)

Nuts and Bolts Family History Problem Solving Through Family Reconstruction Techniques	£3.60	£3.80	£4.45
Record Repositories in Great Britain	£4.65	£4.90	£6.00
Records of the Militia & Volunteer Forces, 1757-1945	£9.00	£9.30	£10.75
Records of the Royal Marines	£10.00	£10.30	£11.65
Records of Merchant Shipping & Seamen	£8.50	£9.20	£10.70
Scottish Roots	£6.00	£6.65	£8.85
The Surname Detective	£12.50	£13.00	£14.75
Tracing Your Ancestors at the PRO (5th ed.)	£16.45	£17.30	£20.50
Tracing Your British Ancestors	£4.75	£5.00	£6.30
Tracing Your Scottish Ancestors	£7.10	£7.80	£10.55
Tudor Taxation Records	£6.90	£7.50	£9.50

Society of Genealogists

14 Charterhouse Buildings, Goswell Road, London EC1M 7BA

Tel: 0171 253 5235 (sales)   Fax: 0171 250 1800

Email: sales@sog.org.uk

Website: http://www.sog.org.uk

Prices do not include postage. Please add 50p per book for postage and packing

General Titles

		Cost
1002	Dates and Calendars for the Genealogist, by C. Webb. 1998 36 pages	£2.70
1046	First steps in Family History, by A. J. Camp. (3rd ed) 1998, 34 pages	£1.95
1082	Making a Pedigree; An Introduction to Sources for Early Genealogy, by J. Unett & A. Tanner. 1997, 112 pages	£5.95
1049	Computers in Genealogy Beginners Handbook, ed. by N. Taylor. 1996, 76 pages	£3.70
1009	Lancashire Association Oath Rolls 1696, by W. Gandy. 1921, reprint 1985, 132 pages	£3.34
1050	Greater London Cemeteries and Crematoria by P.S.Wolfston & C.Webb (4th ed.) 1997, 48 pages	£3.00
1067	Examples of Handwriting 1550-1650, by W.S.B. Buck. 1996,	£3.00
1004	Directory of British Peerages from the Earliest Times to the Present Day, ed by F. Leeson. 1984, 174 pages	£3.34
1047	European Rulers 1060-1981, by C Lake. 1981, 162 pages	£15.00
1105	Registration Districts, by R. Wiggins. 1998, 56 pages	£2.50
1059	An index of wills proved in the Archdeaconry Court of London 1700-1807, by C. Webb. 1996, 100 pages	£8.45
1007	An Index to the wills proved in the Prerogative court of Canterbury 1750-1800, Volume 5 N-Sh, ed by A.J. Camp. 1991	£16.00
1008	An Index to the wills proved in the Prerogative court of Canterbury 1750-1800, Volume 6 Si-Z, ed by A.J. Camp. 1992.	£18.00

Society of Genealogists (continued)

My Ancestors Series:

		Cost
1109	My Ancestor was a Freeman of the City of London, by V. Aldous. 1999, 102 pages	£4.95
1058	My Ancestors were Londoners; how can I find out more about them? By C. Webb. (2nd ed) 1997, 64 pages	£3.55
1017	My Ancestor was in the British Army; how can I find out more about him?, by M.J. Watts & C.T. Watts. 1992, reprinted 1995, 124 pages	£5.50
1019	My Ancestors came with the Conqueror; those who did, and some of those who probably did not, by A.J. Camp. 1997, 84 pages	£3.90
1048	My Ancestors moved in England and Wales; how can I trace where they came from?, by A.J. Camp. 1994, 66 pages	£4.60
1112	My Ancestors were Freemasons, by P Lewis. 1999, 56 pages	£2.95
1020	My Ancestors were Baptists; how can I find out more about them?, by G.R. Breed. (3rd ed) 1995, 98 pages	£4.99
1021	My Ancestors were Congregationalists in England and Wales; how can I find out more about them?, by D. J.H Clifford. (2nd ed.) 1997.	£3.90
1042	My Ancestors were English Presbyterian/Unitarian; how can I find out more about them?, by A. Ruston. 1993, 64 pages	£3.00
1024	My Ancestors were Quakers, by E. Milligan and M. Thomas. (2nd ed) 1999, 64 pages	£2.95
1022	My Ancestors were Manorial tenants; how can I find out more about them?, by P.B. Park, (2nd ed) 1994, 62 pages	£3.60

Library Source Guides

		Cost
1041	Using the Library of the Society of Genealogists, 1999, 20 pages	£1.00
1083	Census Copies and Indexes in the Library of the Society of Genealogists, (3rd ed), 1998, 118 pages	£4.95
1003	Directories and Poll books in the Library of the Society of Genealogists. (6th ed) 1995, 125 pages	£7.60
1051	General Register Office One Name Lists in the Library of the Society of Genealogists, (2nd ed.) 1997, 24 pages	£2.70
1062	How to use the Bernau Index, by H. Sharp. 1996, 24 pages	£2.40
1010	A List of Parishes in Boyds Marriage Index. 1994, 56 pages	£3.25
1081	Maritime Sources in the Library of the Society of Genealogists. 1997.	£2.50
1038	School, University and College Registers and Histories in the Library of the Society of Genealogists. 1996, 52 pages	£3.50
1101	Sources for Irish Genealogy at the Library of the Society of Genealogists compiled by A.J. Camp. (2nd ed) 1998, 56 pages	£4.00
1040	The Trinity House Petitions; a Calendar of the Records of the Corporation of Trinity House, London, in the Library of the Society of Genealogists. 1987, 303 pages	£8.40
1070	Will Indexes and other Probate Material in the Library of the Society of Genealogists, 1996, 164 pages	£9.20

Society of Genealogists (continued)

National Index of Parish Registers

		Price
1026	Vol 4 Part 1 Surrey, 1990, 200 pages.	£5.50
1027	Vol 6 Part 1 Staffordshire, (2nd ed.) 1992, 100 pages.	£4.20
1028	Vol 6 Part 2 Nottinghamshire, (2nd ed.) 1995, 124 pages.	£9.95
1054	Vol 6 Part 3 Leicestershire & Rutland 1995, 117 pages.	£10.40
1055	Vol 6 Part 4 Lincolnshire, 1995, 302 pages.	£16.40
1057	Vol 6 Part 5 Derbyshire, 1995, 104 pages.	£8.20
1030	Vol 8 Part 1 Berkshire, 1989, 128 pages.	£3.80
1031	Vol 8 Part 2 Wiltshire, 1992, 114 pages.	£4.60
1094	Vol 8 Part 3 Somerset, 1997, 144 pages	£7.50
1108	Vol 8 Part 4 Cornwall, 1999, 164 pages	£10.00
1032	Vol 9 Part 1 Bedfordshire & Huntingdonshire, 1991, 120 pages.	£4.00
1033	Vol 9 Part 2 Northamptonshire, 1991, 86 pages	£3.33
1034	Vol 9 Part 3 Buckinghamshire, 1992, 82 pages.	£3.80
1043	Vol 9 Part 4 Essex, 1993, 264 pages.	£7.80
1056	Vol 10 Part 1 Cheshire, 1995, 103 pages	£8.20
1103	Vol 10 Part 2 Lancashire. 1998, 146 pages	£8.00
1111	Vol 10 Part 3 Cumberland & Westmorland. 1999, 68 pages	£6.00
1092	Vol 11 Part 2 Yorkshire; North and East Ridings and York, 1997.	£15.00
1093	Vol 11 Part 3 Yorkshire; West Riding, 1997, 344 pages	£15.00

London Apprentices:
Compiled by C Webb

1063	Volume 1: Brewers Company 1685-1800. 1996, 33 Pages	£5.75
1064	Volume 2: Tylers and Bricklayers Company 1612-44, 1668-1800. 1996, 129 pages	£12.40
1065	Volume 3: Bowyers Company 1680-1806, Fletchers Company 1739-54, 1767-1808, Longbowstringmakers Company 1604-68, 1709, 1714-17. 1996, 36 pages	£5.75
1066	Volume 4: Glovers Company 1675-79, 1735-48, 1766-1804. 1996, 41 pages	£6.00
1074	Volume 5: Glass-sellers Company 1664-1812, Woolmens Company 1665-1828. 1997, 55 pages	£4.20
1075	Volume 6: Broderers Company 1679-1713, 1763-1800, Combmakers Company 1744-50, Fanmakers Company 1775-1805, Frameworkknitters Company 1727-30, Fruiterers Company 1750-1815, Gardeners Company 1764-1850, Horners Company 1731-1800. 1997, 60 pages	£4.60
1076	Volume 7: Glaziers Company 1694-1800. 1997, 55 pages	£4.20
1077	Volume 8: Gunmakers Company 1656-1800. 1997, 60 pages	£4.60
1078	Volume 9: Needlemakers Company 1664-1801, Pinmakers Company 1691-1723. 1997, 72 pages	£5.20

Society of Genealogists (continued)

1084	Volume 10:	Basketmakers Company 1639-1824. 1997, 42 pages	£3.50
1085	Volume 11:	Distillers Company 1659-1811. 1997 46 pages	£3.95
1088	Volume 12:	Makers of Playing Cards Company 1675-1760, Musicians Company 1765-1800, Saddlers Company 1657-1666, 1800, Tobaccopipemakers Company 1800. 1997.	£4.00
1089	Volume 13:	Patternmakers Company 1673-1805, 1997 43 pages	£4.00
1090	Volume 14:	Loriners Company 1722-1731, 1759-1800, 1997 44 pages	£4.00
1091	Volume 15:	Gold and Silver Wyre Drawers Company 1693-1837. 1997, 42 pages	£4.00
1096	Volume 16:	Tinplateworkers Company 1666, 1668, 1676, 1681, 1683-1800. 1998, 68 pages	£5.00
1097	Volume 17:	Innholders Company 1642-1643, 1654-1670, 1670-1800. 1998, 56 pages	£5.00
1098	Volume 18:	Poulters Company 1691-1729, 1754-1800. 1998	£5.00
1099	Volume 19:	Upholders Company 1704-1772. 1998, 46 pages	£5.00
1100	Volume 20:	Paviors Company 1568-1800. 1998, 34 pages	£4.00
1102	Volume 21:	Founders Company 1643-1800. 1998, 90 pages	£8.00
1104	Volume 22:	Armourers and Brasiers Company c1610-1800. 1998. 104 pages	£8.00
1106	Volume 23:	Coachmakers & Coach Harness Makers Company 1677-1800 1998, 102 pages	£8.00
1107	Volume 24:	Ironmongers Company 1655-1800. 1999, 92 pages	£8.00
1110	Volume 25:	Dyers Company 1706-1746,. 1999, 70 pages	£5.00

ENGLAND

BEDFORDSHIRE

Bedfordshire Family History Society

Web Site: http://www.kbnet.co.uk/brian/bfhs

Mrs V.M. Brown, Bookstall Organiser, 90 Devon Rd., Luton, Beds LU2 ORL.

Index to 1851 Census

Vol. 3 Book 1. Tempsford, Blunham, Moggerhanger, Northill, Thorncote, Ickwell, Caldecote, Sandy, Beeston (part).
   Book 2. Everton, Potton, Cockayne Hatley, Wrestlingworth, Dunton, Sutton, Eyeworth.
   Book 3. Edworth, Astwick, Stotfold, Arlesley, Henlow, Clifton, Langford.
   Book 4. Biggleswade
   Book 5. Old Warden, Broom, Southill, Stanford, Chicksands, Campton, Shefford, Shefford Hardwick, Meppershall, Upper Stondon.

Vol. 4 Book 1. Holwell, Shillington, Upper & Lower Gravenhurst, Higham Gobion, Silsoe, Clophill.
   Book 2. Haynes, Houghton Conquest, Ampthill, Maulden.
   Book 3. Flitton, Pulloxhill, Westoning, Flitwick, Steppingley, Milbrook.
   Book 4. Marston Moretaine, Lidlington, Cranfield, Salford, Hulcote and Apsley Guise.

Bedfordshire Family History Society (continued)
Vol. 6 Book 1. Stanbridge, Eggington, Heath & Reach, Leighton Buzzard.
  Book 2. Billington, Eaton Bray, Totternhoe, Houghton Regis.
  Book 3. Whipsnade, Studham, Dunstable, Kensworth.
Vol. 7 Book 1. Caddington, East & West Hyde, Stopsley, Sundon, Streatley & Sharpenhoe, Barton-le-Clay.
  Book 2 & 3 Luton, Limbury-cum-Biscott, Leagrave.
Vol. 8 Book 1 Bedford (part)
  Book 2 Bedford (part).

Each book £2.00, £2.50 incl. UK p&p, £2.50 O/seas p&p.

Miscellaneous
                                                          (a)   (b)
Houghton Conquest Reflections   £1.10   £1.30

BERKSHIRE

Berkshire Family History Society
Web Site: http://www.vellum.demon.co.uk/genuki/BRK/berksfhs
BFHS Bookstall Sales, c/o 6 Meadowside, Tilehurst, Reading, Berks. RG31 5QE
Please make all sterling cheques payable to BFHS & drawn on a UK clearing bank.

Index to 1851 Census
Vol.1.1 Thatcham S.D; Vol.1.2 Newbury S.D; Vol.1.3 Speen S.D; Vol 3. Shrivenham, Faringdon and Buckland S.D.s; Vol 4.1 Abingdon S.D.; Vol 4.2 Fyfield, Cumnor & Sutton Courtney S.D.s; Vol. 6. Cholsey & Wallingford S.D.s Vol. 7 Bradfield R.D.; Vol 8.1 Reading St. Marys S.D.; Vol 8.2 Reading St. Giles & St. Lawrence S.D.s; Vol. 11 Easthampstead R.D.; Vol 12. Windsor R.D.

All Volumes £2.75 each.

Postal Rates:

	1 Vol.	2 Vol.	3 Vol.	4 Vol.	5-6 Vols.	7-9 Vols.	More
U.K.	£0.60	£0.75	£0.95	£1.20	£2.00	£2.60	Enquire
EU & Surface	£0.90	£1.20	£1.50	£1.90	£2.50	£3.30	Enquire
Airmail	£2.00	£2.70	£3.65	£5.00	£6.50	£9.00	Enquire

Miscellaneous
Berkshire outline Parish Maps £0.35 each, p&p UK £0.20, EU £0.30, airmail £0.60

The Birmingham & Midland Society for Genealogy & Heraldry

Web Site: http://www.bmsgh.org/
Mr M Harrison, 121, Rowood Drive, Solihull, West Midlands, B92 9LJ

Staffordshire Registers

	(a)	(b)
Brierley Hill: Round Oak Primitive Methodist Chapel Part 2 Bapts 1850-1864	£2.95	£3.25
Butterton-in-the-Peak: St Bartholomew, BTs 1660-1751	£0.80	£1.00
Darlaston: Non Conformist Registers of Wesleyan Methodist Chapel C1832-1837; B1832-1837 & Wednesbury: Wesleyan Methodist Circuit Register C1795-1837	£4.50	£5.00
Dudley: St Thomas (SPRS) formerly Worcs CMB 1541-1649	£6.00	£7.50
Handsworth: St Mary C1774-1830; B1774-1837	£9.20	£9.80
Mucklestone: St Mary Part 2 CMB 1702-1812	£3.20	£3.70
Norbury: St Peter CB15381812; M1538-1837	£2.50	£2.80
Pensnett Kingswinford Shut End: Primitive Methodist Chapel C1845-1887	£1.25	£1.55
Swynnerton: St Mary Part 2 Bapts Mar. & Bur. 1813-1837	£1.20	£1.40
Walsall Non Conformist - Walsall Unitarian Chapel, Stafford St C 1788-1837 & Bridge Street Independent Chapel C1786-1837 & Wesleyan Methodist Chapel, Ablewell Street C 1811-1837	£4.75	£5.25
Staffordshire County Record Office holdings of Parish Registers	£2.70	£3.00
Tracing Your Ancestors in North Staffordshire (5th edition) by H. Eva Beech.	£3.50	£4.00

Surname Index to 1851 Census

	(a)	(b)
Burton-on-Trent Vol. 9. PRO. Ref HO/107/2011 (Part) & HO/107/2012	£2.10	£2.50
Newcastle-under-Lyme Vol. 3. PRO. Ref HO/107/2001 & HO/107/1996 (part) covers Newcastle-under-Lyme, Chapel Chorlton, Maer, Whitmore, Keele, Madeley, Betley, & Audley together with the Staffordshire part of Market Drayton District, Mucclestone, Ashley & Drayton in Hales	£3.00	£3.50
Penkridge Vol.12. PRO. Ref HO/107/2016	£2.70	£3.00
Stafford / Stone & those parts of the Newport & Shifnal Districts located in Staffordshire - Vol. 1 & 2 PRO Ref HO/107/1999, HO107/2000, HO107/1998 (part) & HO/107/1987 (part)	£4.75	£5.20
West Bromwich Part 2 Vol. 15. PRO Ref HO/107/2026 & HO/107/2027 covers the districts of All Saints, St James & Christchurch & parish of Wednesbury	£3.60	£3.90
Wolverhampton Eastern Vol. 13. PRO. Ref HO/107/2019	£3.50	£3.80

Birmingham & Midland Society for Genealogy & Heraldry (continued)

Warwickshire Registers

	(a)	(b)
Birmingham: The Cathedral Church of St Chad CMB 1807-1837	£8.60.	£9.40
Clifton-upon-Dunsmore: St Mary CB15941855; M 1594-1837	£3.10.	£3.60
Coventry: Holy Trinity Part 2 C1561-1653	£3.00.	£3.40
Part 3: C1653-1745	£3.00	£3.40
Part 4: Banns 1653-1661; M1653-1745; B1653-1674	£6.15	£6.65
Coventry: St Michael Part 1 C1716-1726; M1716-1742; B1715-1726	£3.00	£3.40
Part 2: Bapts 1691-1716; M16921716; B1691-1715	£2.50	£2.90
Part 3: CMB 1640 & 1662-1691	£2.80	£3.40
Part 4: M1742-1837 + Addendum Index	£8.20	£8.80
Edgbaston: St Bartholomew Part 1: M1813-1831	£2.25	£2.65
Part 2: M1832-1837 & Index to Parts 1 & 2	£2.25	£2.65
Part 3 C1813-1837 Late Bapts 1838-1850; B1813-1868	£3.10	£3.50
Wasperton: St John the Baptist: CMB 1538-1837	£1.25	£1.60
Tracing Your Ancestors in Warwickshire (excluding Birmingham) (4th ed). Extensively revised, updated and expanded to over 350 pages.	£10.40	£11.30

Surname Index to 1851 Census

Southam: Vol. 14. PRO. Ref HO/107/2077	£1.90	£2.10
Stratford-on-Avon Vol.11. PRO. Ref HO/107/2074	£2.20	£2.50

Worcestershire Registers

Bromsgrove & Chadwick Meetings — Society of Friends Extracts from 1635-1797	£0.80	£1.10
Bromsgrove & The Poll Tax of 1690	£1.55	£1.80
Clifton upon Teme: St Kenlem CMB 1598-1837	£1.75	£2.15
Droitwich: St Peter de Witton C1544-1840; M1544-1837; B1544-1838	£2.35	£2.80
Dudley: St Thomas (SPRS) now Staffordshire CMB 1541-1649	£6.00	£7.50
Great Whitley: St Michael & All Angels C1538-1874; M1538-1835; B1538-1849; Banns 1754-1812	£1.75	£2.15
Hagley: The Poor Law and Settlement Documents of St John	£1.45	£1.75
Hanbury: St Mary the Virgin: Part 1 CMB 1577-1715	£1.40	£1.70
Little Witley: Chapelry of St Michael & All Angels C1680-1846; M1680-1836; B1680-1744	£1.35	£1.55
Martley: St Peter C1626-1838; MB1626-1837	£3.10	£3.40
Northfield: St Laurence — Register supplement to Part 1 C1742-1757	£0.50	£0.80

Census Books
Transcript & Surname Index of 1851 Census

Bromsgrove-Part 1 Vol.10. PRO. Ref HO/107/2047 incls Stoke Prior & part of Bromsgrove	£6.00	£6.60
Part 2 Vol.10. PRO. Ref HO/107/2047 incls. Belbroughton, Clent, Hagley, Pedmore, Frankley, Hunnington, Romsley, Tutnall & Cobley	£6.00	£6.60

Birmingham & Midland Society for Genealogy & Heraldry (continued)

Part 3 Vol.10. PRO. Ref HO/107/2047 incs. Tardebigg, Tutnall & Cobley, Bentley Pauncefoot, Webheath, Redditch & Alvechurch	£6.00	£6.60
Halesowen - Vol. 1. PRO. Ref HO/107/2034 incs. Cradley, Lutley, Hawne, Hasbury, Cakemore, Ridgeacre, The Hill, Halesowen, Lapal, & Illy	£7.70	£8.40
Kidderminster Part 1Vol. 2. PRO. Ref HO/107/2038-1	£6.60	£7.20
Part 2 Vol. 2. PRO. Ref HO/107/2038-2	£6.60	£7.20
Part 3 Vol. 2. PRO. Ref HO/107/2037 incs. Chaddesley Corbett, Rushock, Stone, Broom, Churchill & Wolverley	£4.30	£4.60
Kingswinford - Part 1 Vol. 1. A-LAD PRO. Ref HO/107/2036	£5.50	£6.00
Part 2 Vol. 1. LADD-Z PRO Ref HO/107/2036	£5.50	£6.00
Stourbridge - Part 1 Vol. 1. PRO. Ref HO/107/2035	£6.00	£6.60

Bristol & Avon Family History Society

Web Site: http://www.CIX.co.uk/%7Ekgroves/ba/index.html

Mrs P Bishop, 8 Benville Avenue, Coombe Dingle, Bristol, BS 9 2 RX

Baptisms	Price Sterling	Post & Packing UK	O/Seas
St Swithins, Walcot, 1800-1812	£3.50	D	G
St Swithins, Walcot, 1812-1826	£3.50	D	G
St Swithins, Walcot, 1827-1837	£3.50	D	G
Census			
Census Returns - Bristol Area 1841-81	£1.20	B	F
Census Returns Guide - Bath	£1.00	A	C
Miscellaneaous			
Finding Index For Avon MIS,			
Part 1 North West Avon	£3.00	B	G
Part 2 Central Bristol	£3.00	D	G
Part 3 South Central Avon	£3.00	D	G
Part 4 South East Avon	£3.00	D	G
Part 5 South West Avon	£3.00	D	G
Part 6 North East Avon	£3.00	D	G
Bristol Apprentice Books			
Vol 1 1566-1573	£4.00	D	G
Vol 2 1573-1579	£4.00	D	G
Vol 13 1579-1586	£4.00	D	G
Vol 14 1586-1593	£4.00	D	G
Bristol Insurance Policy Holders (1714-31)	£1.00	A	C
Somerset Insurance Policy Holders(1714-31)	£2.50	B	F
Wiltshire Insurance Policy Holders (1714-31)	£2.50	B	F
Thornbury Marriages missing from Phillimore	£1.00	A	C
Bristol Marriages 1800-1831 (Errata & addenda to Vols 1-6)	£0.50	A	C

Post & Packing Codes: A=50p; B=75p; C=85p; D=£1.00; E=£1.25; F=£1.40; G=£1.85; H=£2.80.

BUCKINGHAMSHIRE
Buckinghamshire Family History Society
Web Site: http://www.bucksfhs.org.uk/sindex.htm
Buckinghamshire FHS Sales,
3 Swallow Lane Stoke Mandeville, Aylesbury, Bucks. HP22 5UW.

The Society is able to accept both VISA and MASTERCARD when the following information is given: card number and its expiry date, the name on the card, the address of the card holder if different from the one to which the goods are to be sent.

Registers	(a)	(b)	(c)
Baptisms High Wycombe 1775-1812	£5.50	£6.10	£7.00
Baptisms High Wycombe 1813-1837	£2.30	£2.60	£3.30

Buckinghamshire Marriages
A fully indexed transcript with witnesses where applicable

		(a)	(b)	(c)
Aston Clinton	1557-1837 & St Leonards 1739-1754	£3.50	£4.00	£5.00
Aylesbury	1565-1690	£4.50	£5.00	£6.00
Aylesbury	1691-1754	£5.20	£5.80	£6.75
Aylesbury	1754-1806	£4.70	£5.20	£6.20
Aylesbury	1806-1837	£4.50	£5.00	£6.00
Bierton	1561-1837	£3.50	£4.00	£5.00
Buckingham	1559-1682	£5.00	£5.60	£6.60
Buckingham	1682-1754	£5.50	£6.00	£7.00
Buckingham	1754-1796	£3.50	£4.00	£5.00
Buckingham	1796-1837	£4.50	£5.00	£6.00
Buckland	1609-1837 & Hulcott 1539-1840	£2.25	£2.75	£3.25
Drayton Beauchamp 1541-1837 & Cholesbury 1576-1838		£2.50	£3.00	£3.50
Hedsor	1600-1836	£1.80	£2.30	£2.80
Hitcham	1559-1836	£1.80	£2.30	£2.80
Little Marlow	1559-1837	£5.50	£6.00	£7.00
Ludgershall	1570-1836	£2.25	£2.75	£3.25
Olney	1575-1753	£5.70	£6.30	£7.30
Olney	1754-1795	£5.00	£5.50	£6.50
Olney	1796-1837	£5.20	£5.80	£6.75
Taplow	1710-1836	£1.80	£2.30	£2.80
Wendover	1576-1837	£4.75	£5.25	£6.25
Wingrave	1550-1837	£2.50	£3.00	£3.50
Wolverton	1536-1837	£3.00	£3.50	£4.00
Wooburn	1600-1848	£5.20	£5.70	£6.75
Wotton Underwood 1600-1836		£2.00	£2.50	£3.00

1851 Census
A full transcript with index

	(a)	(b)	(c)
Aston Abbots, Cublington, Whitchurch	£4.25	£4.75	£6.00
Aylesbury	£5.50	£6.00	£7.00
Boarstall	£1.25	£1.75	£2.00
Boveney, Dorney, Hitcham & Taplow	£2.90	£3.20	£4,00

Buckinghamshire Family History Society (continued)

Bow Brickhill, Great & Little Brickhill	£3.50	£4.00	£5.00
Buckingham	£5.00	£5.60	£6.50
Buckland, Bierton. Wingrave, Drayton Beauchamp	£3.80	£4.30	£5.30
Burnham	£4.00	£4.40	£5.50
Cheddington & Ivinghoe	£3.80	£4.30	£5.30
Chesham	£5.25	£6.25	£7.50
Chinnor & Hinton	£2.50	£2.80	£3.50
Cuddington, Chearsley	£3.75	£4.25	£4.75
Dinton, Aston Sandford, Hartwell	£3.75	£4.25	£4.75
Edlesborough, Northall, Dagnall, Slapton	£3.50	£4.00	£5.00
Eton	£4.00	£4.50	£5.50
Fingest & Turville	£2.20	£2.50	£3.00
Gawcott, Padbury, Adstock, Addington	£4.50	£5.00	£6.00
Gayhurst Sherrington, Chicheley, Hardmead	£3.60	£4.00	£5.00
Great Kimble, Little Kimble, Monks Risborough	£3.20	£3.70	£4.70
Great Marlow	£6.30	£7.00	£8.50
Great Missenden & The Lee	£3.25	£3.75	£4.75
Haddenham	£3.00	£3.40	£4.25
Hanslope, Castlethorpe, Little Linford, Haversham	£3.25	£3.75	£4.75
Hedgerley Dean, Hedgerley, Fulmer, Denham	£3.00	£3.50	£4.50
Hedsor & Wooburn	£3.70	£4.20	£5.20
High Wycombe	£9.50	£10.50	£12.00
Horton, Wraysbury, Datchet & Ditton	£4.20	£4.60	£5.60
Hughendon & Little Missenden	£3.75	£4.25	£4.75
Iver	£3.00	£3.40	£4.25
Langley Marish	£3.30	£3.80	£4.80
Lewknor Uphill, Ibstone, Stokenchurch	£3.25	£3.75	£4.75
Lillingstone Lovell & Dayrell, Stowe, Shalstone	price on application		
Little Marlow	£2.00	£2.50	£3.00
Nettleden, Pitstone, Marsworth, Long Marston	£3.00	£3.40	£4.25
Newport Pagnell	£5.50	£6.10	£7.00
Newton Blossomville, Lavendon, Clifton Reynes	£3.50	£4.00	£5.00
Olney	£4.00	£4.50	£5.00
Penn, Beaconsfield, Seer Green	£4.60	£5.10	£6.10
Princes Risborough	£4.00	£4.50	£5.00
Quainton, Pitchcott, Oving	£2.25	£2.75	£3.75
Saunderton, Horsen, Ilmer, Bledlow, Radnage	£3.25	£3.75	£4.75
Stoke Mandeville & Ellesborough	£2.75	£3.25	£4.25
Stony Stratford, Calverton	£3.25	£3.75	£4.75
Tingewick, Barton Hartshorn, Chetwode	price on application		
Preston Bissett, Hillesden	price on application		
Upton-cum-Chalvey	£4.00	£4.50	£5.50
Waddesdon, Quarrendon, Fleet Marston	£3.75	£4.25	£5.25
Wendover, Great Hampden, Little Hampden	£4.00	£4.50	£5.00
Westbury, Turweston, Biddleston	£2.00	£2.50	£3.00
Weston Turville, St Leonards, Halton	£4.25	£4.75	£5.75

Buckinghamshire Family History Society (continued)

Weston Underwood, Stoke Goldington & Ravenstone	£3.00	£3.50	£4.25
West Wycombe & Bradenham	£3.25	£3.75	£4.75
Wexham, Stoke Poges, Farnham Royal	£3.80	£4.30	£5.30
Wolverton	£3.00	£3.50	£4.25
Wotton Underwood, Ludgershall, Woodham	£2.25	£2.75	£3.75

1891 Census for Buckinghamshire
A full transcript with index

Aylesbury	£5.50	£6.00	£7.00
Olney	£3.90	£4.50	£5.40
Weston Underwood, Stoke Goldington & Ravenstone	£3.90	£4.50	£5.40
Wooburn, Hedsor, Little Marlow	£4.60	£5.10	£6.10

Monumental Inscriptions

Amersham: St Mary	£1.30	£1.80	£2.30
Aston Sandford: St Michael	£1.30	£1.80	£2.30
Beaconsfield (Old): United Reform	£1.30	£1.80	£2.30
Cadmore End: St Mary-le-Moor	£2.30	£2.80	£3.30
Chalfont St Giles: Methodist Chapel	£1.30	£1.80	£2.30
Dorney: St James	£2.30	£2.80	£3.30
Fawley: St Mary	£2.30	£2.80	£3.30
Lacey Green: Primitive Methodist Chapel	£1.30	£1.80	£2.30
Oakley: St Mary (part only)	£1.30	£1.80	£2.30
Radnage. St Mary the Virgin	£1.30	£1.80	£2.30
Weston Turville. Union Chapel	£0.60	£0.80	£1.30

Miscellaneous

Bucks Wills and Administrations of PCC 1700-1800	£7.50	£8.50	£10.00

CAMBRIDGESHIRE

Cambridgeshire Family History Society

Web Site: http://www.personal.u.net.com/ gaer/cam/cfhs

Carol and Philip Noble, 22 St. Margarets Road Girton Cambridge CB3 OLT

	(a)	(b)
Cambridgeshire Contiguous Parishes	£0.76	£1.10
Cambridgeshire Strays Index	£1.50	£1.75
Cambridgeshire Isle of Ely 1851 Census Surnames Index	£2.50	£2.75

CHANNEL ISLANDS

Société Jersiaise

Web Site: http://www.societe-jersiaise.org
Book Sales, Société Jersiaise, 7 Pier Road, St. Helier, Jersey JE2 4XW.
Email: societe@societe-jersiaise.org

Title	Author	Date	Price
All for the King	Balleine, G.R.	1976	£4.50
Annotated checklist of the birds of Jersey	Allan, J.M.	1997	£4.95
Annual bulletin 1998	Société Jersiaise	1998	£12.50
Biographical dictionary of Jersey Vol.2	Corbet, F.L.M.	1998	£25.00
Brief history of Jersey	Hunt, P.	1998	£6.50
Bulletin index (various years)	Société Jersiaise		£2.00
Coastal towers of Jersey	Davies, W.	1991	£7.50
Dolmens of Jersey	Hunt, P.	1998	£5.95
Elizabeth Castle	Rybot, N.V.L.	1956	£2.85
Fishermans Chapel	Rodwell, W.	1990	£9.95
Flora of Jersey	Le Sueur, F.	1984	£17.50
Geresye to Jersey	Roper, M.	1991	£2.00
German Occupation of Jersey	Mollet, R.	1954	£1.00
Gouvernement particulier de Jersey	De Veulle, P.M.	1974	£0.30
H.M.S. Jersey	Tessier-Yandell, J.	1977	£0.50
La Hougue Bie	Higginbottom, R.W.	1979	£1.00
Introduction to the archaeology of Jersey	Cornwall, I.	1984	£1.50
Jersey : an island on a planet	Nicholson, M.	1989	£2.00
Jersey bird report 1997	Société Jersiaise Ornithology Section	1998	£4.50
Jersey chantry certificate of 1550	Bisson, S.W.	1975	£2.50
Jersey in pre-history	Cunliffe, B.	1995	£2.50
John Ranulph de la Haule Marett	Mourant, A.E.	1981	£0.75
Lillie Langtry	Porter, H.T.	1973	£0.60
Little Master Stonehenge	Hibbs, J.	1985	£1.50
Memories of St Ouen	Bartlett, C.T.	1998	£2.50
Memory and history	Briggs, A.	1997	£2.50
Minerals of Jersey. Rev.ed.	Mourant, A.E.	1978	£0.50
Parish Church of St Helier	Corbet, F.L.M.	1993	£2.00
Past Landscapes of Jersey	Jones, R.	1990	£16.50
Victorian voices	Stevens, J.	1969	£7.95

Postage and packing extra
Purchases can be made by post or by credit card via their web site.

CHESHIRE

Family History Society of Cheshire

Web Site: http://www.users.zetnet.co.uk/blangston/fhsc
Mr D Johnson, 91 Stretford House, Chapel Lane, Stretford. Manchester, M32 9AY

1841 Census Surname and Address Index	(a)	(b)	(c)
Northwich District	£4.60	£5.00	£6.60

1851 Census Surname and Location Index

Vol 7	Northwich	£4.00	£4.50	£5.50
Vol 8	Congleton	£4.00	£4.50	£5.50
Vol 9	Nantwich	£4.00	£4.50	£5.50
Vol 10	Chester	£4.00	£4.50	£5.50
Vol 11	Wirral (part)	£4.00	£4.50	£5.50
Vol 12	Birkenhead	£4.00	£4.50	£5.50

Volumes 1-6 Also available from the Society
See also Family History Society of Cheshire & Liverpool & South West Lancashire FHS

1881 Census Surname and Location Index

Northwich District	£4.60	£5.00	£6.00

1891 Census Surname and Address Index

Northwich District	£4.60	£5.00	£6.00

Miscellaneous

Cheshire Parish Registers - A Summary Guide	£4.60	£5.00	£6.00
Cheshire Place Names: an Index to Census 1841-1891	£4.60	£5.00	£6.60
Guide to the Civil Registration Districts of Cheshire 1837-1974	£4.60	£5.00	£6.00
Research Resources in Macclesfield	£2.85	£3.15	£4.00

North Cheshire Family History Society

Web Site http://www.genuki.org.uk/big/eng/CHS/NorthChesFHS
Mr P. Spivey, 22 Davenport Rd, Hazel Grove, Stockport, SK7 4EZ

1851 Census Surname and Location Index

Vol 1	Stockport Registration District (part)	£3.00	£3.50	£4.50
Vol 2	Stockport Registration District (part)	£3.00	£3.50	£4.50
Vol 3	Macclesfield Registration District (part)	£3.00	£3.50	£4.50
Vol 4	Macclesfield Registration District (part)	£3.00	£3.50	£4.50
Vol 5	Altrincham Registration District (part)	£3.00	£3.50	£4.50

Volumes 6-12 Also available from the Society
See also Family History Society of Cheshire & Liverpool & South West Lancashire FHS

1891 Census Surname and Location Index

Stockport Registration District	£5.70	£6.40	£7.50

CLEVELAND AND DURHAM
Cleveland & Durham Family History Society
Web Site: http://homepages.enterprise.net/pjoiner/cfhs.htm/
Mr D.W. Taylor, 106 The Avenue, Nunthorpe, Middlesbrough TS7 0AH
Costs of the following are based on the number of pages & will be supplied as photocopies

Baptism Registers	Years covered	(a)	(b)
Cornforth: Holy Trinity (Dur)	1868-1876	£1.50	£1.80
Eston Prim.Meth. Circuit (Yks)	1859-1950 A-L	£4.65	£5.30
	1859-1950 M-Z	£3.55	£4.10
Guisborough Prim.Meth. Circuit	1850-1878	£4.80	£5.50
	1878-1903	£5.30	£5.60
Guisborough Wesleyan Circuit (Yks)	1840-1914	£5.00	£5.50
Redcar section	1860-1926	£4.00	£4.50
Skelton section	1869-1957	£2.60	£3.10
Topcliffe: St Columb (Yks)	1570-1588	£2.55	£3.05

Marriage Registers			
Marske: SS Germain & Mark	1570 1984	£2.80	£3.30
Middlesbrough: Wesleyan Meth.	1860-1886	£0.35	£0.65
Redcar: St Peter	1856-1948	£2.10	£2.45
Redcar: Station Rd Prim Meth.	1937-1960	£0.40	£0.65
Redcar: Trinity Meth.	1907-1980	£0.60	£0.85
Saltburn: Albion Tce Meth.	1936-1969	£0.40	£0.65
Saltburn: Regent Circus	1911-1936	£0.40	£0.70
Stockton: St James	1868-1910	£3.05	£3.55
Upleatham Church nr Redcar	1654-1812	£0.75	£1.00
	1813-1947	£0.50	£0.80
West Hartlepool: Christ Church	1854-1865	£2.25	£2.70
	1865-1874	£2.30	£2.75
	1874-1890	£2.30	£2.75
	1890-1900	£2.40	£2.85

Burial Registers			
Coatham: Christ Church	1855-1976	£3.00	£3.35
Kirkleatham: St Cuthbert	1567-1812	£2.75	£3.25
	1813-1875	£1.45	£1.75
	1876-1975	£1.55	£1.80
Marske: SS Germain & Mark	1569-1984	£7.25	£8.35
North Ormesby Cemetery	1870-1899	£3.45	£4.05
Redcar: St Peter	1832-1896	£1.15	£1.35
Thornaby: St Paul	1845-1905	£1.95	£2.35
Upleatham Church nr Redcar	1564-1812	£1.10	£1.30
	1813-1982	£0.90	£1.05
Wilton: St Cuthbert	1601-1718	£0.65	£0.95
	1719-1983	£2.35	£2.80
Yarm Cemetery (updated)	1884-1996	£2.85	£3.30

Parish Registers: CMB		
Embleton: Holy Trinity (Dur) 1650-1760	£1.30	£1.60
Finghall: St Andrew (Yks) 1754-1837	£1.60	£1.90
Middleton Tyas: St Michael (Yks) 1539-1621	£1.45	£1.70
Patrick Brompton: St Patrick (Yks) 1683-1722	£1.75	£2.10
W. Witton: St Bartholomew (Yks) 1665-1696	£1.15	£1.35

Cleveland & Durham Family History Society (continued)

1851 Census Index for Northern Yorkshire & Southern Durham

1	Long Newton & Elton, Redmarshall (part of), Grindon, Whitton Egglescliffe inc Aislaby & Newsham	£1.75	£2.00
2	High & Low Worsall, Kirklevington & Picton, Acklam, Stainton, inc Maltby & Ingleby Barwick, Linthorpe Inc. Ayresome & Newport	£1.75	£2.00
3	Yarm	£1.75	£2.00
4	Thornaby	£1.75	£2.00
5	Easington and Brotton	£1.75	£2.00
6	Skelton	£1.75	£2.00
7	Loftus	£1.75	£2.00
8	Kirkleatham and Upleatham	£1.75	£2.00
9	Redcar and Marske	£1.75	£2.00
10	Great Ayton and Little Ayton	£1.75	£2.00
11	Billingham, Claxton, Cowpen Bewley, Greatham, Haverton Hill, Newton Bewley, Port Clarence, Wolviston	£1.75	£2.00
14a	Middlesbrough: Surnames A-J	£2.25	£2.50
14b	Middlesbrough: Surnames K-Z	£2.25	£2.50
15	E. & W. Rounton, Welbury, Appleton Wiske, Hornby,		
16	Great Smeaton	£1.75	£2.00
16	Norton	£1.75	£2.00
17a	Hartlepool: Surnames A-J	£2.50	£2.75
18	Guisborough, Hutton Lowcross, Morton, Newton, Pinchinthorpe, Tocketts, Upsall	£2.00	£2.25
19	Hemlington, Hilton, Marton, Nunthorpe, Tollesby	£1.50	£1.75
20	Stranton (later known as West Hartlepool)	£2.25	£2.50
21	Deighton, E. & W. Harlsey, E. & S. Cowton, Birkby, Hutton Bonville, Little Smeaton	£1.75	£2.00
22	Hart, Thorp Bulmer, Elwick, Throston, Dalton Piercy, Brierton, Elwick Hall, Seaton Carew	£1.75	£2.00
23	Commondale, Castleton, Danby, Westerdale	£1.75	£2.00
24	Northallerton and Romanby (inc Workhouse)	£2.25	£2.50
25	Stokesley	£2.00	£2.25
26	Faceby, Seamer, Sexhow, Potto, Crathorne, Hutton Rudby, Middleton on Leven, Ingleby Arncliffe, Ingleby Cross	£2.00	£2.25
27	Fylingdales (inc. Robin Hoods Bay)	£1.75	£2.00
28	Hinderwell, Staithes, Roxby, Runswick Bay	£2.00	£2.25
29	Newby, Easby, Carlton, Kildale, Whorlton	£1.75	£2.00
30	Trimdon, Butterwick, Embleton, Fishburn	£2.00	£2.25
31	Barnby, Borrowby, Ellerby, Goldsbrough, Mulgrave, Kettleness, Lythe, Mickleby, Sandsend, Ugthorpe.	£2.00	£2.25
32	Bishopton, Bradbury, Mordon, Woodham, Stillington, Foxton & Shotton, Great & Little Stainton, Elstob & Preston le Skerne, E. & W. Newbiggin, Bp Middleham, Garmondsway & Thrislington, Mainsforth	£2.00	£2.25

Cleveland and Durham Family History Society (continued)

33	Cornforth and Great Chilton	£2.00	£2.25
34	Sleights, Eskdaleside, Glaisdale	£1.75	£2.00
35	Ellerbeck, Nether & Over Silton, Thimbleby, Osmotherley	£1.75	£2.00
36	Ruswarp (use in conjunction with Whitby)	£2.00	£2.25
37a	Whitby: Surnames A-L (see Ruswarp also)	£2.50	£2.75
37b	Whitby: Surnames M-Z (see Ruswarp also)	£2.50	£2.75
38	Egton, Ugglebarnby, Goathland	£2.00	£2.25
39	Brompton (N Allerton), Kirby Sigston, Thornton le Beans	£1.75	£2.00
40	Ingleby Greenhow, Battersby, Kirby & Dromonby, Gt & Little Busby, Skutterskelfe, Gt & Little Broughton	£1.75	£2.00
41a	Darlington (Parish of St John)	£2.50	£2.75
41b	Darlington (Parish of St Cuthbert)	£2.50	£2.75
41c	Darlington (Parish of Holy Trinity)	£2.50	£2.75
42	Hawsker cum Stainsacre	£1.75	£2.00
43	Ferryhill	£1.50	£1.75
44	Sedgefield	£1.75	£2.00
45	Hutton Henry (see also vol 125)	£1.50	£1.75
46	Castle Eden (see also vol 125)	£1.50	£1.75
47	Croft, Eryholme, Dalton, Sockburn, Girsby, Dinsdale, Over Dinsdale	£1.75	£2.00
48	Manfield, Cliffe, Cleasby, Stapleton, Blackwell, Barton, Oxen le Field & Newton Morrell	£2.00	£2.25
49	Killerby, Walworth, School Aycliffe, Coatshaw Moor, Redworth, Great Aycliffe, Brafferton	£2.00	£2.25
50	Hurworth, Neasham, Middleton St George & Middleton One Row (inc Goosepool & Oak Tree)	£2.00	£2.25
51	Middleton in Teesdale	£2.00	£2.25
52a	Barnard Castle: Surnames A-L	£2.00	£2.25
52b	Barnard Castle: Surnames M-Z	£2.00	£2.25
53	Heighington, Barmpton, Whessoe, Coatham Mundeville, Morton Palms, Haughton le Skerne, Sadberge & Gt Burdon	£2.00	£2.25
54	Landmoth with Catto & Gueldable, Borrowby, Crosby, Leake (ex parochial), Cotcliffe (ex parochial), Sowerby u Cotcliffe, Winton & Stank, N. Otterington & Warlaby	£2.00	£2.25
55	Thirsk	£2.00	£2.25
56	Thornton le Street, Thornton le Moor, N. Kilvington, Knayton, Kepwick, Cowesby	£1.75	£2.00
57	Richmond	£2.50	£2.75
58	Staindrop and Walkerfield	£1.75	£2.00
59	Ainderby Quernhow, Catton, Sinderby, Skipton, Howe, Holme, Pickhill with Roxby	£1.75	£2.00
60	Cockfield, Woodland, Langley Dale & Shotton, Raby & Keverstone	£1.75	£2.00
61	Hilton, Morton Tinmouth, Ingleton, Headlam, Langton, Gainford	£1.75	£2.00

Cleveland and Durham Family History Society (continued)

62	Ainderby Steeple, Morton on Swale, Thrintoft, Yafforth, Whitwell, Kiplin, Danby Wiske with Lazenby, Gt & Little Langton	£2.00	£2.25
63	Hutton Sessay, Birdforth, Sessay, Dalton, Eldmire, Fawdington, Topcliffe	£1.75	£2.00
64	Sowerby	£1.75	£2.00
65	S. Kilvington, Bagby, Sutton with Balk, Thirkleby	£1.75	£2.00
66	Cleatham, Winston with Newsham, Barforth, Ovington, Wycliffe, Hutton Magna, Barningham, Scargill, Hope	£1.75	£2.00
67	Kilburn, Felixkirk, Thirlby, Boltby, Upsall, Thornborough, Kirby Knowle	£1.75	£2.00
68	Maunby, Newby Wiske, S. Otterington, Kirby Wiske, Carlton Miniott, Sandhutton, Newsham cum Breckenbrough	£2.00	£2.25
69	Coniscliffe, Carlbury, Piercebridge, Cockerton, Archdeacon Newton, Coldsides, Houghton le Side, Denton, Summerhouses	£1.75	£2.00
70	Downholme, Stainton, Walburn, Marske, Hudswell, Hipswell, Easby, Aske	£1.75	£2.00
71	Skeeby, Gilling, Hartforth, Gatherley Moor, Sedbury	£1.75	£2.00
	Catterick, Brough, Scotton, Colburn, Tunstall, Appleton, Ellerton, Bolton on Swale, Scorton	£2.00	£2.25
73	Brignall, Rokeby, Boldron, Bowes, Streatlam, Stainton, Marwood	£1.75	£2.00
74	Gilmonby, Whorlton, Westwick, Egglestone Abbey, Startforth	£1.75	£2.00
	Egglestone, Newbiggin with Bowlees, Forest & Frith with Harwood	£2.00	£2.25
76	St. Johns Chapel	£2.00	£2.25
77	Middleton Tyas, N. Cowton, Moulton, Uckerby, Brompton on Swale	£1.75	£2.00
78	Aldbrough & Stanwick, Eppleby & Melsonby	£1.75	£2.00
79	Bishop Auckland	£2.75	£3.00
80	Byers Green, Hunwick & Helmington, Newton Cap, Pollards Lands	£2.00	£2.25
81	Kirby Hill with Whashton, Ravensworth, Gayles, New Forest	£1.50	£1.75
82	Auckland St Andrew	£1.75	£2.00
83	Coundon	£1.75	£2.00
84	Lartington, Cotherstone, Hunderthwaite, Romaldkirk, Mickleton, Lundale, Holwick (2 parts: see below)		
84a	Surnames A-J	£1.75	£2.00
84b	Surnames K-Z	£1.75	£2.00
85	Killerby, Kirby Fleetham, Fencote, Ainderby cum Holtby, Hackforth, Scruton, Firby	£1.75	£2.00
86	Bedale	£1.75	£2.00
87	Gatenby, Swainby, Theakston, Burneston, Carthorpe, Kirklington	£1.75	£2.00
88	Well, Snape, Thornton Watlass	£1.75	£2.00
89	Arden (inc Ardenside), Beadlam, Bilsdale Midcable, Bilsdale W. Side, Dale-Town, Hawnby, Laskill-Pasture, Morton (extra parochial), Old Byland, Rievaulx, Snilesworth, Helmsley, Carlton	£1.75	£2.00

Cleveland and Durham Family History Society (continued)

90	Pockley, Harum, Sproxton, Scawton & Cold Kirby, Oldstead & Wass, Thorpe le Willows, Byland Abbey, Ampleforth, Birdforth, Oswaldkirk & W. Newton Grange	£1.75	£2.00
91	Cawton & Grimston, Coulton, E. Ness & Nunnington, N. Holme, Gt & Little Edstone, Gilling E., Muscoates & Wilburn, Normanby & Thornton Riseborough, Salton, Stonegrave & E. Newton, Wombleton	£2.00	£2.25
92	Nawton, Bransdale & Skiplam, Farndale: Low Quarter, E. & W. Side, Gillamoor, Fadmoor, Hutton le Hole	£1.75	£2.00
93	Kirbymoorside, Appleton le Moor	£1.75	£2.00
94a	Aysgarth, Carperby & Thoresby, Burton cum Walden, Newbiggin, Bishopdale	£1.75	£2.00
94b	Thoralby, Thornton Rust, Bainbridge	£1.75	£2.00
95	Askrigg, Abbotside, Burtersett	£1.75	£2.00
96	Reeth, Healaugh, Raw, Fremington, Whitaside, Harkerside, Grinton	£2.00	£2.25
97	Arkengarthdale, Hurst, Marrick, Ellerton Abbey	£2.00	£2.25
98	Gayle, Hawes, Appersett	£1.75	£2.00
99	Thorns & Keld, Stonesdale & Birkdale, Angram & Agill, Thwaite, Muker, Oxnop & Satron, Ivelet	£1.75	£2.00
100	Gunnerside, Lodge Green, Melbecks, Low Row, Kearton, Feetham	£2.00	£2.25
101	Firby, Langthorn, Leeming & Newton, Londonderry, Exelby	£1.75	£2.00
102	Masham, Swinton, Ilton cum Pott	£1.75	£2.00
103	Crakehall, Aiskew & Leeming Bar	£1.75	£2.00
104	Healey & Sutton, Fearby, Ellington, Ellingstring, E. Witton, Colsterdale	£1.75	£2.00
105	Middleham	£1.75	£2.00
106	Dalton, E. and W. Layton, Newsham, Carkin, Caldwell, Forcett	£1.75	£2.00
107	Coverham, Caldbergh, W. Scrafton, Carlton (Highdale), Melmerby, W. Witton	£2.00	£2.25
108	Wensley, Preston, Redmire, Castle Bolton, Leyburn	£2.00	£2.25
109	Spennithorne, Bellerby, Hawkswell, Garriston with Barden, Hornby, Hunton, Patrick Brompton & Arrathorne	£2.00	£2.25
110	Newton le Willows, Burrell, Burton on Ure, Thirn, Thornton Steward, Fingall, Constable Burton	£1.75	£2.00
111	Shildon	£2.00	£2.25
112	Pickering	£2.00	£2.25
113	St Helen Auckland, Middridge, Helmington Row, Crook	£2.00	£2.25
114	Escomb, Coundon Grange	£2.00	£2.25
115	Eldon, Windlestone, E. Thickley	£1.75	£2.25
116	Lastingham, Rosedale E. & W., Cropton, Hartoft, Cawthorne, Aislaby, Middleton	£2.00	£2.25
117	Newton, Marishes, Sinnington, Marton, Kirby Misperton, Gt & Little Barugh, Thornton Dale	£2.00	£2.25

Cleveland and Durham Family History Society (continued)

118	Farmanby, Wilton, Allerston, Ebberston, Lockton, Levisham	£2.00	£2.25
119	Bolam, West Auckland incl Etherley, Evenwood & Barony, Morley, Toft Hill	£2.00	£2.25
120	Merrington, Middlestone, Westerton, Whitworth, Old Park, Binchester, Newfield	£2.00	£2.25
121	Lynesack & Softley, Hamsterley, N. & S. Bedburn	£2.00	£2.25
122	Crook, Billy Row, Witton Le Wear, N. Bitchburn, Witton Pk & Colliery	£2.25	£2.50
123	Monk Hesledon, Church Hesledon, Castle Eden Colliery	£1.75	£2.00
124	Kelloe, Thornley, Deaf Hill, Wingate & Wingate Colliery	£1.75	£2.00
125	South Wingate Colliery, Castle Eden, Hutton Henry, Sheraton	£1.75	£2.00

1881 Census Index

Seaton Carew area of W. Hartlepool	£2.00	£2.25
Dalton Piercy, Brierton, Claxton, Elwick & Hall, Greatham, Hart, Bulmer	£2.00	£2.25
Royal Navy Ships at Sea-extracts for Durham & Yorks	£1.50	£1.75

Workhouse Census Index Years Covered

Bainbridge Workhouse (Yks)	1841-1891	£1.10	£1.30
Bedale (Yks)	1841-1891	£1.00	£1.20
Barnard Castle (Dur)	1841-1891	£2.25	£2.65
Darlington (Dur)	1841-1891	£2.50	£2.90
Easingwold (Yks)	1841-1891	£1.10	£1.30
Guisborough (Yks)	1841-1891	£1.40	£1.90
Hartlepool (Dur)	1871-1891	£1.80	£2.30
Leyburn (Yks)	1841-1891	£1.25	£1.45
Middlesbrough (Yks)	1881	£1.75	£2.00
Middlesbrough (Yks)	1891	£1.75	£2.00
Middlesbrough Nazareth House	1891	£0.70	£1.00
Northallerton (Yks)	1841-1891	£2.10	£2.50
Reeth (Yks)	1841-1891	£1.00	£1.20
Richmond (Yks)	1841-1891	£1.50	£1.75
Stockton (Dur)	1871-1891	£2.20	£2.70
Stokesley (Yks)	1841-1891	£1.00	£1.50
Thirsk (Yks)	1841-1891	£1.35	£1.55
Northallerton (House of Correction)	1841-1891	£1.95	£2.20

Monumental Inscriptions
Costs of the following are based on the number of pages & will be supplied as photocopies
    (Yks) = North Riding   (Dur) = Durham

Acklam: St Mary (Yks)	£4.00	£5.00
Ainderby Steeple: St Helen (Yks)	£2.10	£2.45
Ampleforth: St Hilda (Yks)	£1.40	£1.70
Appleton Wiske: St Mary (Yks)	£1.35	£1.55

Cleveland and Durham Family History Society (continued)

Arkletown,Wesleyan Chapel & St Mary, Arkengarthdale (Yks)	£1.20	£1.45
Arkendale: St Bartholomew (Yks)	£0.50	£0.75
Auckland St Helen: (Dur)	£3.00	£3.50
Aycliffe: St Andrew (Dur)	£2.30	£2.70
Aysgarth: St Andrew (Yks)	£5.85	£6.60
Bagby: St Mary (Yks)	£0.90	£1.25
Bainbridge Quaker Burial Ground (Yks)	£0.70	£1.00
Barnard Castle: St Mary (Dur)	£2.40	£2.90
Baldersby: St James (Yks)	£1.50	£1.75
Barningham: St Michael & All Angels (Yks)	£1.85	£2.10
Barton: St Cuthbert (Yks)	£1.45	£1.70
Barton: St Mary (Yks)	£0.55	£0.80
Bedale: St Gregory (Yks)	£5.45	£6.20
Bellerby: St John (Yks)	£0.85	£1.05
Bilsdale: St Hilda (Yks)	£2.60	£3.10
Bilsdale Midcable: St John (Yks)	£0.85	£1.25
Birkby: St Peter (Yks)	£0.60	£0.85
Bishop Middleham: St Michael (Dur)	£1.35	£1.55
Bishopton: St Peter (Dur)	£1.65	£1.90
Boltby: Holy Trinity (Yks)	£0.55	£0.80
Bolton on Swale: St Mary (Yks)	£1.90	£2.20
Boosbeck: St Aidan (Yks)	£1.70	£1.95
Bransdale: St Nicholas with Carlton: St Aiden (Yks)	£0.60	£0.90
Brignall: Old Church (Yks)	£0.50	£0.75
Brignall: St Mary (Yks)	£0.60	£0.85
Brompton nr Northallerton: St Thomas (Yks)	£1.45	£1.70
Brotton: St Peter (Yks)	£6.40	£7.10
Burneston: St Lambert (Yks)	£1.80	£2.10
Carlton in Cleveland: St Botolph (Yks)	£4.10	£4.70
Carlton Miniott: St Lawrence (Yks)	£1.85	£2.10
Castle Bolton cum Redmire: St Mary(Yks)	£1.30	£1.60
Castle Eden: St James (Dur)	£1.35	£1.55
Castleton: Friends Burial Ground (Yks) (free with others)		
Catterick: St Anne & Cemetery (Yks)	£1.80	£2.05
Cleasby: St Peter (Yks)	£0.55	£0.80
Coatham: Christ Church (Yks)	£3.40	£4.15
Cockfield: St Mary the Virgin (Dur)	£1.30	£1.50
Cold Kirby: St Michael (Yks)	£0.55	£0.80
Commondale: St Peter (Yks)	£0.55	£0.80
Coniscliffe Cemetery (Dur)	£0.65	£0.95
Cotherstone: Quaker Burial Ground (Yks)	£0.50	£0.75
Coverham: Holy Trinity (Yks)	£2.45	£2.85
Cowesby: St Michael and All Angels (Yks)	£0.65	£0.95
Coxwold: St Michael (Yks)	£3.10	£3.55
Crakehall: St Gregory (Yks)	£0.65	£0.95
Crathorne: All Saints (Yks)	£1.55	£1.80

Cleveland and Durham Family History Society (continued)

Croft on Tees: St Peter (Yks)	£2.75	£3.25
Cundall: All Saints (Yks)	£0.65	£0.95
Dalby: St Peter (Yks)	£0.50	£0.75
Dalton in Topcliffe: St John (Yks)	£0.60	£0.85
Danby: St Hilda (Yks)	£5.05	£6.60
Danby Wiske: (Yks)	£1.35	£1.55
Darlington: Holy Trinity (Dur)	£1.30	£1.50
Darlington: St Cuthbert (Dur)	£4.50	£5.10
Deaf Hill cum Langdale: St Paul (Dur)	£1.60	£1.90
Deighton: All Saints (Yks)	£0.60	£0.85
Denton: St Mary the Virgin (Dur)	£1.10	£1.40
Dinsdale St John the Baptist (Dur)	£1.25	£1.50
Dishforth Cemetery (Yks)	£1.85	£2.10
Downholme: St Michael & All Angels (Yks)	£0.85	£1.25
Easby: St Agatha (Richmond) (Yks)	£3.10	£3.55
Easington,near Loftus: All Saints (Yks)	£3.10	£3.55
Easington: St Mary the Virgin (Dur)	£1.35	£1.55
E. Cowton: All Saints & Cemetery (Yks)	£1.50	£1.75
E. Harlsey: St Oswald (Yks)	£1.75	£2.05
E. Loftus Cemetery (old part) (Yks)	£5.25	£5.95
E. Witton nr Leyburn: St Martin (Yks)	£0.60	£0.85
E.Witton nr Leyburn: St John (Yks)	£1.70	£1.95
Egglescliffe: St John (Dur)	£6.95	£7.80
Eggleston: Old Church & Holy Trinity (Dur)	£1.65	£1.90
Egton: St Hilda (Yks)	£1.95	£2.25
Elton: St John (Dur)	£1.35	£1.55
Elwick Hall: St Peter (Dur)	£1.10	£1.30
Embleton: Holy Trinity (Dur)	£0.50	£0.75
Eryholme: St Mary (Yks)	£0.60	£0.85
Faceby: St Mary Magdalene (Yks)	£0.80	£1.00
Farndale: St Mary (Yks)	£1.65	£1.90
Felixkirk: St Felix (Yks)	£2.10	£2.45
Forcett: St Cuthbert (Yks)	£1.65	£1.95
Forest & Frith: St James the Less (Yks)	£0.90	£1.10
Gayle: Sandemanians Burial Ground (Yks)	£0.60	£0.85
Gilling West: St Agatha (Yks)	£1.80	£2.05
Girsby: All Saints (Dur)	£0.55	£0.80
Glaisdale: St Thomas & Glaisdale Head Wslyn Chapel (Yks)	£2.80	£3.30
Great Ayton: All Saints (Yks)	£3.80	£4.30
Great Ayton: Friends Burial Ground (Yks)	£0.80	£1.10
Great Fencote: St Andrew (Yks)	£1.50	£1.75
Great Langton: St Wilfred (Yks)	£0.65	£0.95
Great Smeaton: St Eloy (Yks)	£1.75	£2.00
Great Stainton: All Saints (Dur)	£0.55	£0.80
Greatham: St John the Baptist & Cemeteries (Dur)	£4.00	£5.00
Greatham: Ind Methodist Church (Dur)	£0.50	£0.75

Cleveland and Durham Family History Society (continued)

Grindon: see Thorpe Thewles: St James (Dur)	£0.60	£0.85
Grinton: St Andrew Swaledale (Yks)	£1.60	£1.90
Grosmont: St Matthew (Yks)	£1.00	£1.30
Guisborough Cemetery (Yks)	£5.75	£6.50
Guisborough: Quaker Burial Ground (Yks)	£0.50	£0.75
Guisborough: St Nicholas (Yks)	£3.00	£3.50
Gunnerside: Methodist Church, Swaledale (Yks)	£0.60	£0.85
Hamsterley: St James & Baptist Chapel (Dur)	£1.90	£2.20
Hardraw: SS. Mary & John (Yks)	£0.70	£1.00
Hart: Mary Magdalene (Dur)	£2.80	£3.30
Hartlepool: St Hilda (Dur)	£2.10	£2.45
Hartlepool: Spion Kop Cemetery (Dur)	£5.95	£6.70
Haughton le Skerne: St Andrew (Dur)	£3.00	£3.50
Hauxwell: St Oswald (Yks)	£1.20	£1.50
Haverton Hill: St John (Dur)	£3.00	£3.50
Hawes: St Margaret & Quaker Burial Ground (Yks)	£2.10	£2.50
Heighington: St Michael (Dur)	£2.80	£3.30
High Coniscliffe: St Edwin (Dur)	£2.10	£2.45
High Worsall: St John (Yks)	£0.60	£0.85
High Worsall: St John (addition) (Yks)	£0.50	£0.75
Hilton: St Peter (Yks)	£0.95	£1.15
Hinderwell: St Hilda (Yks)	£2.60	£3.10
Hipswell: St John the Evangelist (Yks)	£1.65	£1.95
Horsehouse in Coverdale: St Botolph (Yks)	£0.65	£0.95
Hudswell: St Michael & All Angels (Yks)	£0.85	£1.25
Hurworth: All Saints (Dur)	£6.65	£7.40
Hutton Bonville: St Laurence (Yks)	£0.60	£0.85
Hutton Henry: St Francis/Station Town (Dur)	£0.90	£1.10
Hutton juxta Rudby: All Saints (Yks)	£3.40	£3.90
Hutton Magna: St Mary (Yks)	£0.90	£1.10
Ingleby Arncliffe: All Saints (Yks)	£1.35	£1.55
Ingleby Greenhow: St Andrew (Yks)	£1.85	£2.10
Ingleton: St John (Dur)	£1.05	£1.25
Kelloe: St Helen & Cemetery (Dur)	£2.60	£3.10
Kilburn: St Martin (Yks)	£1.35	£1.55
Kildale: St Cuthbert & St Gregory (Yks)	£1.35	£1.55
Kirby in Cleveland: St Augustine (Yks)	£3.00	£3.50
Kirby Fleetham: St Mary (Yks)	£1.75	£2.00
Kirby Hill: (Kirby Ravensworth) St Peter & St Felix (Yks)	£2.10	£2.45
Kirby Knowle: St Wilfred (Yks)	£0.85	£1.25
Kirby Sigston: St Lawrence (Yks)	£0.95	£1.15
Kirby Wiske: St John the Baptist (Yks)	£2.10	£2.45
Kirkleatham: St Cuthbert (Yks)	£2.75	£3.25
Kirklevington: St Martin (Yks)	£1.75	£2.00
Laithkirk: (Yks)	£1.65	£1.90
Langthwaite: St Mary (see Arkletown)		

Cleveland and Durham Family History Society (continued)

Lartington: R.C. Cemetery (Yks)	£0.55	£0.80
Leake: St Mary (Yks)	£3.40	£3.90
Lealholm: Catholic Church (Yks)	£0.55	£0.80
Leeming: St John (Yks)	£1.95	£2.10
Leyburn: Cemetery (Yks)	£1.60	£1.90
Liverton: St Michael (Yks)	£2.10	£2.45
Loftus: Newton Memorial Church (Yks)	£0.60	£0.85
Loftus: St Leonard (Yks)	£1.65	£1.90
Longnewton: St Mary (Dur)	£2.10	£2.45
Lynesack & Softley: St John the Evan.(Dur)	£2.10	£2.45
Manfield: All Saints (Yks)	£1.35	£1.55
Marrick Priory: Swaledale (Yks)	£0.55	£0.80
Marske: St Germain (Yks)	£2.90	£3.30
Marske (nr Richmond): St Edmund (Yks)	£0.65	£0.95
Marton: St Cuthbert (Yks)	£2.90	£3.30
Maunby: St Michael & All Angels (Yks)	£0.55	£0.80
Melsonby: St James the Great (Yks)	£2.60	£3.10
Middlesbrough: Ayresome Gardens (Yks)	£3.20	£3.75
Middlesbrough: St Hilda (Yks)	£0.40	£0.65
Middleton in Teesdale: St Mary (Yks)	£3.60	£3.90
Middleton One Row: St George (Dur)	£1.80	£2.05
Middleton Tyas: St Michael & All Angels (Yks)	£3.00	£3.50
Monk Hesleden: St Mary with St John (Dur)	£0.90	£1.10
Moorsholm: St Mary (Yks)	£1.30	£1.50
Muker: St Mary (Yks)	£0.90	£1.10
Nether Silton: All Saints (Yks)	£0.60	£0.85
Newton under Roseberry: St Oswald (Yks)	£1.65	£1.90
Normanby: St Helen (Yks)	£1.25	£1.45
N. Ormesby: Protestant Cemetery (Yks)	£2.10	£2.45
N. Ormesby: St Josephs R.C. Cemetery (Yks)	£1.60	£1.90
N. Otterington: St Michael & All Angels (Yks)	£1.90	£2.20
Norton on Tees: St Mary (Dur)	£5.85	£6.60
Nunthorpe: St Mary (Yks)	£1.40	£1.60
Old Byland: All Saints (Yks)	£0.55	£0.80
Ormesby: St Cuthbert (Yks)	£4.10	£4.70
Osmotherley: Cemetery (Yks)	£1.25	£1.45
Osmotherley: Quaker Burial Ground (Yks) (free with others)		
Osmotherley: St Peter (Yks)	£2.10	£2.45
Over Silton: St Mary (Yks)	£1.35	£1.55
Pickhill: All Saints (Yks)	£1.80	£2.05
Piercebridge: St Mary (Dur)	£0.55	£0.80
Preston on Tees: Cemetery (Dur)	£1.30	£1.50
Quarrington Hill: (Dur)	£1.35	£1.55
Redcar: Cemetery (Main Part) (Yks)	£4.50	£5.10
Redcar: St Peter (Yks)	£1.75	£2.00
Redmarshall: St Cuthbert (Dur)	£0.85	£1.00

Cleveland and Durham Family History Society (continued)

Redmire (See Castle Bolton)	£1.30	£1.60
Reeth: Congregational Chapel (Yks)	£0.55	£0.80
Richmond: St Mary (Yks)	£5.95	£6.80
Richmond: Cemetery (Yks)	£5.10	£5.85
Rievaulx & Scawton (Yks)	£0.60	£0.90
Rokeby: (Dur)	£0.85	£1.00
Romaldkirk: St Romald (Yks)	£3.10	£3.55
Rosedale Abbey: St Mary & St Lawrence (Yks)	£2.45	£2.90
Rounton E: St Laurence (Yks)	£0.60	£0.85
Rounton W: St Oswald (Yks)	£0.90	£1.10
Roxby: St Nicholas (Yks)	£1.35	£1.55
Sadberge: St Andrew (Dur)	£1.20	£1.40
Saltburn: Cemetery (Yks)	£5.00	£5.65
Sandhutton: St Leonard (Yks)	£0.85	£1.00
Scawton: St Mary (Yks)	£0.50	£0.75
Scruton: St Radegund (Yks)	£1.50	£1.75
Seamer: St Martin (Yks)	£1.55	£1.80
Seaton Carew: Holy Trinity (Dur)	£2.75	£3.25
Sedgefield: St Edmund (Dur)	£1.60	£1.90
Sedgefield: Old Cemetery (Dur)	£0.60	£0.85
Sessay: St Cuthbert (Yks)	£1.30	£1.50
Skelton: All Saints nr Saltburn (Yks)	£5.50	£6.20
Skipton on Swale: St John (Yks)	£0.65	£0.95
S. Cowton: St Mary (Yks)	£1.60	£1.90
S. Kilvington: St Wilfred (Yks)	£1.30	£1.50
S. Otterington: St Andrew (Yks)	£1.55	£1.80
Sowerby: St Oswald (Yks)	£2.10	£2.45
Staindrop: St Mary incl Quaker Burial ground (Dur)	£3.70	£4.35
Stainton: St Peter & Paul (Yks)	£2.00	£2.35
Stalling Busk: St Matthew (Yks)	£0.95	£1.15
Stanwick St John (Aldbrough) & Caldwell (Yks)	£2.10	£2.45
Startforth: Holy Trinity (Yks)	£1.70	£1.95
Stillington: St John (Dur)	£1.35	£1.55
Stockton: St Thomas (Dur)	£0.90	£1.10
Stockton: Holy Trinity (Dur)	£0.50	£0.75
Stokesley: SS Peter & Paul (Yks)	£3.25	£3.75
Stokesley: Churchyard extension (Yks)	£2.00	£2.35
Stranton: All Saints (Dur)	£1.75	£2.00
Thirkleby: All Saints (Yks)	£1.35	£1.55
Thirsk: St Mary (Yks)	£2.80	£3.30
Thornaby: St Peter Ad Vincula (Yks)	£0.90	£1.10
Thornley: St Bartholomew (Dur)	£1.65	£1.90
Thornton le Street: St Leonard (Yks)	£0.65	£0.95
Thorpe Thewles: St James (Dur)	£0.60	£0.85
Topcliffe: St Columba & Cemetery (Yks)	£2.15	£2.50
Trimdon: St Mary & Cemetery (Dur)	£1.55	£1.80

Cleveland and Durham Family History Society (continued)

Tunstall: Holy Trinity (Yks)	£0.65	£0.95
Ulshaw Bridge: St Simon & St Jude R.C. (Yks)	£0.50	£0.80
Upleatham: St Andrew (Yks)	£1.50	£1.75
Welbury: St Leonard (Yks)	£0.55	£0.80
West Auckland: Cemetery (Dur)	£3.85	£4.10
Westerdale: Christ Church (Yks)	£1.50	£1.75
Whorlton nr Swainby: Holy Cross (Yks)	£2.00	£2.25
Whorlton: St Mary (Dur)	£1.65	£1.90
Wilton: St Cuthbert (Yks)	£1.90	£2.20
Wingate: Churchyard (Dur)	£2.60	£3.10
Winston: St Andrew (Dur)	£1.50	£1.75
Wolviston: St Peter (Dur)	£1.65	£1.90
Worsall: All Saints (see High Worsall) (Yks)	£0.65	£0.95
Wycliffe: St Mary (Yks)	£0.85	£1.00
Yafforth: All Saints (Yks)	£0.65	£0.95
Yarm: St Mary (Yks)	£5.40	£6.10

Miscellaneous

1871 Norfolk Immigrants to Cleveland	£1.35	£1.65
Beginners Start Here	£1.00	£1.50
Children of Middlesbrough Workhouse 1876-1919	£3.30	£3.80
Family History Research Facilities in North. Yorks, Cleveland & South. Durham (2nd ed)	£2.30	£2.50
Genealogical Sources in Hartlepool	£0.65	£0.95
Genealogical Study of the Family of Captain James Cook RN	£4.65	£5.30
Guide to Genealogical Sources in the Borthwick Institute	£3.45	£3.75
In Memoriam Cards for Hartlepool Area 1839-1916	£2.30	£2.50
Middlesbrough Volunteer Corps 1877-1885	£2.10	£2.50
Place Names: 19th Century Gazetteer for North Riding of Yorkshire	£2.75	£3.25
Resources at the Family History Centre, Billingham	£1.00	£1.50
Ships in Port at Hartlepool Census 1881	£1.40	£1.70
Yorkshire Family History Societies Addresses and Details	£1.00	£1.30

CORNWALL

Cornwall Family History Society
Web Site: http://www.cfhs.demon.uk/Society/
5 Victoria Square, Truro, Cornwall TR2 5DX

Marriage Indexes pre 1813

	(a)	(b)			
Advent	£1.28	£1.94	Landulph	£3.34	£4.68
Blisland	£3.34	£4.68	Laneast	£1.28	£1.94
Bodmin	£7.66	£10.36	Lanherne Roman Catholic	£1.28	£1.94
Botus Fleming	£3.34	£4.68	Lanhydrock	£1.28	£1.94
Boyton	£2.28	£3.12	Lanivet	£3.34	£4.68
Budock	£4.41	£6.02	Lanlivery	£3.34	£4.68
Camborne	£7.66	£10.36	Lanteglos by Camelford	£3.34	£4.68
Cardinham	£2.28	£3.12	Launcells	£3.34	£4.68
Colan	£2.28	£3.12	Launceston:		
Constantine	£4.41	£6.02	St Mary Magdelene	£6.66	£9.36
Cornelly	£1.28	£1.94	Lelant	£3.34	£4.68
Crantock	£3.34	£4.68	Lesnewth	£1.28	£1.94
Creed	£3.34	£4.68	Lewannick	£2.28	£3.12
Crowan	£4.41	£6.02	Lezant	£3.34	£4.68
Cubert	£2.28	£3.12	Linkinhorne	£4.41	£6.02
Cuby with Tregony	£3.34	£4.68	Little Petherick	£1.28	£1.94
Davidstow	£1.28	£1.94	Lostwithiel	£3.34	£4.48
Egloshayle	£3.34	£4.68	Ludgvan	£4.41	£6.02
Egloskerry	£2.28	£3.12	Luxulyan	£3.34	£4.68
Endellion	£2.28	£3.12	Madron	£8.66	£11.36
Falmouth	£9.66	£12.36	Manaccan	£2.28	£3.12
Forrabury	£1.28	£1.94	Marhamchurch	£3.34	£4.68
Fowey	£5.58	£7.56	Mawgan in Meneage	£3.34	£4.68
Germoe	£2.28	£3.12	Mawgan in Pydar	£2.28	£3.12
Gerrans	£4.41	£6.02	Mawnan	£3.34	£4.68
Gorran	£3.34	£4.48	Menheniot	£4.41	£6.02
Grade	£1.28	£1.94	Michaelstow	£2.28	£3.12
Gulval	£3.34	£4.68	Minster	£1.28	£1.94
Gwennap	£6.66	£9.36	Morvah	£1.28	£1.94
Gwinear	£3.34	£4.68	Morwenstow	£4.41	£6.02
Gwithian	£2.28	£3.12	Mylor	£4.41	£6.02
Helland	£1.28	£1.94	Newlyn East	£4.41	£6.02
Helston	£5.58	£7.56	Otterham	£1.28	£1.94
Jacobstow	£2.28	£3.12	Padstow	£4.41	£6.02
Kea	£3.34	£4.68	Paul	£5.58	£7.56
Kenwyn	£7.66	£10.36	Perranarworthal	£2.28	£3.12
Kilkhampton	£4.41	£6.02	Perranzabloe	£4.41	£6.02
Ladock	£2.28	£3.12	Phillack	£3.34	£4.68
Landewednack	£1.28	£1.94	Philleigh	£2.28	£3.12
Landrake	£3.34	£4.68	Pillaton	£3.34	£4.68
			Poughill	£3.34	£4.48

Cornwall Family History Society (continued)

Poundstock	£2.28	£3.12	St. Wenn	£2.28	£3.12
Probus	£3.34	£4.68	St. Winnow	£3.34	£4.68
Redruth	£7.66	£10.36	Sancreed	£3.34	£4.68
Roche	£3.34	£4.68	Sennen	£2.28	£3.12
Ruan Lanihorne	£2.28	£3.12	Sheviock	£3.34	£4.68
Ruan Major	£1.28	£1.94	Sithney	£4.41	£6.02
Ruan Minor	£1.28	£1.94	South Petherin	£3.34	£4.68
St. Agnes	£5.58	£7.56	Stithians	£3.34	£4.68
St. Allen	£2.28	£3.12	Stratton	£3.34	£4.68
St. Anthony-in-Meneage	£1.28	£1.94	Tintagel	£3.34	£4.68
St. Breock	£4.41	£6.02	Towednack	£2.28	£3.12
St. Breward	£3.34	£4.68	Tremaine	£1.28	£1.94
St. Buryan	£3.34	£4.68	Treneglos	£1.28	£1.94
St. Cleer	£3.34	£4.68	Trevalga	£1.28	£1.94
St. Clement	£5.58	£7.56	Truro: St. Mary	£9.66	£12.36
St. Clether	£1.28	£1.94	Tywardreath	£3.34	£4.68
St. Columb Minor	£4.41	£6.02	Veryan	£3.34	£4.68
St. Dennis	£2.28	£3.12	Warbstow	£1.28	£1.94
St. Enoder	£3.34	£4.68	Warleggan	£2.28	£3.12
St. Erme	£2.28	£3.12	Week: St. Margaret	£3.34	£4.68
St. Erney	£2.28	£3.12	Wendron	£6.66	£9.36
St. Erth	£3.34	£4.68	Withiel	£2.28	£3.12
St. Ervan	£2.28	£3.12	Zennor	£2.28	£3.12
St. Eval	£1.28	£1.94			
St. Ewe	£4.41	£6.02	**1813-1837 Marriage Index**		
St. Gluvias	£6.66	£9.36	Advent	£1.28	£1.94
St. Hilary	£4.41	£6.02	Altarnun	£1.28	£1.94
St. Issey	£3.34	£4.68	Antony	£2.28	£3.12
St. Ives	£5.58	£7.56	Blisland	£1.28	£1.94
St. Juliot	£1.28	£1.94	Boconnoc	£1.28	£1.94
St, Just-in-Penwith	£6.66	£9.36	Bodmin	£2.28	£3.12
St. Keverne	£5.58	£7.56	Botus Fleming	£1.28	£1.94
St. Kew	£4.41	£6.02	Boyton	£1.28	£1.94
St. Levan	£1.28	£1.94	Braddock	£1.28	£1.94
St. Mabyn	£3.34	£4.68	Breage	£3.34	£4.48
St. Martin in Meneage	£2.28	£3.12	Budock	£2.28	£3.12
St. Mellion	£3.34	£4.68	Callington	£1.28	£1.94
St. Meryn	£2.28	£3.12	Calstock	£2.28	£3.12
St. Michael Penkevil	£2.28	£3.12	Camborne	£3.34	£4.68
St. Minver	£4.41	£6.02	Cardinham	£1.28	£1.94
St. Sampson also known as Golant	£2.28	£3.12	Colan	£1.28	£1.94
			Constantine	£1.28	£1.94
St. Stephen in Brannel	£4.41	£6.02	Cornelly	£1.28	£1.94
St. Stephen by Launceston	£3.34	£4.68	Crantock	£1.28	£1.94
St. Teath	£3.34	£4.68	Creed	£1.28	£1.94
St. Tudy	£3.34	£4.68	Crowan	£1.28	£1.94

Cornwall Family History Society (continued)

Parish			Parish		
Cubert	£1.28	£1.94	Lawhitton	£1.28	£1.94
Cuby with Tregony	£1.28	£1.94	Lelant	£1.28	£1.94
Cury	£1.28	£1.94	Lesnewth	£1.28	£1.94
Davidstow	£1.28	£1.94	Lewannick	£1.28	£1.94
Duloe	£1.28	£1.94	Lezant	£1.28	£1.94
Egloshayle	£1.28	£1.94	Linkinhorne	£1.28	£1.94
Egloskerry	£1.28	£1.94	Liskeard	£2.28	£3.12
Endellion	£1.28	£1.94	Little Petherwick	£1.28	£1.94
Falmouth	£4.41	£6.02	Lostwithiel	£1.28	£1.94
Feock	£1.28	£1.94	Ludgvan	£2.28	£3.12
Forrabury	£1.28	£1.94	Luxulyan	£1.28	£1.94
Fowey	£1.28	£1.94	Mabe	£1.28	£1.94
Germoe	£1.28	£1.94	Madron	£4.41	£6.02
Gerrans	£1.28	£1.94	Maker	£3.34	£4.68
Gorran	£1.28	£1.94	Manaccan	£1.28	£1.94
Grade	£1.28	£1.94	Marhamchurch	£1.28	£1.94
Gulval	£1.28	£1.94	Mawgan In Meneage	£1.28	£1.94
Gunwalloe	£1.28	£1.94	Mawgan in Pydar	£1.28	£1.94
Gwennap	£3.34	£4.68	Mawnan	£1.28	£1.94
Gwinear	£2.28	£3.12	Menheniot	£1.28	£1.94
Gwithian	£1.28	£1.94	Merther	£1.28	£1.94
Helland	£1.28	£1.94	Mevagissey	£2.28	£3.12
Helston	£2.28	£3.12	Michaelstow	£1.28	£1.94
Illogan	£3.34	£4.68	Minster	£1.28	£1.94
Isles of Scilly	£2.28	£3.12	Morvah	£1.28	£1.94
Jacobstow	£1.28	£1.94	Morval	£1.28	£1.94
Kea	£2.28	£3.12	Morwenstow	£1.28	£1.94
Kenwyn	£4.41	£6.02	Mullion	£1.28	£1.94
Kilkhampton	£1.28	£1.94	Mylor	£2.28	£3.12
Ladock	£1.28	£1.94	Newlyn East	£1.28	£1.94
Lamorran	£1.28	£1.94	North Hill	£1.28	£1.94
Landewednack	£1.28	£1.94	North Petherwin	£1.28	£1.94
Landrake	£1.28	£1.94	North Tamerton	£1.28	£1.94
Landulph	£1.28	£1.94	Otterham	£1.28	£1.94
Laneast	£1.28	£1.94	Padstow	£1.28	£1.94
Lanhydrock	£1.28	£1.94	Paul	£3.34	£4.48
Lanivet	£1.28	£1.94	Pelynt	£1.28	£1.94
Lanlivery	£1.28	£1.94	Perranarworthal	£1.28	£1.94
Lanreath	£1.28	£1.94	Perranuthnoe	£1.28	£1.94
Lansallos	£1.28	£1.94	Perranzabuloe	£2.28	£3.12
Lanteglos by Camelford	£1.28	£1.94	Phillack	£2.28	£3.12
Lanteglos by Fowey	£1.28	£1.94	Philleigh	£1.28	£1.94
Launcells	£1.28	£1.94	Pillaton	£1.28	£1.94
Launceston:			Poughill	£1.28	£1.94
St. Mary Magdalene	£2.28	£3.12	Poundstock	£1.28	£1.94
St. Thomas	£1.28	£1.94	Probus	£1.28	£1.94

Cornwall Family History Society (continued)

Quaker	£1.28	£1.94	St. Levan	£1.28	£1.94
Quethiock	£1.28	£1.94	St. Mabyn	£1.28	£1.94
Rame	£1.28	£1.94	St. Martin by Looe	£1.28	£1.94
Redruth	£4.41	£6.02	St. Martin in Meneage	£1.28	£1.94
Roche	£1.28	£1.94	St. Mellion	£1.28	£1.94
Ruan Lanihorne	£1.28	£1.94	St. Merryn	£1.28	£1.94
Ruan Major	£1.28	£1.94	St. Mewan	£1.28	£1.94
Ruan Minor	£1.28	£1.94	St. Michael Caerhayes	£1.28	£1.94
St. Agnes	£3.34	£4.68	St. Michael Penkevil	£1.28	£1.94
St. Allen	£1.28	£1.94	St. Minver	£1.28	£1.94
St. Anthony-in-Meneage	£1.28	£1.94	St. Neot	£1.28	£1.94
St. Anthony-in-Roseland	£1.28	£1.94	St. Pinnock	£1.28	£1.94
St. Austell	£3.34	£4.68	St. Sampson or Golant	£1.28	£1.94
St. Blazey	£2.28	£3.12	St. Stephen in Brannel	£2.28	£3.12
St. Breock	£1.28	£1.94	St. Stephen by Launceston	£1.28	£1.94
St. Breward	£1.28	£1.94	St. Stephens by Saltash	£2.28	£3.12
St. Buryan	£1.28	£1.94	St. Teath	£1.28	£1.94
St. Cleer	£1.28	£1.94	St. Tudy	£1.28	£1.94
St. Clement	£2.28	£3.12	St. Veep	£1.28	£1.94
St. Clether	£1.28	£1.94	St. Wenn	£1.28	£1.94
St. Columb Major	£2.28	£3.12	St. Winnow	£1.28	£1.94
St. Columb Minor	£1.28	£1.94	Sancreed	£1.28	£1.94
St. Day	£1.28	£1.94	Sennen	£1.28	£1.94
St. Dennis	£1.28	£1.94	Sheviock	£1.28	£1.94
St. Dominick	£1.28	£1.94	Sithney	£2.28	£3.12
St. Enoder	£1.28	£1.94	South Hill	£1.28	£1.94
St. Erme	£1.28	£1.94	South Petherwin	£1.28	£1.94
St. Erth	£1.28	£1.94	Stithians	£2.28	£3.12
St. Ervan	£1.28	£1.94	Stoke Climsland	£1.28	£1.94
St. Eval	£1.28	£1.94	Stratton	£1.28	£1.94
St. Ewe	£1.28	£1.94	Talland	£1.28	£1.94
St. Gennys	£1.28	£1.94	Tintagel	£1.28	£1.94
St. Germans	£1.28	£1.94	Towednack	£1.28	£1.94
St. Giles in the Heath	£1.28	£1.94	Tremaine	£1.28	£1.94
St. Gluvias	£3.34	£4.68	Treneglos	£1.28	£1.94
St. Hilary	£2.28	£3.12	Tresmeer	£1.28	£1.94
St. Issey	£1.28	£1.94	Trevalga	£1.28	£1.94
St. Ive	£1.28	£1.94	Trewen	£1.28	£1.94
St. Ives	£3.34	£4.68	Truro: St. Mary	£2.28	£3.12
St. John	£1.28	£1.94	Tywardreath	£1.28	£1.94
St. Juliot	£1.28	£1.94	Veryan	£1.28	£1.94
St. Just-in-Penwith	£3.34	£4.68	Virginstow	£1.28	£1.94
St. Just-in-Roseland	£1.28	£1.94	Warbstow	£1.28	£1.94
St. Keverne	£1.28	£1.94	Warleggan	£1.28	£1.94
St. Kew	£1.28	£1.94	Week: St. Mary	£1.28	£1.94
St. Keyne	£1.28	£1.94	Wendron	£3.34	£4.68

Cornwall Family History Society (continued)

Werrington	£1.28	£1.94	**Census Indexes**			
Whitstone	£1.28	£1.94	Trewen 1841	£1.28	£1.94
Withiel	£1.28	£1.94	Trewen 1861	£1.28	£1.94
Zennor	£1.28	£1.94	Trewen 1871	£1.28	£1.94
			Trewen 1891	£1.28	£1.94

1851 Census (Woodbine)

Each parish fully transcribed and printed in schedule order by Ray Woodbine. All information included and indexed by surname. Please order this particular census from Ray Woodbine, 5 Priory Close, Tywardreath, Par, Cornwall PL24 2PG. The numbers printed refer to volume and part number.

St. Austell 7-1; St. Blazey 6-3; Blisland 4-7; Boconnoc 3-5; Bodmin 4-8; Braddock 3-5; St. Breock 5-1; Callington 1-3; Calstock1-2; Cardinham 4-5; St. Cleer 2-1; Colan 5-4; St. Columb Major 5-3; St. Columb Minor 5-4; Crantock 5-5; Creed 8-3; Cubert 5-5; St. Dennis 7-2; St. Dominick 1-1; Duloe 3-1; Egloshayle 4-13; Endellion 4-11; St. Enoder 5-5; St. Ervan 5-2; St. Eval 5-2; St. Ewe 8-1; Fowey 6-1; Gorran 8-2; Grampound (see also Creed) 8-3; Helland 4-6; St. Issey 5-1; St. Ive 1-4; St. Kew 4-10; St. Keyne 2-3; Lanhydrock 4-9; Lanivet 4-9; Lanlivery 4-3; Lanreath 3-5; Lansallos 3-4; Lanteglos by Fowey 3-4; Linkinhorne1-4; Liskeard 2-3; Liskeard Borough 2-2; Little Petherick 5-1; WeSt. Looe (Talland) 3-3; Lostwithiel 4-2; Luxulyan 4-4; St. Mabyn 4-6; St. Martin by Looe 3-2; Mawgan in Pydar 5-3; Menheniot 2-1; St. Merryn 5-2; Mevagissey 8-1; St. Mewan 8-3; St. Michael Caerhays 8-2; St. Minver 4-12; Morval 3-2; St. Neot 2-3; Newlyn EaSt. 5-5; Padstow 5-2; Pelynt 3-1; St. Pinnock 2-3; Roche 7-2; St. Sampson (also known as Golant) 6-1; South Hill 1-3; St. Stephen in Brannel 8-2; Talland 3-3; Temple 4-5; St. Tudy 4-7; Tywardreath 6-2; St. Veep 3-5; Warleggan 4-5; St. Wenn 5-4; St. Winnow 4-1; Withiel 4-9.

Postage is as follows:
 Vol 1 pt. 1- £3.50, £4.00. pt 2 £5.00, £5.50. pt 3 £4.25, £4.75. pt 4 £4.25 £4.75.
 Vol 2 pt 1- £4.50, £5.00. pt 2 £4.50, £5.00. pt 3 £4.50, £5.00.
 Vol 3 pt 1- £4.25, £4.75. pt 2 £4.25, £4.75. pt 3 £4.25, £4.75. pt 4 £4.25, £4.75
 Pt 5 £4.25, £4.75.
 Vol 4 pt 1- £3.50, £4.00. pt 2 £3.50, £4.00. pt 3 £3.50, £4.00. pt 4 £3.50, £4.00
 Pt 5 £3.50, £4.00. pt 6 £3.50, £4.00. pt 7 £3.50, £4.00 pt 8 £5.00, £5.50
 Pt 9 £3.50, £4.00. pt 10 £3.50, £4.00. pt 11 £3.50, £4.00. pt 12 £3.50, £4.00. pt 13 £3.50, £4.00.
 Vol 5 pt 1- £4.25, £4.75. pt 2 £4.50, £5.00. pt 3 £4.50, £5.00. pt 4 £4.25, £4.75
 Pt 5 £5.00, £5.50.
 Vol 6 pt 1- £4.25, £4.75. pt 2 £4.25, £4.75. pt 3 £4.25, £4.75.
 Vol 7 pt 1 (a,b,&c) £8.75, £9.50. pt 2 £4.25, £4.75.
 Vol 8 pt 1- £4.25, £4.75. pt 2 £4.50, £5.00. pt 3 £3.50, £4.00.

The prices include p & p, UK and Overseas surface mail.

Cornwall Family History Society (continued)

1851 Census (N.Z. Society of Genealogists)
Advent 4; St. Agnes 18; St. Agnes (see also Isles of Scilly) 30; St. Allen 19; Altarnun 6; St. Anthony in Meneage 32; St. Anthony in Roseland 17; Antony 8; Botus Fleming Boyton 6; Breage 33; St. Breward (also known as Simonward) 4; Budock 22; St. Buryan 30; Camborne 37; St. Clement 19; St. Clether 4; Constantine 23; Cornelly 17; Crowan 33; Cuby with Tregony 17; Cury 32; Davidstow 4; St. Day 34; Egloskerry 6; St. Elwyn (see Hayle 38; St.Erme 19; St. Erth 24; Falmouth 22; Feock 21; St. Gennys 5; St.Germans 9; Germoe 33; Gerrans 17; St. Gluvias 23; Godolphin 33; Grade 32; Gulval 27; Gunwalloe 32; Gwennap 34; Gwinear 38; Gwithian 38; Helston 32; St. Hilary 26; Illogan 36; Isles of Scilly 30; St. Ives 25; Jacobstow 5; St. John 8; St. Juliot 4; St. JuSt. in Penwith 29; St. JuSt. in Roseland 17; Kea 21; Kenwyn 20; St. Keverne 32; Kilkhampton 5; Ladock 17; Lamorran 17; Landewednack 32; Landrake 9; Landulph 9; LaneaSt. 6; Lanteglos by Camelford 4; Launcells 5; Launceston: St. Mary Magdalene 7; St. Stephen by Launceston 6; Launceston St. Thomas 6 & 7; Lawhitton 7; Lelant 24; Lesnewth 4; St. Levan 30; Lewannick 6; Lezant 7; Ludgvan 24; Mabe 23; Madron 28; Maker 8; Manaccan 32; Marazion 26; Marhamchurch 5; St. Martin in Meneage 32; Mawgan in Meneage 32; Mawnan 23; St. Mellion 9; Merther 17; St. Michael Penkivel 17; St. Michaels Mount 26; Michaelstow 4; Minster 4; Morvah 29; Morwenstow 5; Mullion 32; Mylor 22; North Hill 7; North Petherwin 6; Otterham 4; Paul 27; Penryn 23; Penzance, St. Mary 28; Perranarworthal 22; Perranuthnoe 26; Perranzabuloe 18; Phillack 38; Philleigh 17; Pillaton 9; Porthleven 31; Poughill 5; Poundstock 5; Probus 17;Quethiock 9; Rame 8; Redruth 35; Ruan Lanihorne 17; Ruan Major 32; Ruan Minor 32; Saltash 9; Sancreed 29; Sennen 30; Sheviock 8; Sithney 31; South Petherwin 7; St. Stephens by Saltash 9; Stithians 34; Stoke Climsland 7; Stratton 5; St. Teath 4; Tintagel 4; Towednack 25; Tremaine 6; Treneglos 6; Tresmere 6; Trevalga 4; Trewen 6; Truro: St. Mary 19; Veryan 17; Warbstow 6; Week: St. Mary 5; Wendron 31;Werrington 6;Whitstone 5; Zennor 25.

1871 Census Index

	(a)	(b)			
Advent	£2.28	£3.12	St. Clement	£9.66	£12.36
St. Agnes	£9.66	£12.36	Colan	£2.28	£3.12
St. Allen	£3.34	£4.68	St. Colum Minor	£6.66	£9.36
Altarnun	£4.41	£6.02	Cornelly	£1.28	£1.94
St. Antony	£8.66	£11.36	Crantock	£2.28	£3.12
St. Anthony in Roseland	£1.28	£1.94	Creed	£2.28	£3.12
Blisland	£3.34	£4.68	Cuby with Tregony	£1.28	£1.94
Boconnoc	£2.28	£3.12	Cury	£3.34	£4.68
Botus Fleming	£2.28	£3.12	Davidstow	£2.28	£3.12
Boyton	£3.34	£4.68	St. Dennis	£4.41	£6.02
Braddock	£2.28	£3.12	St. Dominick	£3.34	£4.68
St. Breward	£3.34	£4.68	St. Enoder	£4.41	£6.02
Budock	£6.66	£9.36	St. Erme	£3.34	£4.68
St. Buryan	£4.41	£6.02	St. Ervan	£2.28	£3.12
Calstock	£9.66	£12.36	St. Eval	£2.28	£3.12
Camborne	£9.66	£12.36	Falmouth	£9.66	£12.36
Cardinham	£3.34	£4.68	Forrabury	£2.28	£3.12
			St. Gennys	£3.34	£4.68

Cornwall Family History Society (continued)

Gulval	£5.58	£7.56	Ruan Major		£1.28	£1.94
Gwennap	£9.66	£12.36	Ruan Minor		£2.28	£3.12
Gwithian	£3.34	£4.68	Saltash		£6.66	£9.36
Helland	£2.28	£3.12	South Hill		£3.34	£4.68
St. John	£2.28	£3.12	St. Stephens by Saltash		£4.41	£6.02
St. Juliot	£2.28	£3.12	Temple		£1.28	£1.94
St. JuSt. in Roseland	£4.41	£6.02	Towednack		£3.34	£4.68
St. Kew	£4.41	£6.02	Trewen		£1.28	£1.94
St. Keyne	£1.28	£1.94	Truro: St. Mary		£7.66	£10.36
Kilkhampton	£4.41	£6.02	St. Tudy		£3.34	£4.68
Ladock	£3.34	£4.68	St. Veep		£3.34	£4.68
Lamorran	£1.28	£1.94	St. Wenn		£3.34	£4.68
Landewednack	£3.34	£4.68	Zennor		£3.34	£4.68
Landrake	£3.34	£4.68				
Landulph	£3.34	£4.68	**1813-1837 Burial Index**			
Lanhydrock	£2.28	£3.12	Advent		£1.28	£1.94
Lanlivery	£4.41	£6.02	Altarnun		£2.28	£3.12
Lanreath	£3.34	£4.68	Antony		£4.41	£6.02
Lansallos	£3.34	£4.68	Blisland		£1.28	£1.94
Lanteglos by Fowey	£4.41	£6.02	Boconnoc		£1.28	£1.94
St. Stepehen by Launceston:	£3.34	£4.68	Bodmin		£4.41	£6.02
Lawhitton	£3.34	£4.68	Botus Fleming		£1.28	£1.94
Lesnewth	£1.28	£1.94	Boyton		£1.28	£1.94
St. Levan	£3.34	£4.68	Braddock		£1.28	£1.94
Lezant	£3.34	£4.68	Breage		£5.58	£7.56
Little Petherick	£2.28	£3.12	Budock		£3.34	£4.68
WeSt. Looe (Talland)	£3.34	£4.68	Callington		£2.28	£3.12
St.Mabyn	£3.34	£4.68	Calstock		£3.34	£4.68
Maker	£7.66	£10.36	Cardinham		£2.28	£3.12
Manaccan	£2.28	£3.12	Chacewater		£3.34	£4.68
Marazion	£4.41	£6.02	Colan		£1.28	£1.94
Mawgan in Pydar	£3.34	£4.68	Constantine		£3.34	£4.68
St. Mellion	£2.28	£3.12	Cornelly		£1.28	£1.94
Merther	£2.28	£3.12	Crantock		£1.28	£1.94
St. Mewan	£4.41	£6.02	Creed		£2.28	£3.12
St. Michael Penkivel	£2.28	£3.12	Crowan		£4.41	£6.02
St. Michaels Mount	£1.28	£1.94	Cubert		£1.28	£1.94
St. Minver	£4.41	£6.02	Cuby with Tregony		£3.34	£4.68
Morvah	£2.28	£3.12	Cury		£1.28	£1.94
Mylor	£6.66	£9.36	Davidstow		£1.28	£1.94
Perranarworthal	£5.58	£7.56	Duloe		£2.28	£3.12
Philleigh	£2.28	£3.12	Egloshayle		£2.28	£3.12
Pillaton	£2.28	£3.12	Egloskerry		£1.28	£1.94
Poughill	£2.28	£3.12	Gervans		£2.28	£3.12
Rame	£3.34	£4.68	Endellion		£2.28	£3.12
Ruan Lanihorne	£2.28	£3.12	Falmouth		£8.66	£11.36

Cornwall Family History Society (continued)

Parish			Parish		
Feock	£2.28	£3.12	Luxulyan	£2.28	£3.12
Forrabury	£1.28	£1.94	Mabe	£1.28	£1.94
Fowey	£3.34	£4.68	Madron	£3.34	£4.68
Germoe	£2.28	£3.12	Maker	£4.41	£6.02
Gerrans	£2.28	£3.12	Manaccan	£1.28	£1.94
Gorran	£2.28	£3.12	Marhamchurch	£2.28	£3.12
Grade	£1.28	£1.94	Mawgan in Meneage	£2.28	£3.12
Gulval	£3.34	£4.68	Mawgan in Pydar	£2.28	£3.12
Gunwalloe	£1.28	£1.94	Mawnan	£1.28	£1.94
Gwennap	£8.66	£11.36	Menheniot	£3.34	£4.68
Lamorran	£1.28	£1.94	Merther	£1.28	£1.94
Gwinear	£3.34	£4.68	Mevagissly	£3.34	£4.68
Gwithian	£1.28	£1.94	Michaelstow	£1.28	£1.94
Helston	£4.41	£6.02	Minster	£1.28	£1.94
Illogan	£6.66	£9.36	Morvah	£1.28	£1.94
Isles of Scilly	£3.34	£4.68	Morval	£2.28	£3.12
Jacobstow	£2.28	£3.12	Morwenstow	£2.28	£3.12
Kea	£3.34	£4.68	Mullion	£2.28	£3.12
Kenwyn	£5.58	£7.56	Mylor	£3.34	£4.68
Kilkhampton	£2.28	£3.12	Newly East	£2.28	£3.12
Ladock	£2.28	£3.12	North Hill	£2.28	£3.12
Lamorran	£1.28	£1.94	North Petherwin	£2.28	£3.12
Landewednack	£1.28	£1.94	North Tamerton	£1.28	£1.94
Landrake	£2.28	£3.12	Otterham	£1.28	£1.94
Landulph	£2.28	£3.12	Padstow	£3.34	£4.68
Laneast	£1.28	£1.94	Paul	£5.58	£7.56
Lanivet	£2.28	£3.12	Pelynt	£2.28	£3.12
Lanlivery	£2.28	£3.12	Penzance: St. Mary	£6.66	£9.36
Lanreath	£1.28	£1.94	Perranarworthal	£3.34	£4.68
Lansallos	£2.28	£3.12	Perranuthnoe	£2.28	£3.12
Lanteglos by Camelford	£2.28	£3.12	Perranzabuloe	£3.34	£4.68
Lanteglos by Fowey	£2.28	£3.12	Phillack	£1.28	£1.94
Launcells	£2.28	£3.12	Pillaton	£1.28	£1.94
Launceston:			Poughill	£1.28	£1.94
St. Mary Magdalene	£3.34	£4.68	Poundstock	£2.28	£3.12
St. Thomas	£1.28	£1.94	Philleigh	£1.28	£1.94
Lawhitton	£1.28	£1.94	Probus	£3.34	£4.48
Lelant	£3.34	£4.68	Quaker	£5.58	£7.56
Lesnewth	£1.28	£1.94	Quethiock	£2.28	£3.12
Lewannick	£2.28	£3.12	Redruth	£8.66	£11.36
Lezant	£2.28	£3.12	Roche	£3.34	£4.68
Linkinhorne	£2.28	£3.12	Ruan Lanihorne	£1.28	£1.94
Liskeard	£4.41	£6.02	Ruan Minor	£1.28	£1.94
Little Petherick	£1.28	£1.94	St. Agnes	£6.66	£9.36
Lostwithiel	£3.34	£4.68	St. Allen	£2.28	£3.12
Ludgvan	£3.34	£4.68	St. Anthony-in-Meneage	£1.28	£1.94

Cornwall Family History Society (continued)

St. Anthony-in-Roseland	£1.28	£1.94	St. Minver	£2.28	£3.12
St. Austell	£6.66	£9.36	St. Neot	£2.28	£3.12
St. Blazey	£3.34	£4.68	St. Pinnock	£1.28	£1.94
St. Breock	£2.28	£3.12	St. Sampson	£1.28	£1.94
St. Breward	£1.28	£1.94	St. Stephen in Brannel	£3.34	£4.68
St. Buryan	£3.34	£4.68	St. Stephens in Saltash	£4.41	£6.02
St. Cleer	£2.28	£3.12	St. Teath	£2.28	£3.12
St. Clement	£3.34	£4.68	St. Tudy	£1.28	£1.94
St. Clether	£1.28	£1.94	St. Veep	£2.28	£3.12
St. Columb Major	£3.34	£4.68	St. Wenn	£1.28	£1.94
St. Columb Minor	£2.28	£3.12	St. Winnow	£2.28	£3.12
St. Day	£1.28	£1.94	Saltash	£1.28	£1.94
St. Dennis	£2.28	£3.12	Sancreed	£2.28	£3.12
St. Dominick	£2.28	£3.12	Sennen	£1.28	£1.94
St. Enoder	£2.28	£3.12	Sheviock	£1.28	£1.94
St. Erme	£1.28	£1.94	Sithney	£3.34	£4.68
St. Erth	£3.34	£4.68	South Hill	£1.28	£1.94
St. Ervan	£1.28	£1.94	South Petherwin	£2.28	£3.12
St. Eval	£1.28	£1.94	Stithians	£4.41	£6.02
St. Ewe	£3.34	£4.68	Stoke Climsland	£3.34	£4.68
St. Gennys	£2.28	£3.12	Stratton	£2.28	£3.12
St. Germans	£3.34	£4.68	Talland	£3.34	£4.68
St. Giles in the Heath	£1.28	£1.94	Tintagel	£2.28	£3.12
St. Gluvias	£5.58	£7.56	Towednack	£2.28	£3.12
St. Hilary	£4.41	£6.02	Tremaine	£1.28	£1.94
St. Issey	£2.28	£3.12	Tresmere	£1.28	£1.94
St. Ive	£2.28	£3.12	Trevalga	£1.28	£1.94
St. Ives	£4.41	£6.02	Truen	£1.28	£1.94
St. John	£1.28	£1.94	Truro: St. Mary	£5.58	£7.56
St. Juliot	£1.28	£1.94	Tywardreath	£3.34	£4.68
St. JuSt. in Penwith	£5.58	£7.56	Veryan	£3.34	£4.68
St. JuSt. in Roseland	£3.34	£4.68	Virginstow	£1.28	£1.94
St. Keverne	£3.34	£4.68	Warleggan	£1.28	£1.94
St. Kew	£2.28	£3.12	Week: St. Mary	£2.28	£3.12
St. Keyne	£1.28	£1.94	Wendron	£4.41	£6.02
St. Stephen by Launceston	£2.28	£3.12	Werrington	£2.28	£3.12
St. Levan	£1.28	£1.94	Whitstone	£1.28	£1.94
St. Mabyn	£2.28	£3.12	Withiel	£1.28	£1.94
St. Martin by Looe	£2.28	£3.12	Zennor	£2.28	£3.12
St. Martin in Meneage	£1.28	£1.94	Burials in the period		
St. Mellion	£1.28	£1.94	1-15 July 1837	£1.28	£1.94
St. Merryn	£1.28	£1.94			
St. Mewan	£3.34	£4.68	**Monumental Inscriptions**		
St. Michael Caerhayes	£1.28	£1.94	Bal West: Methodist		
St. Michael Penkivel	£1.28	£1.94	(Germoe)	£1.28	£1.94
St. Michaels Mount	£1.28	£1.94	Blisland	£3.34	£4.68

Cornwall Family History Society (continued)

Boconnoc	£2.28	£3.12		Isles of Scilly Bryher	£1.28	£1.94
Bodmin; Methodist	£1.28	£1.94		St. Ives	£2.28	£3.12
Boyton:	£2.28	£3.12		St. Ives Barnoon Cem.	£9.66	£12.36
Breage	£5.58	£7.56		Kea	£5.58	£7.56
Budock	£6.66	£9.36		Kilkhampton	£5.58	£7.56
Calestock:				Landewednack	£3.34	£4.68
Methodist Perranzabuloe	£2.28	£3.12		Lanhydrock	£2.28	£3.12
Callington	£4.41	£6.02		Launceston-Dock Acre Ce.	£2.28	£3.12
Calstock: BaptiSt. Chapel	£1.28	£1.94		Lewannick	£3.34	£4.68
Carbis Bay	£1.28	£1.94		Liskeard Cemetery	£5.58	£7.56
Carnmenellis	£3.34	£4.68		Lostwithiel	£3.34	£4.68
Chacewater	£4.41	£6.02		Lostwithiel:		
Chynhale;				Castle Hill Cemetery	£3.34	£4.48
Methodists (Sithney)	£1.28	£1.94		Lost. Withiel:		
Come to Good:				Restormel Rd. Cemetery	£3.34	£4.68
Quaker (Kea)	£1.28	£1.94		Ludgvan	£6.66	£9.36
Connon:				Madron	£3.34	£4.68
Methodist (St.Pinnock)	£2.28	£3.12		Madron Cemetery	£4.41	£6.02
Crowlas:				Manacan	£2.28	£3.12
Methodist (Ludgvan)	£1.28	£1.94		Marazion	£2.28	£3.12
Crows-an-Wra:				Mawgan in Meneage	£4.41	£6.02
Methodist St. Bryan	£1.28	£1.94		Merther	£1.28	£1.94
Cubert	£2.28	£3.12		Mithian	£3.34	£4.68
Cubert: Methodist.	£2.28	£3.12		Morvah	£1.28	£1.94
Cury	£2.28	£3.12		Morval	£4.41	£6.02
Cury: Cemetery	£2.28	£3.12		Mullion	£2.28	£3.12
Delabole (St. Teath)	£3.34	£4.68		Mullion Cemetery	£3.34	£4.68
Devoran	£4.41	£6.02		Nancegollan:		
Duloe	£3.34	£4.68		Methodist. Crowan	£2.28	£3.12
Egloshayle	£2.28	£3.12		Newlyn	£1.28	£1.94
Edgcumbe:				North Tamerton	£3.34	£4.68
Methodist (Mabe)	£3.34	£4.68		Paul	£3.34	£4.68
Egloskerry	£3.34	£4.68		Paul: Cholera Cemetery	£2.28	£3.12
Escalls:				Paul: Sheffield Rd. Cem.	£9.66	£12.36
Bible Christian (Sennen)	£1.28	£1.94		Pendeen	£5.58	£7.56
Flushing	£1.28	£1.94		Penponds	£3.34	£4.46
Germoe	£2.28	£3.12		Pensilba (St. Cleer)	£3.34	£4.68
Gerrans	£4.41	£6.02		Penzance: Jewish Cem.	£1.28	£1.94
Godolphin	£3.34	£4.68		Penzance; St. John	£1.28	£1.94
Gunwalloe	£2.28	£3.12		Penzance: St. Mary	£3.34	£4.68
Gunwen:				Penzance; St. Paul	£1.28	£1.94
Methodist. (Luxulyan)	£1.28	£1.94		Perranarworthal	£4.41	£6.02
Gwennap	£5.58	£7.56		Perranuthnoe	£3.34	£4.68
Halsetown	£1.28	£1.94		Perranzabuloe	£7.66	£10.36
Hayle: (St. Elwyn)	£1.28	£1.94		Polyphant Methodist		
Helston	£3.34	£4.48		(Lewannick)	£1.28	£1.94

Cornwall Family History Society (continued)

Port Isaac	£1.28	£1.94
Porthleven	£8.66	£11.36
Port Catho Unt Ref. (Gerrans)	£1.28	£1.94
Probus	£4.41	£6.02
Redruth	£4.41	£6.02
Ruan Major	£1.28	£1.94
St. Allen	£2.28	£3.12
St. Allen Cemetery	£2.28	£3.12
St. Anthony-in-Meneage	£2.28	£3.12
St. Austell: Baptist	£1.28	£1.94
St. Buryan	£4.41	£6.02
St. Day	£5.58	£7.56
St. Gluvias	£9.66	£12.36
St. Just-in-Penwith	£3.34	£4.68
St. Just-in-Penwith Cemetery	£4.41	£6.02
St. Just-in-Penwith: Wesleyan	£5.58	£7.56
St. Levan	£2.28	£3.12
St. Martin in Meneage	£2.28	£3.12
St. Nectan; Chapel (St. Winnow)	£3.34	£4.48
St. Teath	£4.41	£6.02
St. Teath: Methodist	£1.28	£1.94
St. Veep	£3.34	£4.68
St. Winnow	£3.34	£4.68
Sennen	£3.34	£4.48
Sheviock	£3.34	£4.68
Sithney	£3.34	£4.68
South Petherwin: Methodist	£2.28	£3.12
Towednack	£2.28	£3.12
Townshend: Methodist (Crowan)	£3.34	£4.68
Tregadillet: Methodist (Launceston St.Thomas)	£1.28	£1.94
Tregerest: Methodist. (Sancreed)	£1.28	£1.94
Treleigh	£7.66	£10.36
Truro: St. John	£1.28	£1.94
Truro: Cemetery	£9.66	£12.36
Truro: St. George	£1.28	£1.94
Truro: St. Paul	£1.28	£1.94
Tywardreath	£4.41	£6.02
Tywardreath Cemetery	£3.34	£4.68
Week: St. Mary	£3.34	£4.68
Wendron	£4.41	£6.02
Zennor	£3.34	£4.68

Miscellaneous

500 year Calendar	£2.54	£3.73
Apprentices' Index	£4.41	£6.02
Index, Pigots 1830 Directory	£6.66	£9.36
Local Research Sources for Baptisms, Marriages & Burials with maps	£4.41	£6.02
Masters' Index	£4.41	£6.02
Pascoes Around the World	£5.58	£7.56
Principal Holdings for Family Historians	£1.34	£2.48
Some Sources for Historians of Cornish Families	£4.41	£6.02
Strays Index -1991	£4.41	£6.02
Strays Index -1992	£4.41	£6.02
Strays Index-1993	£5.58	£7.56
Strays Index -1994	£5.58	£7.56

CUMBRIA

Cumbria Family History Society
Web Site: http://www.genuki.org.uk/big/eng/CUL/cumbFHS
Mrs.M.M.Russell, Ulpha, 32, Granada Rd., Denton, Manchester M34 2LJ
Postage code: (a) U.K; (b) sea; (c) Air Canada & USA; (d) Air Australia & New Zealand

Census 1851

	(a)	(b)	(c)	(d)
Allithwaite, Cartmel Fell, Staveley, Broughton E. & Upper Holker	£4.00	£4.25	£5.00	£5.25
Dalton, Ireleth, Lindale, Rampside, New Barnes, N. Scales	£4.00	£4.25	£5.00	£5.25
Ulverston Pt.1, Mansrigg, Osmotherly (HO107/2274:Fol 369-492)	£4.00	£4.25	£5.00	£5.50
Appleby	£4.75	£5.25	£5.75	£5.85
Hugill, Kentmere, Over & Nether Staveley	£1.80	£2.10	£2.40	£2.50
Grasmere, Langdale, Rydal & Loughrigg	£1.60	£2.00	£2.30	£2.40.
Undermillbeck, Nth.& Sth.Crook	£1.80	£2.10	£2.40	£2.50
Killington, Middleton, Barbon & Casterton	£1.80	£2.10	£2.40	£2.50
Burton in Kendal, Holme & P.Patrick	£3.50	£3.90	£4.70	£4.80
Kendal Part 2	£4.00	£4.25	£5.00	£5.20
Helsington, Underbarrow, Levens, Crosthwaite & Lyth	£3.75	£4.00	£4.90	£5.00
Hutton Old & New, Mansergh, K.Lonsdale, Firbank, Lupton, Hutton Roof & Farleton	£3.75	£4.00	£4.90	£5.00
Orton, Newbiggin, Tebay, Raisbeck, Longdale & Asby	£3.75	£4.00	£4.90	£5.00
Ambleside, Troutbeck, & Applethwaite	£3.75	£4.00	£4.90	£5.00
Brougham, Lowther, Askham, Eamont Bridge, Stockbridge, Tirril & Patterdale	£3.75	£4.00	£4.90	£5.00
Fawcett Forest, Whitwell, Selside, Docker, Lambrigg, Skelsmergh & Strickland Kettle	£3.75	£4.00	£4.90	£5.00
Heversham, Milnthorpe, Beetham, Meathop & Witherslack etc.	£3.75 £4.00		£4.90	£5.00
Crosby Ravensworth, Maulds Meaburn, Shap, Bolton, Morland,Cliburn	£4.00	£4.25	£5.00	£5.10
Garsdale and Dent	£4.00	£4.25	£5,00	£5.10
Wasdale, Eskdale, Irton, Drigg, Muncaster & Waberthwaite	£2.70	£3.00	£3.50	£3.60
Cockermouth Part 2	£3.50	£3.90	£4.80	£4.90
Alston	£3.80	£4.10	£4.90	£5.00
Carlisle Part 1	£3.80	£4.10	£4.90	£5.00
Carlisle Part 2	£3.80	£4.10	£4.90	£5.00
Carlisle Part 3	£3.80	£4.10	£4.90	£5.00
Carlisle Part 4	£3.80	£4.10	£4.90	£5.00
Carlisle Part 5	£3.80	£4.10	£4.90	£5.00
Carlisle Part 6	£4.00	£4.25	£5.00	£5.10
Carlisle Part 7	£4.75	£5.25	£5.75	£5.85
Upperby, Harraby, pt of Botchergate	£3.50	£3.90	£4.80	£4.90

Cumbria Family History Society (continued)

Wetheral, Warwick, Scotby	£3.50	£3.90	£4.80	£4.90
Burtholm, Waterend, Kingwater, Askerton, Irthington, Laversdale, Newby, Newtown & Walton.	£4.00	£4.25	£5.00	£5.10
Longtown, Arthuret, Netherby, Moat, Kirkandrews Middle, Kirkandrews Nether (HO107/2428; Fols.122-262)	£4.00	£4.25	£5.00	£5,20
Wigton Part 1	£3.50	£3.90	£4.80	£4.90
Wigton Part 2	£3.50	£3.90	£4.80	£4.90
All Hallow, Bolton	£1.70	£2.00	£2.30	£2.40
Brocklebank, Rosley, Seberham & Westward	£2.70.	£3.00	£3.40	£3.50
Workington Part 1	£3.80	£4.10	£4.90	£5.00
Arlecdon, Frizington, Lamplugh, Ennerdale, Kinniside, Moresby & Parton	£4.00	£4.25	£5.00	£5.10
Whitehaven Part 1	£3.80	£4.10	£4.90	£5.00
Whitehaven Part 2	£3.80	£4.10	£4.90	£5.00
Whitehaven Part 3	£3.80	£4.10	£4.90	£5.00
Whitehaven Part 4	£3.50	£3.90	£4.80	£4.90
Holme Cultram, Holme St. Cuthbert & Holme Abbey	£4.75	£5.25	£5.75	£5.85
Harrington & Distington	£3.80	£4.10	£4.90	£5.00
Hensingham & Preston Qtr. Part 1	£3.80	£4.10	£4.90	£5.00
Preston Qtr.Part 2, Sandwith & St.Bees	£3.80	£4.10	£4.90	£5.00
Cleator & Egremont	£4.00	£4.25	£5.00	£5.10
Corney, Bootle, Whitbeck,Whicham, Millom & Ulpha	£3.80	£4.10	£4.90	£5.00
Penrith Leath Ward				
Part 1 (Index)	£3.80	£4.30	£4.80	£5.00
Part 2 (Index)	£3.00	£3.30	£3.90	£4.00
Part 3 (Index)	£3.30	£3.90	£4.30	£4.40
Part 4 (Index)	£3.30	£3.90	£4.30	£4.40

Cumbrians in Liverpool 1851 Census

Part 2	£2.90	£3.30	£3.80	£4.90
Part 3	£2.90	£3.30	£3.80	£4.90
Part 4	£3.20	£3.70	£4.20	£4.30
Colton, Blawith, Subberthwaite, Lowick & Egton cum Newland	£4.75	£5.25	£5.75	£5.85
Torver, Church & Monk Coniston, Hawkshead, Skelwith, Claife & Satterthwaite	£4.75	£5.25	£5.75	£5.85

Miscellaneous

Marriage Bonds (Diocese of Carlisle) Vol.1 (1668-1739)	£7.00	£8.00	£11.00	£12.00
Vol. 2 (1740-1752)	£7.00	£8.00	£11.00	£12.00
Index to the Place Names of Cumberland	£4.75	£5.25	£5.75	£5.85
Window Tax for North Westmorland 1777	£2.45	£2.65	£2.75	£2.85
Window Tax for South Westmorland 1777	£2.45	£2.65	£2.75	£2.85

Cumbria Family History Society (continued)

Monumental Inscriptions

Cleator & Haile	£2.20	£2.50	£3.00	£3.10
Burton in Kendal	£2.70	£3.00	£3.40	£3.50

Cheques made payable to Cumbria FHS please.

British Record Society

For details of publications relating to Cumbria published by the British Record Society see their entry on page 200.

Furness Family History Society

Web Site: http://members.aol.com/FurnessFHS/pw0.htm

Mrs M Bland, 5 Cherrytree Way, Barrow in Furness, Cumbria LA13 0LG

Combined Census Index / Transcriptions 1851-1891 for the following places
Blawith, Church Coniston South, Claife, Colton East, Colton West, Egton, Egton District, Finsthwaite, Haverthwaite, Hawkshead, Lowick North, Lowick South, Monk Coniston, Newland, Nibthwaite, Russland, Satterthwaite, Skelwith, Spark Bridge, Subberthwaite, Torver.

Genealogy Sources in Furness
(a)

Burial Index / Transcript	£2.50
Aldingham: St. Cuthbert & Barsea St. 1836-1996	£1.50
Dalton St. Mary 1837-1926	£2.50
Dendron: St. Matthew 1837-1995 & Pennington St. Michael 1837 1993	£1.50
Rampsgill: St. Michael 1877-1995	£1.50
Urswick: St. Mary & St. Michael 1813-1995	£1.50
Walney: St. Mary the Virgin 1856-1994	£2.50
Barrow Borough Cemetery ESt. Ch. 1873-1900	£4.50
Barrow Borough Cemetery Non Conf. Ch. 1873-1900	£1.50
Barrow Borough Cememetery R.C. Ch. 1873-1900	£1.50
Ulverston: St. Mary 1839-1950	£2.50
Ulverston: Holy Trinity 1835-1972	£1.50
Kirkby Ireleth: St. Cuthbert 1813-1997	£1.00
Askham with Ireleth St. Peter 1866-1997	apply

Memorial Inscriptions

War Memorials in Furness	£3.50
Furness Parish Map (laminated)	£1.50

(All above prices include local postage)

Further prices on application

DERBYSHIRE
Derbyshire Family History Society
Web Site: http://web.ukonline.co.uk/Members/gj/hadfield/dbyfhs.htm

Mrs L.I. Bull 17, Penrhyn Avenue Littleover Derby DE23 6LB
Please send payment with order in Sterling currency, preferably cheques made out to DFHS & allow three weeks for delivery. All prices include postage.

1851 Census Name Index

		(a)	(b)	(c)
Vol 2.1	Measham, Hartshorne, Ashby & Whitwick Sub Districts (Dbys.parts only)	£4.00	£4.50	£5.20
Vol 3.1	Bakewell Sub District incl. Edensor, Beeley, Chatsworth etc.	£5.50	£5.90	£6.95
Vol 3:2	Matlock Sub. District	£3.15	£3.45	£4.50
Vol 3.3	Tideswell	£4.55	£4.85	£5.90
Vol 4.1	Greasley & Ilkeston (Derbyshire parts only)	£5.40	£5.80	£6.80
Vol 5:3	Belper Sub District	£4.55	£4.75	£5.75
Vol 5.5	Alfreton Sub district (incl.Swanwick, Ironville Somercotes etc.	£4.60	£4.90	£5.90
Vol 6:1	Tutbury & Repton Sub Dist. (Derbys.parts only)	£3.00	£3.40	£4.15
Vol 6.2	Gresley & Burton (Derbyshire parts only)	£3.50	£3.75	£4.40
Vol 8.1	Ashover	£4.55	£4.85	£5.90
Vol 8.2	Chesterfield	£6.90	£7.45	£9.15
Vol 8.3	Bolsover & Dronfield Sub Districts of Chesterfield	£4.00	£4.50	£5.20
Vol 8:4	Eckington Sub District	£3.70	£3.90	£4.75
Vol 9:1	Derby: St. Alkmund	£5.15	£5.70	£7.60
Vol 9.2	Derby: St. Peter	£5.90	£6.35	£7.85
Vol 9.3	Derby: St. Werburgh	£5.00	£5.40	£6.30
Vol 10.1	Upper Hallam, Ecclehall, Beighton, Norton, Area of Rotherham sub-district	£3.00	£3.20	£3.90
Vol 11:1	Glossop Sub District	£5.30	£5.75	£7.65
Vol.11.2	Hayfield Sub-District	£4.00	£4.50	£5.20
Vol 12:1	Carburton, Pleasley, Blackwell Sub Dists	£3.40	£3.60	£4.60
Vol 14:4	Spondon Sub Districts	£2.40	£2.85	£3.35

Memorial Inscriptions

Vol 2	South Normanton	£4.65	£5.05	£6.60
Vol 3	Ockbrook	£2.95	£3.30	£4.30
Vol 4	Ashbourne St Oswald	£4.65	£5.05	£6.60
Vol 5	Elvaston & Weston-on-Trent	£3.10	£3.45	£4.35
Vol 6	Eckington & Handley	£3.10	£3.45	£4.35
Vol 7	Repton: St Wystans	£3.70	£4.05	£5.35

Derbyshire Family History Society (continued)

Miscellaneous

Derbyshire Strays 2	£2.40	£2.60	£3.70
Derbyshire Strays 3	£2.40	£2.60	£3.70
Derbyshire Strays 4	£2.80	£3.00	£3.70
Derbyshire Strays 5	£2.65	£2.85	£3.95
Derbyshire Strays 6	£3.10	£3.40	£4.50
Derbyshire Strays 7	£3.60	£3.95	£5.00
Derbyshire Strays 8	£3.65	£3.85	£4.90
The Free & Voluntary Present 1661	£3.55	£3.85	£4.80
Ripley & Pentrich Non Conformist Reg. Bapt. 1753-1805	£2.30	£2.50	£3.60
Overseers of Poor Vol 1: Tibshelf	£2.15	£2.30	£2.95
Employment of children in Mines and Manufactories DBY	£2.25	£2.45	£3.05
Dr Williams Library-Derbyshire Extracts	£2.05	£2.25	£2.85
Members Interests Book 1993	£3.30	£3.70	£5.20
Derbyshire Names in Miscellaneous Lists Vol. 1	£4.00	£4.25	£5.05
Derbyshire Names in Miscellaneous Lists Vol. 2	£3.45	£3.55	£4.20
D.F.H.S. Library Contents	£3.40	£3.70	£4.45

DEVON

Devon Family History Society

Web Site: http://www.devonfhs.org.uk/

Mrs J. Bennett, 334 St. Peters Rd., Mandon, Plymouth Devon PL5 3DR

	(a)	(b)	(c)	(EEC)
Burial Books (1813-1837)	£2.00	£3.00	£3.00	£2.50
Marriage Books (1813-1837)	£2.00	£3.00	£3.00	£2.50
Sherford Marriage Banns (1824-1929)	£2.00	£3.00	£3.00	£2.50
Occupations & Descriptions of Yesteryear Folk	£2.00	£3.00	£3.00	£2.50
Stoke Damerel Indexed Records in W.Devon R.O.	£2.00	£3.00	£3.00	£2.50
1851 Surname Indexes Nos.1-39 (price each)	£2.50	£3.00	£3.00	£3.00
Library Listing & Tree House Resources	£4.25	£5.25	£5.50	£4.50
Stoke Damerel Monumental Inscriptions Surname Index	£3.50	£4.50	£4.50	£4.00
Devon Extracts London Gazette				
North Devon Vol. 1 1665-1850	£12.00	£16.50	£17.50	£13.50
Plymouth Vol. 2 1665-1765	£7.50	£10.75	£11.50	£8.50
Of Chirche-Reves and of Testamentes (Barnstaple Consistory Courts 1579-1750)	£7.95	£9.00	£9.00	£8.45
An Introduction to Shopping through the ages	£1.75	£2.70	£2.75	£2.15

Obtain up-to-date list of places named for all books from the above address. Please make cheques out to the Devon Family History Society.

DORSET
Dorset Family History Society
Available from: Miss S. Lawrence, 179 Victoria Road, Ferndown, Dorset BH22 9HY
Please make all cheques out to Dorset Family History Society.

Dorset Parishes & Neighbouring Parishes (2nd edition)	U.K.£1.75		O/s £3.00	

Dorset 1891 Census Indexes

	(a)	(b)	(c)	(d)
Vol.1. Shaftesbury, Cann & Motcombe	£3.00	£3.25	£3.40	£4.10
Vol.2. Cranborne Area	£3.00	£3.25	£3.40	£4.10
Vol.3. Wimborne Area	£4.00	£4.25	£4.70	£5.85
Vol.4. Weymouth & Melcombe Regis	£4.00	£4.25	£4.70	£5.85
Vol.5. Fontmell & Gillingham	£4.00	£4.25	£4.70	£5.85
Vol.6. Stalbridge & Sturminster Newton	£4.00	£4.25	£4.70	£5.85
Vol.7. Portland & Abbotsbury	£4.00	£4.25	£4.70	£5.85
Vol.8. Lyme Regis & Neighbouring Parishes	£4.00	£4.25	£4.70	£5.85
Vol.9. Purbeck District	£4.00	£4.25	£4.70	£5.85
Vol.10. The Parishes around Weymouth (Wyke Regis & Upwey Reg. Sub Dists.)	£4.00	£4.25	£4.70	£5.85

Note:
Indexing of the 1891 Census of Dorset is a Joint Project with Somerset & Dorset FHS. Copies can also be obtained from Mrs Murial Monk, 65 Wyke Road, Weymouth, Dorset DT4 9QN

Monumental Inscriptions
Wareham United Reformed Church	£1.00	£2.00

The above publication is available from:
Mr M.Blakeston, 7 Miles Avenue, Sandford Woods, Wareham BH20 7AS

ESSEX (See also Greater London)
Essex Society for Family History
Web Site: http://midas.ac.uk/genuki/big/eng/ESS/efhs
R.E. Henrys, 56 The Paddocks, Ingatestone, Essex CM4 0BH

Most of the Societys publications are in microfiche form but up-to-date lists can be found on their website or by writing to the above address.

Monumental Inscriptions
	(a)	(b)
Finding Essex Monumental Inscriptions by Clayton Lewis	£2.00	£3.00

GREATER LONDON

East of London Family History Society
David Philby, 19 Cavendish Gardens, Ilford, Essex IG1 3EA

All Cheques/Postal orders/Bankers Draft payable to East of London FHS.UK deliveries, send the listed price as cheque or postal order. Australia, Canada, N.Z., send Sterling postal order. U.S.A. send Sterling or Dollar notes or Bankers Draft in sterling drawn on the banks London Branch. Please note this address is for the receipt of postal orders only and with no facilities for callers.

	(a)	(b)
A Guide to the Parish Registers of Newham	£3.30	£3.80

Parish Returns Series

		(a)	(b)
No.1	Hackney 1811	£3.30	£3.80
No.2	Hackney 1821 Part 1 Surnames A-K	£3.30	£3.80
No.2	Hackney 1821 Part 2 Surnames L-Z	£3.30	£3.80
No. 3	Poplar 1821	£3.30	£3.80

1851 Census Index Series

Vol. 1. Havering & Barking & Dagenham. HO107/1772
   (Giving surname, forename, age, birth code, & fol.nbr) A5 book form.
   Part 1. Hornchurch;
   Part 2. Havering & Romford;
   Part 3. Dagenham & Great Ilford ;
   Part 4. Barking.
Each part £3.30 UK p&p and £3.80 O/seas surface mail.

Vol. 2. Bethnal Green sub-district Town HO107/1542. Four parts, A-D, E-K, L-R, S-Z Priced as above.

Vol.3. Bethnal Green S.D. Church HO107/1541.
   4 parts (as Vol 2), prices as Vol. 1.

Vol.4. Bethnal Green S.D. Hackney Road HO107/1539.
   Four parts (as Vol 2), prices as Vol.1.

Vol.5. Bethnal Green S.D. HO107/1540.
   Four parts (as Vol 2), priced as Vol.1.

	U.K. price	O/seas
For any four parts of Vol.1-5, purchased together	£12.50	£14.00

Vol.6. St. George in the East (giving surname & folio nbr only)
   Part 1. St. Paul HO107/1548;
   Part 2. St. Mary HO107/1547;
   Part 3. St. John HO107/1549
Each part £3.30 UK p&p and £3.80 O/seas surface mail.

(All three parts ordered together)	£9.50	£11.00
Bethnal Green Enumeration Districts given in the 1851 census returns with Index of Streets	£1.75	£2.00

East of London Family History Society (continued)

Vol.7. Shoreditch (giving surname & fol.nbr only)
　　　Part 1. Hoywell & Moorfield HO107/1533,
　　　Part 2. St. Leonard HO107/1534;
　　　Part 3. Hoxton New Town HO107/1535;
　　　Part 4. Hoxton Old Town HO107/1536;
　　　Part 5. Haggerston West HO107/1537;
　　　Part 6. Haggerston East HO107/1538.
Each part £3.30 UK p&p and £3.80 O/seas surface mail.
(All six parts ordered together) £18.50 £20.00
Vol.8. Wanstead & Woodford HO107/1769 (giving surname
　　　forename, age birth & fol.nbr) £3.30 £3.80
Vol.9 Whitechapel sub-districts, Artillery & Spitalfields
　　　(giving surname, forename, age & fol. nbr)
　　　HO107/1543.
　　　Parts 1-3, A-F, G-M, N-Z. £3.30 £3.80
(All three parts ordered together) £9.50 £11.00
Vol.10 Whitechapel sub-district, Mile End New Town
　　　HO107/1544 (giving surname, forename, age & fol.nbr.)
　　　Parts 1-2, A-J, K-Z. £3.30 £3.80
　　　(Purchased together) £6.55 £7.55
Vol.11 Whitechapel sub-district, Church & North HO107/1545
　　　(giving surname, forename, age & fol.nbr.)
　　　Parts 1-3, A-F, G-M, N-Z £3.30 £3.80
　　　(Purchased together) £9.50 £11.00
Vol.12 Whitechapel sub-district, Goodman Field & Aldgate
　　　HO107/1546 (giving surname, forename, age & fol.nbr.)
　　　Parts 1-3 A-F, G-M, N-Z. £3.30 £3.80
　　　(Purchased together) £9.50 £11.00
All 11 parts of Vols. 9, 10, 11, and 12 purchased together £34.00 £40.00

1861 Census Index Series
Vol.1. Part 1. Havering Romford area RG9/1068, 1069 (part)
　　　and 1072. (giving surname, film nbr. & fol.nbr) £3.30 £3.80
Vol. 2. East Ham & Little Ilford RG9/1058 (details as above) £3.30 £3.80

1871 Census Index Series
(compiled by Clive Ayton)
Bethnal Green sub-district Green, Part 1. RG10/481-485
　　　(giving surname, piece nbr, fol nbr A5 book form) £4.90 £5.40
Bethnal Green sub-district Green Part 2 RG10/486-490
　　　(details as above) £4.90 £5.40
Shoreditch sub-district Haggerston West RG10/461-467
　　　(details as above) £4.90 £5.40
Poplar Part 1 RG10/580-584 (details as above) £4.90 £5.40

East of London Family History Society (continued)

1891 Census Index Series
Vol.1 Part 1, Bethnal Green sub-district East RG12/267
    (giving surname, forename & fol.nbr A5 book form)   £3.30   £3.80
Vol.1 Part 2, Bethnal Green sub-district East RG12/268
    (giving details as above)   £3.30   £3.80
1891 Census Index of Heads of Family. From the census project of
    Spitalfields, by the University of Leicester in association
    with the Jewish Historical Society. A5 book form   £3.30   £3.80

Hillingdon Family History Society

Web Site: http://gold.ac.uk/genuki/MDX/Hillingdon__FHS.txt
Gill May, 20 Moreland Drive, Gerrards Cross, Bucks SL9 8BB

Beginning Genealogy

Part 1. Why, What & Where?	£1.50	£1.75	£2.43
Part 2. Civil Registration	£1.25	£1.50	£2.18
Part 3. English & Welsh Census Returns 1841-1891	£1.25	£1.50	£2.18
Part 4. Wills & Administrations	£1.25	£1.50	£2.18
Part 5. Parish Registers	£1.25	£1.50	£2.18
Part 6. Parish Officers, Records & Surveys	£1.25	£1.50	£2.18
Part 7. Useful Civil Records	£1.25	£1.50	£2.18
Part 8. Military & Naval Records	£1.25	£1.50	£2.18
Part 9. Tudor & Stuart Sources	£1.25	£1.50	£2.18
Part 10. Writing & Presentation	£1.50	£1.75	£2.43
Part 11. Searching in London	£1.50	£1.75	£2.43
Part 12. Surnames & One-Name Studies	£1.25	£1.50	£2.18
Family History in Hillingdon, A Guide to Sources	£1.75	£2.00	£2.68

Please make all cheques out in sterling and to:- Hillingdon Family History Society.

Westminster & Central Middlesex Family History Society

Mr. G.A. Drewe, 6 Treve Avenue, HARROW, Middx., HA1 4AJ

Getting Around London Record Offices &
Repositories (map & guide) 2nd edition   £0.75

Information Leaflets
1. The area covered by the Society   £0.50
2. Parish records of Paddington   £1.75
3. School records of Paddington   £1.25
4. Census returns of Paddington   £1.25

Westminster and Central Middlesex Family History Society (continued)

Maps

Westminster Parish Boundaries (1900 & 1851 Census Districts, with list of Streets)	£1.75
Paddington Boundaries (before/after 1910 & Wards with list of 1851 Census Streets)	£0.75

Research Guides

Researching in Wembley - Doris Jones	£2.25
Researching in Willesden - Michael Fountain (Published by London & North Middlesex FHS)	£2.25
A Brief Parish Guide to St Anne, Soho	£1.50
A Brief Parish Guide to St George, Hanover Square 1998	£2.00

Postage & Packing Rates:

Order Value	UK	Overseas Surface	Overseas Air Mail
£4.00 or under	£0.50	£0.60	£1.10
£4.01-£7.99	£0.60	£0.80	£1.60
£8.00-£9.99	£0.80	£1.00	£2.00
£10.00 & over	£1.00	£2.00	£3.00

British Record Society

For details of publications relating to London published by the British Record Society see their entry on page 200.

HAMPSHIRE

Hampshire Genealogical Society

Web Site: http://www.hantsgensoc.demon.co.uk/

Jan & Alan Bridger, 50 Ernest Road, Portsmouth, Hants P01 5RB,

1851 Census Surname Index for Hampshire including the Isle of Wight.
Volumes 1 to 68 Hampshire 1851 Census
Books £3.00 each + postage; 40p UK, 60p sea mail, £1.40 air mail. For postal orders only members may deduct 10% from the price. (Membership number must be quoted for discount).

Volume
1. East Dean, East Wellow, Lockerley, Michelmersh, Mottisfont, Nursling, Sherfield English, Timsbury
2. Basingstoke, Nateley Scures, Newham, Upper Nateley, Upton Grey, Weston Corbett, Weston Patrick, Tunworth.

Hampshire Genealogical Society (continued)

3. Avington, Crawley, Easton, East Stratton, Headbourne Worthy, Itchen Abbas, Kingsworthy, Littleton, Martyr Worthy, Micheldever, Sparsholt, Stoke Charity, Wonston.
4. Abbotts Ann, Amport, Barton Stacey, Bullington, Chilbolton, Goodworth Clatford, Longparish, Upper Clatford. Wherwell.
5. Bramley, Church Oakley, Deane, Monk Sherborne, Pamber, Silchester. Wootton St Lawrence, Worting.
6. Andwell, Basing, Eastrop, Hartley, Wespall, Mapledurwell, Sherborne St John, Sherfield on Loddon, Stratfield Saye, Stratfield Turgis, Winslade
7. Bradley, Cliddesden, Dummer, Ellisfield. Farleigh Wallop, Herriard, North Waltham, Nutley. Preston Candover, Popham, Steventon, Woodmancott
8. Andover, Foxcott, Knights Enham, Monxton, Penton Grafton, Penton Mewsey.
9. Baughurst. Ecchinswell, Ewhurst, Hannington, Kingsclere, Sydmonton, Wolverton.
10. Ashmansworth, Burghclere, Crux Easton, East Woodhay, Highclere, Litchfield. Tadley, Woodcott.
11. Chilcomb, Compton, Morestead, Owlesbury, Twyford.
12. Bishopstoke, Farley Chamberlayne, Hursley, North Baddesley, Otterbourne.
13. Romsey Extra, Romsey Infra.
14. Botley, Bursledon, Chilworth, Hamble-le-Rice, Hound, North Stoneham, St Mary Extra.
15. Beauworth, Bishops Sutton, Bramdean, Cheriton, Hinton Ampner, Itchen Stoke, Kilmeston, Ovington, Ropley, Tichborne, West Tisted.
16. South Stoneham.
17. Ashe, Freefolk, Hurstbourne Priors, Laverstoke, Overton, Tufton, St Mary Bourne, Whitchurch.
18. Bedhampton, Farlington, Havant, Hayling North, Hayling South, Warblington.
19. Colemore, East Meon, Empshot, Froxfield, Greatham, Hawkley, Liss, Priors Dean, Privett, Sheet, Steep.
20. Alton, Bentworth. Chawton, East Tisted, Farringdon, Lasham, Medstead, Newton Valence, Shalden, Wield.
21. Bishops Waltham, Durley, Exton, Meonstoke, Upham, West Meon, Warnford.
22. Bighton, Brown & Chilton Candover, Nether & Over Wallop, New & Old Alresford, Northington, Swarraton, Plaitford, West Wellow.
23. Beech Hill, Crondall,. Dogrmersfield, Odiham, Stratfield Mortimer.
24. Bentley, Binsted, East Worldham, Froyle, Hartley Mauditt, Holyborne, Neatham, Selborne, West Worldham.
25. Blendworth, Buriton. Catherington, Chalton, Clanfield, Idsworth, Petersfield, Waterlooville.
26. Corhampton, Droxford, Hambledon, Soberton.
27. Beaulieu, Bramshaw, Dibden, Exbury, Lyndhurst, Minstead, Normansland.
28. Holdenhurst, Ringwood. Sopley.
29. Millbrook.
30. Ashley, Bossington, Broughton, East Buckholt, East Tytherley, Frenchmoor, Houghton, Kings Somborne, Leckford, Little Somborne, Longstoke, Stockbridge, West Dean, West Tytherley.
31. Boarhunt, Fareham, Porchester, Rowner.
32. Southwick, Tichfield, Wickham, Widley, Wymering.
33. Eling, Fawley.

Hampshire Genealogical Society (continued)
34. Elvetham, Eversley, Greywell, Hartley Wintney, South Warnborough, Winchfield.
35. Alverstoke Vol. 1
36. Alverstoke Vol. 2
37. Alverstoke Vol. 3
38. Burley, Christchurch, Ellingham, Harbridge, Ibsley.
39. Winchester Vol. 1
40. Winchester Vol. 2
41. Winchester Vol. 3
42. Appleshaw, Chute, Faccombe, Fifield, Hurstbourne Tarrant, Grateley, Linkenholt, Ludgershall, Kimpton, Quarley, Redenham, Shipton Bellinger, Tangley, Thruxton, Tidworth, Vernham Dean.
43-51. Portsea Island if sold as book set (including index) £23.00 including UK postage (overseas + £5.00)
52. Breamore, Damerham, Damerham South, Fordingbridge, Godshill, Hale, Martin, New Ground, North Charford, Rockbourne. South Charford, Tidfit, Toyd (Extra Parochial), Tything of East Martin, Whitsbury, Woodgreen.
60. Lymington, Milford.
61. Boldre, Brockenhurst. Hordle, Milton.
62. Southampton-A-DeGage
63. DeGee-Keeves
64. Keinway-Renne
65. Rennie-Z
66. Index (free)
67. Aldershot Cove, Coombe, Farnborough, Hawley, Long Sutton, Newtown. Yateley
68. Bramshott, Dockenfield, Headley, Kingsley.

Isle of Wight 1851 Census
53. Northwood, Whippingham.
54. Binstead. Ryde.
55. Adgestone (with Horton and Yarbridge), Alverstone, Bembridge, Brading, Lake, Nettlestone, Newchurch, Oakfield, Sandown, Sea View, Shanklin, St Helena, Yaverland.
56. Arreton, Carisbrook. Gatcombe, Wootton.
57. House of Industry, Newport, Parkhurst Prison and Barracks, St Nicholas.
58. Bonchurch, Brighstone. Brixton, Brook, Freshwater, St. Lawrence, Newchurch, Whitwell.
59. Calborne, Chale, Godshill, Kingston, Mottistone, Niton, Shalfleet, Shorwell, South Chale, Thorley, Yarmouth.

1891 Census Surname Index for Hampshire completed to date
Books £3.50 each + postage; 40p UK, 60p sea mail, £1.40 air mail.
Vols. 1 to 4 Covers Portsea Island
Vol. 1 Portsea Town:
    Part 1.A to D,
    Part 2 .E to K,
    Part 3. L to R,
    Part 4. S to Z

Hampshire Genealogical Society (continued)
Vol. 2 Portsmouth Town
   Part 1. A to J,
   Part 2. K to Z
Vol. 3 Kingston:
   Part 1 .A;
   Part 2. B;
   Part 3 .C;
   Part 4. D to E.
   Part 5. F to G,
   Part 6. H.
   Part 7. I to L,
   Part 8. M to O,
   Part 9. P to R,
   Part. 10 S,
   Part 11.T to V.
   Part 12. W to Z.
Vol. 4 Landport
   Part 1 -- to Behr.
   Part 2 Beirnstein to Burroughs,   Part 3 Burrows to Cooley,
   Part 4 Coombe to Dumper.   Part 5 Dunbar to Gatrall.
   Part 6 Gatteral to Hartt,   Part 7 Harvey to Hursley.
   Part 8 Hurst to Lanksford,   Part 9 Lanning to McDougall
   Part 10 McDow to Ollis.   Part 11 Olliver to Quew,
   Part 12 Quick to Shorland,   Part 13 Short to Tawsey,
   Part 14 Tayler to Welles.   Part 15 Welling to Zuhlcke
Vol. 5 Havant & Hayling: Bedhampton, Brockhampton, Durrants, East Leigh. Emsworth, Farlington, Havant, Homewell, Langstone, North Hayling, Purbrook, Redhill, Stoke, Stokes, South Hayling.Warblington. Waterloo, West Leigh
   Part 1 A to K,   Part 2 J toZ
Vol. 6 Alverstoke: Alverstoke, Anglesey, Anns Hill, Bridgemary, Brockhurst, Bury, Elson, Ewer Common, Forton, Hardway & Burrow Island or Rat Island, Leesland, Stoke Road.
   Part 1 Abbatt to Coonan,   Part 2 Cooper to Harries.
   Part 3 Harrington to Milledge.   Part 4 Miller to Sizer,
   Part 5 Skeats to Youngman
Vol. 7 Fareham & Titchfield: Boarhunt, Cosham, Crofton, Fareham, Great Horsea Island, Hilsea, Hook, Lee on Solent. Little Horsea Island, Portchester, Rowner, Sarisbury, Southwick. Swanwick, Tichfield, Wallington, Warsash, Widley, Wickham, Wymering.
   Part 1 A to Didymus,   Part 2 Dieper to Keller,
   Part 3 Kellow to Robertson,   Part 4 Robins to Young
Vol. 11 Lymington: Ashley, Barton, Bashley, Boldre, Brockenhurst, Buckland, Everton, Hordle, Keyhaven, Lymington, Milford, Milton, Norley Wood, Pennington, Pilley Street. Rhinefield, Sway, Tiptoe, Walhampton.
   Part 1--to G,   Part 2 H to P,
   Part 3 R to Z

56

Hampshire Genealogical Society (continued)

Vol. 13 Ringwood & Fordingbridge: Ashley Walk, Bicton, Blashford, Breamore, Broomy, Burley, Ellingham, Fordingbridge, Frogham, Godshill, Hale, Harbridge, Hunton, Hyde, Ibsley, Kingston, North Charford, North Gorley, Poulner, Ringwood,Rockbourne, South Charford, South Damerham, Stuckton, Toyd Farm with Allenford (Wil), Upper Street, Whirsbury (Wil),Woodgreen.
Part 1 Abbott to Guy,   Part 2 Habgood to Rytes,
Part 3 Sainsbury to Zebedee

Special Army Volume (Portsea Island Only)   Apply for price.

Miscellaneous

The Cemeteries of Hampshire: Their History and Records	£3.90	£4.10	£4.90
A Guide to Genealogical Sources for Hampshire	£3.90	£4.10	£4.90
Dogmersfield 1841 to 1891 Census Index	£3.90	£4.10	£4.90

HERTFORDSHIRE

Hertfordshire Family & Population History Society

Book Sales, 56 Dalkeith Road, Harpenden, Hertfordshire AL5 5PW

Miscellaneous

		(a)	(b)	(c)
Transported Beyond the Seas		£8.80	£9.40	£11.50
Vol. 2	Directory of Members Interests	£1.21	£1.40	£2.10
Vol. 3	Directory of Members Interests	£1.46	£1.65	£ 2.35
Vol. 4	Directory of Members Interests	£1.96	£2.15	£2.85
Vol. 5	Directory of Members Interests	£1.96	£2.15	£2.85
Vol. 2	Hertfordshire Strays: Out of Area & Late Baptisms	£3.28	£3.60	£4.30
Vol. 3	Hertfordshire Strays: Out of Area & Late Baptisms	£3.41	£3.60	£4.30
Vol. 4	Hertfordshire Strays: Out of Area & Late Baptisms	£3.41	£3.60	£4.30
Vol. 5	Hertfordshire Strays: Out of Area & Late Baptisms	£3.41	£3.60	£4.30
Vol. 6	Hertfordshire Strays: Out of Area Marriages	£3.41	£3.60	£4.30

Militia Lists

2	Sandridge Ayot St Peter & Ayot St Lawrence	£2.78	£3.10	£3.80
3	St Albans-St Peters Ward	£3.21	£3.40	£4.10
4	St Albans-Holywell Ward	£3.21	£3.40	£4.10
5	Offley	£2.35	£2.65	£3.35
6	Lilley & Hexton	£2.46	£2.65	£3.35
7	Pirton & Ickleford	£2.71	£2.90	£3.60
8	Stevenage	£3.53	£3.85	£4.55
9	Great Amwell	£3.21	£3.40	£4.10
10	Little Amwell & St Margarets	£3.21	£3.40	£4.10
11	Knebworth & Shephall	£2.46	£2.65	£3.35
12	Harpenden	£3.53	£3.85	£4.55
13	Watford (1) A-E	£3.41	£3.60	£4.30

Hertfordshire Family & Population History Society (continued)

14	St Albans-Sleap & Smallford	£2.96	£3.15	£3.85
15	Watford (2) F-0	£3.41	£3.60	£4.30
16	Layston	£2.96	£3.15	£3.85
17	Watford (3) P-Z	£2.96	£3.15	£3.85
18	St Albans Windridge Ward St Stephens	£2.96	£3.15	£3.85
19	Wyddial Anstey Meesden & Throcking	£2.96	£3.15	£3.85
20	Kings Walden	£2.46	£2.65	£3.35
21	Caldecote Newnham Radwell & Hinxworth	£2.71	£2.90	£3.60
22	Letchworth Norton & Willian	£2.71	£2.90	£3.60
23	Codicote	£2.71	£2.90	£3.60
24	Bramfield Sacomb & Stapleford	£3.21	£3.40	£4.10
25	Ware (1) A-C	£3.41	£3.60	£4.30
26	Ware (2) D-I	£3.41	£3.60	£4.30
27	Ware (3) J-R	£3.41	£3.60	£4.30
28	Ware (4) S-Z	£3.41	£3.60	£4.30
29	Braughing	£4.03	£4.35	£5.05
30	Graveley & the Wymondleys	£3.21	£3.40	£4.10
31	Great & Little Hormead	£2.71	£2.90	£3.60
32	Brent Furneux & Stocking Pelham	£3.41	£3.60	£4.30
33	Hertingfordbury	£3.41	£3.60	£4.30
34	St Pauls Walden & Stagenhoe	£3.21	£3.40	£4.10
35	Aspenden	£2.46	£2.65	£3.35
36	Reed & Buckland	£2.46	£2.65	£3.35
37	Bygrave Clothall & Wallington	£2.96	£3.15	£3.85
38	Westmill & Wakeley Hamlet	£2.46	£2.65	£3.35
39	Datchworth	£2.10	£2.40	£3.10
40	Barley	£2.46	£2.65	£3.35
41	Bushey	£3.21	£3.40	£4.10
42	Baldock	£3.46	£3.65	£4.35
43	Hitchin (1) A-E	£3.71	£3.90	£4.60
44	Hitchin (2) F-O	£3.71	£3.90	£4.60
45	Hitchin (3) P-Z	£3.71	£3.90	£4.60
46	Ardeley & Cottered	£3.41	£3.60	£4.30
47	St Albans-Middle Ward	£3.41	£3.60	£4.30
48	Ashwell	£3.21	£3.40	£4.10
49	St Albans-Fishpool Ward	£3.21	£3.40	£4.10
50	Weston	£2.96	£3.15	£3.85
51	Kelshall & Therfield	£3.71	£3.90	£4.60
52	St Albans-St Michaels Ward	£3.21	£3.40	£4.10
53	Hertford (1) A-F	£3.48	£3.80	£4.50
54	Hertford (2) G-O	£3.41	£3.60	£4.30
55	Hertford (3) P-Y	£3.48	£3.80	£4.50
56	Digswell & Tewin	£3.21	£3.40	£4.10
57	Rushden & Sandon incl. Broadfield	£3.21	£3.40	£4.10
58	Bayford & Little Berkhampstead	£3.28	£3.60	£4.30
59	Aston & Walkern	£3.21	£3.40	£4.10

Hertfordshire Family & Population History Society (continued)

60	Barkway & Nuthampstead	£3.21	£3.40	£4.10
61	Great Berkhamstead & Frithsden	£4.48	£4.80	£5.70
62	Flaunden & Sarratt	£2.46	£2.65	£3.35
63	Ippollitts	£2.35	£2.65	£3.35
64	Welwyn	£3.41	£3.60	£4.30
65	Bishops Stortford (1) A- J	£4.48	£4.80	£5.50
66	Bishops Stortford (2) K-Y	£4.48	£4.80	£5.70
67	St Albans St Stephens Park Ward	£3.21	£3.40	£4.10
68	Wheathampstead	£3.71	£3.90	£4.60
69	Great & Little Munden	£3.21	£3.40	£4.10
70	Hoddesdon	£5.03	£5.35	£6.40
71	Kimpton	£2.46	£2.65	£3.35
72	Much Hadham	£4.28	£4.60	£5.50
73	Benington & Watton at Stone	£3.71	£3.90	£4.60
74	Aldbury	£2.46	£2.65	£3.35
75	Thorley	£2.46	£2.65	£3.35
76	Little Hadham	£2.71	£2.90	£3.60
77	Broxbourne & Wormley	£3.71	£3.90	£4.60
78	Standon (1) A-H	£3.71	£3.90	£4.60
79	Standon (2) I-Y	£3.71	£3.90	£4.60
80	Eastwick, Gilston & Widford	£3.71	£3.90	£4.60
81	Sawbridgeworth (1) A-H	£3.21	£3.40	£4.10
82	Sawbridgeworth (2) J-Z	£3.71	£3.90	£4.60
83	Thundridge	£2.96	£3.15	£3.90
84	Bengeo	£3.21	£3.40	£4.10
85	Hunsdon	£3.21	£3.40	£4.10
86	Ridge & Tyttenhanger	£3.21	£3.40	£4.10

Monumental Inscriptions

3	Bovingdon	£1.71	£1.90	£2.60
4	Shephall St Mary	£1.10	£1.40	£2.10
6	Datchworth	£1.46	£1.65	£2.35
7	Ashwell	£1.46	£1.65	£2.35
9	Bramfield, Stapleford & Waterford	£2.46	£2.65	£3.25
10	London Colney St Peter	£1.46	£1.65	£2.35
12	Digswell	£1.71	£1.90	£2.60
13	Letchworth St Mary & Willian All Saints	£1.96	£2.15	£2.85
14	Knebworth St Mary also St Martin	£2.21	£2.40	£3.10
15	Stanstead Abbotts & Stanstead St Margarets	£2.78	£3.10	£4.00
16	Great Amwell	£2.46	£2.65	£3.35
18	Hemel Hempstead St Mary	£2.71	£2.90	£3.60
19	Harpenden St Nicholas	£3.41	£3.60	£4.30
20	St Pauls Walden	£2.46	£2.65	£3.35
21	Tewin	£2.46	£2.65	£3.35
22	Graveley & Great & Little Wymondley	£3.21	£3.40	£4.10
23	Apsley St Marys	£2.10	£2.40	£3.10

Hertfordshire Family & Population History Society (continued)

24	Great Gaddesden St John the Baptist	£2.46	£2.65	£3.35
25	Flamstead St Leonard	£3.41	£3.60	£4.30
26	Sawbridgeworth Great St Marys	£2.96	£3.15	£3.85
27	Aston	£2.46	£2.65	£3.35
28	Gilston St Mary & Eastwick St. Botolph	£2.46	£2.65	£3.35
29	Great Munden St Nicholas	£1.85	£2.15	£2.85
30	Hertingfordbury St Mary	£2.96	£3.15	£3.85
31	Watton at Stone St Andrew & St Mary	£2.71	£2.90	£3.60
32	Boxmoor St John	£1.60	£1.90	£2.60
33	Non-Conformists Burial Grounds in Dacorum	£1.60	£1.90	£2.60
34	Sandridge St Leonard	£2.96	£3.15	£3.85
35	Codicote St Giles	£3.41	£3.60	£4.30
36	Walkern	£2.71	£2.90	£3.60
37	Frogmore	£3.21	£3.40	£4.10
38	Weston	£2.21	£2.40	£3.10
39	Abbots Langley St Lawrence	£3.48	£3.80	£4.50
40	Pirton St Mary	£2.46	£2.65	£3.35
41	Ridge St Margarets	£2.96	£3.15	£3.85
42	Hinxworth Newham Caldecote & Radwell	£2.71	£2.90	£3.60
43	Leverstock Green Holy Trinity	£2.96	£3.15	£3.85
44	Norton & Bygrave	£2.71	£2.90	£3.60
45	Little Munden All Saints	£2.96	£3.15	£3.85
46	Benington St Peter	£2.71	£2.90	£3.60
47	Hitchin Tilehouse Street Baptist Church	£2.71	£2.90	£3.60
48	Colney Heath St Marks	£3.41	£3.60	£4.30
49	Little Gaddesden St Peter & St Paul	£3.46	£3.65	£4.35
50	Redbourn St Marys	£3.46	£3.65	£4.35
51	Baldock	£3.46	£3.65	£4.35
52	Wheathampstead St Helens & United Reformed Church	£4.48	£4.80	£5.50
53	Radlett Christ Church	£4.03	£4.35	£5.05
55	Hunsdon St Dunstan & Widford St John the Baptist	£3.71	£3.90	£4.60
56	St Albans St Stephens	£3.71	£3.90	£4.60
57	Kings Langley All Saints	£3.71	£3.90	£4.60
58	Bourne End St John the Evangelist	£2.71	£2.90	£3.60
59	Sunnyside (Berkhampstead)	£2.71	£2.90	£3.60
60	Northaw	£3.71	£3.90	£4.60
61	St Albans St Michaels & Childwick Green St Marys	£2.96	£3.15	£3.85
62	Potten End Holy Trinity & Nettleden St Lawrence	£2.96	£3.15	£3.85
63	Sarratt Holy Cross	£3.21	£3.40	£4.10

Royston & District Family History Society

Mrs. D. Oakman, 34 Whitecroft Road, Meldreth, Royston, Herts SG8 6LR

Monumental Inscriptions	U.K.	O/s
Barkway Church	£3.60	£3.80
Buckland Church	£3.10	£3.30
Reed Church	£3.10	£3.30
Barley Church	£3.60	£3.80
Royston Church	£3.10	£3.30
Royston Additional Burial Ground	£6.95	£7.20
Melbourn Road Cemetery, Royston	£4.20	£4.40
United Reformed Church, Melbourn	£3.10	£3.30
Redhill United Reformed Church, Rushen	£2.00	£2.20

Miscellaneous

Index of Births, Marriages & Deaths from 'The Royston Crow	(U.K.)	(O/s)
1876-1886	£5.00	£5.50
1887-1899	£5.60	£6.00

ISLE OF MAN

Isle of Man Family History Society

David Christian, Treasurer, 3 Minorca Hill, Laxey, Isle Of Man IM4 7DN, British Isles Via U.K. Tel. 01624 862088

Ordering Information
Please note that postage and packing are extra; unless stated do not send payment with order unless p&p. is quoted you will be invoiced for the order later

I.O.M. - U.K. & Sterling Payment orders to above address.

Or To: Area Representatives -

Australian Orders to:
David W. Paterson, 2 Verdant Court, Wynn Vale, So. Australia 5127. (Tel. 08-8251-1558)
Email Address: patodw@tne.net.au

Canadian Orders to:
James B. Phillips, 3073 Donald Street, Victoria, B.C. V9A 1Y1 (Tel. 250-360-2823)
Email Address: jbphilli@iname.com

New Zealand Orders to:
Phil Skelley, 15 Edgewater Grove, Orewa 1461 New Zealand (Tel. 09-426-7450)

U.S.A. Orders to:
Shirley C. Hogensen, 2352 West 4600 South, Roy, UT 84067-1848 (Tel. 801-825-6391) Email Address: schogen@popd.ix.netcom.com

Isle of Man Family History Society (continued)
Burial Registers
Please note: For early Douglas Burials refer to Braddan or St Georges Burial Registers

			(Price)
Andreas Parish	1800-1849	(To be revised)	£3.00
Arbory Parish	1729-1988		£ 7.30
Ballaugh Parish	1595-1986		£ 8.50
Braddan Parish-Book 1,	1624-1699 & 1700- 1799		£ 8.50
Braddan Parish-Book 2,	1800-1849		£10.90
Braddan Parish-Book 3,	1849-1981	A-C	£11.50
Braddan Parish-Book 4,	1849-1981	D-L	£11.20
Braddan Parish-Book 5,	1849-1981	M-Z	£10.60
Douglas Borough Cemetery	1899-1989	A-J	£11.00
Douglas Borough Cemetery	1899-1989	K-Z	£10.20
Douglas St Georges Church	1790-1994		£ 4.60
German Parish-Book 1,	1665-1865		£ 9.90
German Parish-Book 2,	1866-1979		£ 9.60
Jurby Parish	1606-1989		£ 6.00
Lonan Parish	1718-1996		£10.60
Malew Parish-Book 1,	1649-1989	A-Cav	£11.80
Malew Parish-Book 2,	1649-1989	Cha-Cut	£12.20
Malew Parish-Book 3,	1649-1989	D-Ju	£11.00
Malew Parish-Book 4,	1649-1989	K-Miz	£11.40
Malew Parish-Book 5,	1649-1989	Moa-Ry	£11.60
Malew Parish-Book 6,	1649-1989	S-You	£10.20
Maughold Parish	1642-1849		£7.80
Maughold Parish	1849-1950	(In four sections)	£ 9.50
Michael Parish	1610-1981		£8.80
Patrick Parish	1714-1986		£11.50
Patrick Parish, St Pauls	1882-1995		£2.60
Church, Foxdale	1882-1995		£2.60
Rushen Parish	1712-1968		£14.40
Santan Parish	1656-1985		£ 4.40

Census

Andreas	1851	£7.00	1881	£5.40
Arbory	1851	£3.50	1881	£4.90
Ballaugh	1851	£4.80	1881	£4.40
Braddan	1851	£7.50	1881	£6.60
Bride	1851	£4.30	1881	£3.30
Bride	1861	£3.80	1871	£3.70
Douglas Town	1851	£13.10		
Douglas Town Index A-J	1881	£10.20		
Douglas Town Index K-Z	1881	£9.20		
District 1 To 8	1881	£12.30		
District 9 to 19	1881	£13.30		
German	1851	£4.40	1881	£5.60

Isle of Man Family History Society (continued)

Jurby	1851	£4.00	1881	£3.40
Lezayre	1851	£7.40	1881	£5.70
Lonan	1851	£8.40	1881	£8.30
Malew & Castletown	1851	£9.20	1881	£13.80
Marown	1851	£5.00	1881	£4.10
Maughold	1851	£5.80	1881	£4.10
Michael	1851	£3.10	1881	£4.80
Onchan	1851	£10.50	1881	£5.70
Patrick	1851	£9.10	1881	£7.70
Peel Town	1851	£4.00	1881	£11.20
Ramsey Town	1851	£8.30	1881	£11.60
Rushen	1851	£5.10	1881	£9.20
Santan	1851	£3.60	1881	£3.10
Santan	1861	£3.60	1871	£3.00
Manx Fishing Fleets	1871&1881	£12.80		

Monumental Inscriptions
PLEASE NOTE: For early Douglas MIs refer to Braddan, St Georges or Onchan MIs

	(Price)
Andreas: Old Yard, with Index	£8.50
Andreas: East & West Yards, with Indexes	£9.40
Andreas: St Judes	£2.40
Arbory: All Yards, with Index	£13.50
Ballaugh: Old & New Yards, with Indexes	£12.70
Braddan: Old Yard, North Side with Index	£6.40
Braddan: Old Yard, South Side with Index	£7.00
Braddan New: Index A-J for all Sections	£10.00
Braddan New: Index K-Z for all Sections	£8.30
Braddan New: Section 1, Block 1 & 2	£10.00
Braddan New: Section 1, Block 3 to 6	£12.00
Braddan New: Section 2	£9.40
Braddan New: Section 3	£11.50
Braddan New: New Section	£5.20
Braddan: St Lukes, Baldwin	£4.70
Bride: Old & New Yards, with Indexes	£8.60
Douglas Borough: Index AJ for all Books	£8.10
Douglas Borough: Index KZ for all Books	£7.40
Douglas Borough: Book 1, Blocks A-E	£10.00
Douglas Borough: Book 2, Blocks G-N	£10.30
Douglas Borough: Book 3, Blocks P-Px & Na - Nf	£9.80
Douglas Borough: Book 4, Blocks Ng-Nn	£10.50
Douglas Borough: Book 5, Blocks No-Nv & Oa-Ob	£9.80
Douglas Borough: Crematoria Index	£5.50
Douglas Borough: Crematoria Plaques	£12.60
Douglas -St Georges Churchyard	£9.10
Jurby: Old & New Yards with Indexes	£7.50
Lezayre: Old Yard with Index	£10.70

Isle of Man Family History Society (continued)

Lezayre: Middle Yard with Index	£8.40
Lezayre: New West Yard & New Section with Index	£9.70
Lonan: Old Yard with Index	£7.80
Lonan: 1871 Yard with Index	£9.40
Lonan: 1920 & 1958 Yards with Index	£6.80
Lonan: St Adamnans Old Yard	£2.20
Malew: Old Yard Index	£6.30
Malew: Old Yard plus Abbey Church, St Marys and K.W.C.	£14.90
Malew: Glebe Yard with Index (c-1865)	£7.50
Malew: 1895 Yard with Index	£8.70
Malew: 1935 Yard with Index	£6.80
Malew: St Marks Churchyard	£3.90
Marown: New Yard with Index	£9.60
Marown: St Runius Old Churchyard	£3.10
Maughold: Old Yard Index	£5.60
Maughold: Old Yard	£14.80
Maughold: New Yard with Index	£4.80
Maughold: St Marys, Ballure Churchyard	£3.60
Michael: Old and New Yards	£9.20
Onchan: Index for all Yards	£5.50
Onchan: Old Yard, 1877 Yard and New Yard	£12.40
Patrick: Old & New Yards with Indexes	£9.20
Patrick: St Pauls Churchyard, Foxdale	£5.20
Peel Town Cemetery (German, 1852) Section 1	£9.20
Peel Town Cemetery (German Section) 2	£10.70
"Old" Peel: St Peters Churchyard, Trans. (German)	£4.30
Rushen: Index for all Yards	£8.60
Rushen: Old Yard & 1869 Yard	£11.20
Rushen: 1899 & 1926 Yards	£11.20
Rushen: 1967 & Crematoria Plaques	£3.40
Santan: Old & New Yards with Indexes	£7.20

ISLE OF WIGHT

Isle of Wight Family History Society

Web Site: http://www.dina.clara.net/iowfhs/

Janet Few, 12 Ranelagh Road, Lake, Sandown, Isle of Wight PO36 8NX

Census

	Price	Band
Name index to 1891 census West Wight Part 1 surnames A-K	£2.50	C
Name index to 1891 census West Wight Part 2 surnames L-M	£2.50	C
Name index to 1891 census West Wight surnames Part 1 & 2 together	£4.50	E

Isle of Wight Family History Society (continued)

Miscellaneous

Quigley Indexes:	Price	Band
I.W County Press Marriage Announcements Dec 1884-Dec 1896	£2.00	B
I.W County Press Marriage Announcements Jan 1897-Dec 1902	£2.00	B
Coroners Inquests 1850-1864	£1.75	A
Coroners Inquests 1886-1906	£2.00	B
The I.of W. Apprenticeship Register 1802 1833	£1.75	A
Gurnard Church Burial Register 1902-1994	£1.75	A
Princess Beatrices I.of W. Rifles Gallipolli Nominal roll	£2.00	B
I.of W. Volunteer Artillery Militia 1852-1872	£2.50	B
Index to the Burial Record of W.G.Thomas (Cowes undertaker) Part 1 1912-1928	£3.00	C
Index to the Burial Record of W.G. Thomas Part 2 1928-1943	£3.00	C
Index to the Burial Record of W.G.Thomas Part 3 1943-1955	£3.00	C
Index to the Burial Record of W.G.Thomas Part 4 1955-1971	£3.00	C
Index to the Burial Book for Fairlee (Newport) Cemetery 1859-1892	£2.50	C
Index to the Burial Book for Fairlee (Newport) Cemetery 1892-1934	£2.50	C
Index to burials in Northwood Cemetery Part 1 1856-1880	£2.50	C
Index to burials in Northwood Cemetery Part 2 1880-1892	£2.50	B
Index to burials in Northwood Cemetery Part 3 1892-1904	£2.50	B
Index to burials in East Cowes Cemetery 1877-1918	£2.50	C
Index to burials in Barton St. Pauls 1872-1954	£2.50	C
Index to burials at Binstead 1857-1978	£2.50	B
Newchurch Burial Register 1865-1980	£2.50	B
Index to burials at Wroxall 1910-1934	£1.50	A
Index to Carisbrooke (Mount Joy) Cemetery Part 1 1859-1877	£2.50	B
Index to Carisbrooke (Mount Joy) Cemetery Part 2 1878-1897	£2.50	B
Index to Carisbrooke (Mount Joy) Cemetery Part 3 1897-1915	£2.50	B
Index to Carisbrooke (Mount Joy) Cemetery Part 4 1915-1924	£2.50	B
Index to Carisbrooke (Mount Joy) Cemetery Part 5 1924-1934	£2.50	B
An Atlas of Northwood Cemetery (plot numbers only - no names)	£6.00	F
Index to the burial order books for the Newport area 1934-1938	£2.50	A
Index to burial registers of Sandown Cemetery Part 1 1926-1954	£2.50	A
Index to burial registers of Sandown Cemetery Part 2 1954-1973	£2.50	A
Index to burial registers of Ryde Cemetery Part 1 1862-1874	£2.50	B
Index to burial registers of Ryde Cemetery Part 2 1874-1884	£2.50	B
Index to burial registers of Ryde Cemetery Part 3 1884-1895	£2.50	B
Index to burial registers of Ryde Cemetery Part 4 1895-1903	£2.50	B
Members of the Royal Yacht Squadron July 1832	£1.25	A
Index to County Petty Sessions 1878-1879	£2.50	A
Index to C18th Recognizances	£2.50	B
Shanklin Cemetery Part 1 1877-1918	£2.50	B
Shanklin Cemetery Part 2 1918-1948	£2.50	C
Shanklin Cemetery Part 3 1948-1970	£2.50	B

Isle of Wight Family History Society (continued)

Shanklin Cemetery Part 4 1970-1989	£2.50	A
Ventnor Cemetery Part 1 1870-1887	£2.50	B
Ventnor Cemetery Part 2 1887-1907	£2.50	C
Ventnor Cemetery Part 3 1907-1934	£2.50	C
Ventnor Cemetery Part 4 1934-1948	£2.50	C
Directory of Members Interests 1990	£0.50	B
Big R booklet of research interests 1994	£0.75	B
Big R booklet of research interests 1997	£1.50	A
Index to the Isle of Wight County War memorial Carisbrooke Castle	£1.00	A
A4 map of I.O.W. Pre-Victorian parishes	£0.20	A

Postage and Packing Prices:
Please add the following amounts to your payment. Air mail prices are available on request.

Price Band	U.K. 2nd class	Overseas Surface
A	£0.22	£0.52
B	£0.33	£0.52
C	£0.40	£0.69
E	£0.57	£1.02
F	£0.66	£1.19

KENT (see also Greater London)

North West Kent Family History Society

Web Site: http://users.ox.ac.uk/~malcolm/NWKFHS/

Mrs Barbara Attwaters, 141 Princes Road, Darford, Kent DA1 3HJ

Payment with order please, in sterling and cheques made out to:- NWK FHS.

1851 Census Index Series

		Price	p&p U.K.	O/s
Vol 4 Lewisham R.D.	35,000 names	£5.95	.65	£1.90
Vol 5 Dartford R.D.	27,000 names	£4.95	.57	£1.60
Vol 6 Sevenoaks R.D.	22,000 names	£4.95	.57	£1.60

West Kent Sources (3rd ed.) (A Genealogical Guide to research in the Diocese of Rochester)	£5.95	.47p	£1.30
Memories Of Lewisham in the late 19th and early 20th Centuries	£3.75	.38p	£1.00
Bromley Settlement Examinations Index 1747-1787 & 1816-1831	£1.00p	.00	£1.60

LANCASHIRE
Lancashire Family History & Heraldry Society
Web Site: http://www.lfhs.mcmail.com/
Mr. John Griffiths, 21 Priory Crescent, Penwortham, Preston, PR1 0AC
(all books shown exclude postage. Add the weights of all the items you wish to purchase, and enquire at the Post Office for current prices for whichever rate of postage you require.) Please make all cheques payable to L.F.H.&.H.S.

1851 Census Surname Indexes

			Weight	Price
Vol.21	Rochdale, Butterworth & Castleton.	HO107/2244 (LFH&HS)	50gms	£2.50
Vol.22	Spotland Near-Side & FurtherSide	HO107/2245 (LFH&HS)	40	£1.25
Vol 23	Wardleworth & Wardle	HO107/2246 (LFH&HS)	55	£1.75
Vol.24	Whitworth & Blatchinworth	HO107/2247 (LFH&HS)	40	£1.25
Vol.25	Holcombe, Tottington Lower End & Walmersley	HO107/2212 (LFH&HS)	40	£1.25
Vol.27	South Bury	HO107/2214 (LFH&HS)	45	£1.25
Vol.28	North Bury & Elton	HO107/2215 (LFH&HS)	50	£1.25
Vol.30	Newchurch in Rossendale	HO107/2248 (LFH&HS)	45	£1.25
Vol.31	Rossendale & Edenfield	HO107/2249 (LFH&HS)	30	£1.25
Vol.32	Haslingden & Accrington	HO107/2250 (LFH&HS)	50	£1.25
Vol.35	Colne & Pendle	HO107/2254 (LFH&HS)	70	£2.50
Vol.36	Mellor, Harwood & Billington	HO107/2257(LFH&HS)	50	£2.50
Vol.37	Blackburn (Western)	HO107/2258 (LFH&HS)	45	£2.50
Vol.38	Blackburn (Eastern)	HO107/2259 (LFH&HS)	60	£2.70
Vol.39	Oswaldtwistle	HO107/2260 (LFH&HS)	40	£1.70
Vol.40	Darwen & Witton	HO107/2261 (LFH&HS)	55	£2.50
Vol.41/2	Clitheroe & Stoneyhurst College	HO107/2255 (LFH&HS)	60	£2.50
Vol.43	Fylde	HO107/2269 (LFH&HS)	60	£2.50
Vol.44	Garstang	HO107/2270 (LFH&HS)	40	£1.70

Vols. 1-20 and 45-58 also available from the Society (see list as under Manchester & Lancashire FHS)

Index to Townships in 1851 Census-Surname Index of Lancashire		35gms	£1.50

1851 Census Surname Index of Lancashire- Full Transcription

F1	Caton	HO107/2273 Folio 1-78	115gms	£5.25
F2	Wray	HO107/2273 Folio 79-18	150	£6.50
F3	Tunstall & Arkholme	HO107/2273 Folio 333-415	115	£5.25
F4	Bentham	HO107/2277 Folio 1-112	150	£6.50
F5	Warton	HO107/2273 Folio 242-332	120	£5.50
F6	Warton & Lancaster	HO107/2272 Folio 1-49	140	£5.95
F7	Lancaster (Outer Townships)	HO107/2272 Folio 50-107, 526-558	180	£6.75

Lancashire Family History & Heraldry Society (continued)

Miscellaneous

Lancashire Graveyards: Location of Transcibed M.I.s (4th ed) by W. Taylor	120gms	£2.00
Rev. Peter Walkden Diary & Early Nonconformist Baptisms G.A. Foster	340	£9.95
Whalley Church M.I.s	300	£3.50
Routes to your Roots: A Guide to Local Sources	75	£2.95
Family History in Preston: A guide to Sources in the Harris Library	160	£2.50
Lancashire Strays	40	£0.50

Lancashire Parish Register Society

Web Site: http://www.genuki.org.uk/big/eng/LAN/prs
Hon. Treasurer Mr. Tom O'Brien, L.P.R.S. 16 Rothay Drive, Penketh, Warrington WA5 2PG

Parish Registers

Vol.114*	Prescot, St. Mary	1632-1666
Vol.120*	Hollinfare, St.Helen (Bap)	1654-1837
	(Mar)	1705-1744
	(Bur)	1709-1837
Vol.121	Heaton Norris, St. Thomas	1767-1850
Vol.122	Childwall, All Saints	1681-1753
Vol.124*	Chorlton cum Hardy, St Clement	1737-1837
	Holme in Cliviger, St.John the Divine	1742-1841
	(formerly St. John the Evangelist)	1742-1841
Vol.125	Warrington, St.Elphin	1680-1706
Vol.126	Halton, St. Wilfred	1727-1837
Vol.129	Ashton under Lyne, St Peter	1824-1837
	Blackley, St. Peter	1754-1783
	Chorley, St. Lawrence	1653-1708
Vol.131	Eccles, St.Mary	1632-1666
Vol.132	Urswick, St.Mary (Baps, Mar & Bur)	1696-1837
Vol.133	Colton, Holy Trinity (Baps, Mar & Bur)	1813-1837
	Lancaster, St.Mary (Mar)	1754-1777
	Rusland, St.Paul (Bap)	1781-1827
	Rusland, St.Paul (Bur)	1781-1851
Vol.134*	Manchester, St. James, George St. (Bap & Bur)	1788-1837
Vol.135	Egton cum Newland, St.Mary the Virgin (Bap & Bur)	1792-1841
	Finsthwaite, St.Peter (Bap)	1726-1840
	(Mar)	1727-1839
	(Bur)	1725-1840
	Satterthwaite, All Saints (Bap)	1766-1840
Vol.136	Rivington, (Bap, Mar & Bur)	1702-1837

Lancashire Parish Refister Society (continued)

Vol.137	Prescot, St. Mary (Bap)	1540-1595
	(Mar)	1538-1595
	(Bur)	1524-1592
Vol.138	Hindley, All Saints (Bap)	1644-1814
	(Mar)	1644-1813
	(Bur)	1642-1814
Vol.139	Haslingden, St.James the Great (Bap)	1603-1683
	(Mar)	1603-1698
	(Bur)	1603-1679
Vol.140	Todmorden, St.Mary (Bap, Mar & Bur)	1781-1812
Vol.141	Ashton-in-Makerfield, St.Thomas (Bap)	1810-1827
	(Bur)	1806-1844
Vol.142	Ashton-in-Makerfield, St.Thomas) (Bap)	1828-1873
Vol.143	St.Michael on Wyre, (Bap, Mar & Bur)	1707-1837
	Copp Chapel, St.Annes (Mar)	1737
	(Bap)	1728-1837
Vol.144	Clitheroe, St.Mary Magdalene (Bap)	1570-1725
	(Mar)	1570-1727
	(Bur)	1570-1724

* Denotes low stocks.

1998 Handbook, this lists the registers of Lancashire, those published by the Society and those published by other organisations along with the years covered. Within its covers will also be found a list of unpublished transcripts belonging to the Society, a list of parishes, no part of which has been published along with their dates, when registers began and a list of libraries both in the UK and overseas where our registers may be consulted. £2.00 including 2nd class/surface mail.

Back numbers held by the Lancashire Parish Register Society. Prices are £21.50 to non members. Please add postage of £1.50 per volume for non U.K. addresses.

Liverpool and South West Lancashire Family History Society

Web Site: http://www.lswlfhs.freeserve.co.uk
Mr. J. D. Griffiths, 9 Manor Road, Lymm, Cheshire, WA13 0AY

1851 Cenusus Surname Index	(a)	(b)	(c)
Runcorn	£2.05	£1.95	£3.00
Outer Warrington	£1.55	£1.75	£2.50
Warrington	£2.05	£1.95	£3.00

Monumental Inscriptions

Burtonwood	£1.30	£1.35	£2.20
Christchurch, Croft	£2.00	£1.95	£3.00
Daresbury All Saints	£3.50	£3.90	£5.20

Miscellaneous

St.James / St.Albans / Friends, Monumental Inscriptions	£1.05	£1.20	£1.50
St.Pauls (Bewsey Road) Monumental Inscriptions	£1.80	£2.00	£2.50
St Lewis (Croft) Monumental Inscriptions	£1.05	£1.20	£2.50
Bank St. Methodist Births & Baptisms 1809-1837	£2.00	£1.95	£2.50
King St. 1798-1837 / Winwick St. 1806-1837	£1.80	£2.00	£2.50
Hill Cliffe Burials 1802-1839	£1.80	£2.00	£2.50
Hill Cliffe Children Dedicated-God 1793-1837	£1.80	£2.00	£2.50
St Marys, Lymm, Cheshire Monumental Inscriptions 1630-1990	£2.50	£2.75	£4.70
Places Of Worship; History, School & Register	£1.80	£2.00	£2.50
Family Historians Guide to Warrington Library	£1.80	£2.00	£2.50
St.Wilfrids Grappenhall, Baptisms 1813-1837	£2.00	£1.95	£3.00
Warrington Epidemic Victims 1832 & 1892/3	£1.50	£1.75	£2.50
Warrington Photographers 1854-1992	£1.80	£2.00	£2.50

Warrington's Great War Heroes (References in The Warrington Guardian)

Sick/Injured Excluding South Lancs. Regiment	£2.00	£2.25	£3.00
As Above But the South Lancs. Regiment	£1.90	£2.10	£2.60
Fatalities Excluding South Lancs. Regiment	£2.10	£2.25	£2.95
Fatalities of The South Lancs Regiment	£1.70	£2.00	£2.70

Wigan Area

St.Paul's Chapel Standishgate Baptisms 1777-1837	£2.50	£2.80	£3.75
St.Paul's Chapel Burials 1786-97/1827-1837	£1.50	£1.75	£1.95
St.Paul's Chapel Monumental Inscriptions 1788-1943	£1.50	£1.75	£1.95

Liverpool Area

Beginners Guide To F.H. In The Liverpool Record Office (Compiled by the Liverpool Group)	£1.60	£1.75	£2.45
Genealogists Handbook of S. W. Lancashire	£1.50	£1.65	£2.00
St.Oswalds R.C. Old Swan Marriages 1846-55	£1.50	£1.65	£2.05
St.Austins R.C. Grassendale Marriages 1858-95	£1.70	£1.85	£2.25

Liverpool and South West Lancashire Family History Society (continued)

1851 Census of Liverpool Inner Districts

The Society has published a series of volumes indexing the 1851 Census of Liverpool. (Municipal Wards only, 258,346 residents). The Indexes list surnames, first names, place of birth, occupations and folio numbers. Each P.R.O. piece number is issued in 3 or 4 volumes (34 in total).

Volume	Ward	Section	ED	Folios
Volume 1	Scotland Ward	Section 1.	ED1 - 6.	Folios 1 - 206
Volume 2	Scotland Ward	Section 2.	ED1 - 7.	Folios 207 - 422
Volume 3	Scotland Ward	Section 3.	ED1 - 6.	Folios 423 - 626
Volume 4	Scotland Ward	Section 4.	ED1 - 6.	Folios 627 - 647
Volume 5	Scotland Ward	Section 1.	ED1 - 6.	Folios 1 - 229
Volume 6	Scotland Ward	Section 2.	ED1 - 4.	Folios 230 - 431
Volume 7	Scotland Ward	Section 3.	ED1 - 7.	Folios 432 - 694
Volume 8	Scotland Ward	Section 4.	ED1 - 4.	Folios 695 - 967
Volume 9	Vauxhall Ward	Section 1.	ED1 - 7.	Folios 1 - 198
Volume 10	Vauxhall Ward	Section 2.	ED1 - 5.	Folios 199 - 385
Volume 11	Vauxhall Ward	Section 3.	ED1 - 8.	Folios 386 - 594
Volume 12	Vauxhall Ward	Section 4.	ED1 - 6.	Folios 595 - 814
Volume 13	St Paul's/Exchange	Section 1.	ED1 - 7.	Folios 1 - 246
Volume 14	St Paul's/Exchange	Section 2.	ED1 - 7.	Folios 247 - 456
Volume 15	St Paul's/Exchange	Section 3.	ED1 - 8.	Folios 457 - 672
Volume 16	St Paul's/Exchange	Section 4.	ED1 - 7.	Folios 673 - 928
Volume 17	Castle St/St Peter	Section 1.	ED1 - 4.	Folios 1 - 179
Volume 18	Castle St/St Peter	Section 2.	ED1 - 6.	Folios 180 - 359
Volume 19	Castle St/St Peter	Section 3.	ED1 - 6.	Folios 360 - 563
Volume 20	Pitt St/Gt. George	Section 1.	ED1 - 6.	Folios 1 - 220
Volume 21	Pitt St/Gt. George	Section 2.	ED1 - 7.	Folios 221 - 468
Volume 22	Pitt St/Gt. George	Section 3.	ED1 - 5.	Folios 469 - 721
Volume 23	Pitt St/Gt. George	Section 4.	ED1 - 6.	Folios 722 - 941
Volume 24	Rodney St. Ward	Section 1.	ED1 - 6.	Folios 1 - 216
Volume 25	Rodney St. Ward	Section 2.	ED1 - 7.	Folios 217 - 389
Volume 26	Rodney St. Ward	Section 3.	ED1 - 5.	Folios 390 - 596
Volume 27	Rodney St. Ward	Section 1.	ED1 - 7.	Folios 1 - 231
Volume 28	Rodney St. Ward	Section 2.	ED1 - 7.	Folios 232 - 475
Volume 29	Rodney St. Ward	Section 3.	ED1 - 8.	Folios 476 - 676
Volume 30	Lime St./St. Ann's	Section 1.	ED1 - 8.	Folios 1 - 273
Volume 31	Lime St./St. Ann's	Section 2.	ED1 - 7.	Folios 274 - 508
Volume 32	Lime St./St. Ann's	Section 1.	ED1 - 6.	Folios 1 - 251
Volume 33	Lime St./St. Ann's	Section 2.	ED1 - 7.	Folios 252 - 495
Volume 34	Lime St./St. Ann's	Section 3.	ED1 - 8.	Folios 496 - 731

COMPANION PUBLICATION,
"A Guide To The Enumeration Districts In The 1851 Census" (Includes Street Index and Enumerators walks, enables the correct volume to be identified if the Street is known) ALL at, U.K. £2.85: O/S Surface £3.00: O/S Air £4.00 (per volume)

Manchester & Lancashire Family History Society

Web Site: http://www.mlfhs.demon.co.uk/
Clayton House, 59 Piccadilly, Manchester M1 2AQ
Tel: 0161-236-9750 Fax: 0161-237-3812

(Payment may be made by VISA/ACCESS/EUROCARD/MASTERCARD. Please give your number, date of expiry of card and signature.)

1851 Census Surname Index of Manchester

				(a)	(c)
1101	Vol.1	Newton, Beswick & Bradford	HO107/2231	£2.00	£2.45
1102	Vol.2	Market St., Manchester	HO107/2229	£2.60	£3.25
1103	Vol.3	London Rd., Manchester	HO107/2228 unfilmed	£2.00	£2.45
1104	Vol.4	St. George, Manchester	HO107/2230	£2.90	£3.30
1105	Vol.5	Ancoats, Manchester	HO107/2225/6	£3.20	£3.95
1106	Vol.6	Deansgate, Manchester	HO107/2227	£2.60	£3.10
1107	Vol.7	Cheetham & Failsworth, Manchester	HO107/2232	£2.10	£2.65
1108	Vol.8	Hulme, Manchester	HO107/2221	£3.10	£3.75
1109	Vol.9	Didsbury & Ardwick, Manchester	HO107/2219	£2.10	£2.60
1110	Vol.10	Chorlton on Medlock & Ardwick,	HO107/2220	£2.50	£2.95
1111	Vol.11	Salford	HO107/2222/4	£3.10	£3.75
1112	Vol.12	Barton, Stretford & Worsley	HO107/2217/18	£3.10	£3.75
1113	Vol.13	Droylsden, Audenshaw & Denton	HO107/2234/5	£2.00	£2.45
1114	Vol.14	Standish & Aspull	HO107/2198	£2.00	£2.45
1115	Vol.15	Wigan	HO107/2199	£3.60	£4.10
1116	Vol.16	Hindley, Pemberton, Up Holland & Ashton in Makerfield	HO107/2200/1	£2.10	£2.65
1117	Vol.17	Leigh	HO107/2204/5	£2.10	£2.60
1118	Vol.18	Ashton Under Lyne	HO107/2233	£2.00	£2.45
1119	Vol.19	Newton & Dukinfield	HO107/2236/7	£3.10	£3.75
1120	Vol.20	Hartshead, Mottram & Staly	HO107/2238/9	£3.10	£3.60
1145	Vol.45	Ellel & Heaton	HO107/2271	£2.00	£2.45
1146	Vol.46	Lancaster; Slyne & Hest Halton with Aughton, Bulk/Skerton Lancaster Castle/Aldcliffe, Ashton with Stodday & Scotforth.	HO107/2272	£3.10	£3.45
1147	Vol.47	Oldham	HO107/2240/1	£3.20	£4.20
1148	Vol.48	Middleton, Chadderton, Royton, & Crompton	HO107/2242/3	£2.50	£2.95
1149	Vol.49	Preston	HO107/2265/7	£3.70	£4.55

Manchester & Lancashire Family History Society (continued)

1150	Vol.50	Longton	HO107/2264	£2.00	£2.45
1151	Vol.51	Chorley & Croston	HO107/2263	£2.50	£2.95
1153	Vol.53	London Road, Manchester	HO107/2228	£3.05	£3.45
1154	Vol.54	Brindle, Leyland & Rivington	HO107/2262	£2.60	£3.10
1156	Vol.56	Bolton District	HO107/2206/8	£3.70	£4.55
1157	Vol.57	Caton, Wray, Tunstall Arkholme & Warton	HO107/2273	£2.50	£2.95
1158	Vol.58	Walton-le-Dale, Alston & Broughton	HO107/2268	£3.20	£3.70
1199		Index to Townships in the 1851 Census Surname Index of Lancashire		£2.05	£2.30

Volumes 21-44 can also be purchased from the Society (see list as under Lancashire Family History & Heraldry Society).

1861 Census (a) (c)

Directory of Irish born people & resident in Manchester in The 1861 Census:

1015	Vol.1	Ancoats sub-district	£10.10	£13.00

Miscellaneous

1003	A Guide to the Registration Districts of Manchester	£2.00	£2.45
1005	A Case Study in Early Genealogy: The Ravalds of Manchester & Kersal 1381-1600	£3.40	£4.00
1006	A Dictionary of Scottish Emigrants, Vol.1	£1.90	£2.75
1007	A Dictionary of Scottish Emigrants, Vol.2	£1.90	£2.75
1008	A Dictionary of Scottish Emigrants, Vol.3	£1.90	£2.75
1009	A Dictionary of Scottish Emigrants, Vol.4	£1.90	£2.75
1010	A Dictionary of Scottish Emigrants, Vol.5	£4.45	£5.20
1011	Scottish Genealogy: A Digest of Library Sources	£0.80	£1.25
1004	Registers in the Local Studies Unit of Manchester Central Library	£5.50	£6.90
1901	Bolton Directory for 1818 (reprint)	£3.00	£3.10
1902	Bolton Directory for 1829 (reprint)	£2.25	£3.00
1903	Dukes Alley Chapel, Bolton: History & Seatholders 1837-1854	£1.15	£1.85
1904	Handlist of Registers held at Bolton Library & Archives	£2.50	£3.25
1905	Bolton Wills Transcripts 1545-1600 Surnames A-M	£8.35	£10.20
1906	Bolton Wills Transcripts 1545-1600 Surnames N-Z	£8.35	£10.20

North Meols Family History Society

Jennie Gregson, 1 Dukes Avenue, Southport PR8 5EW
(Prices are (A) Members; (B) Non Members; (C) P&P)

Parish Registers

	(a)	(b)	(c)
S.CH.1: Christ Church, Southport Baptisms (1821-1838).	£2.50	£3.00	50p
S.CH.2: Churchtown Congregational Church, Baptisms (1825-1840), Marriages (1853-1900).	£0.75p	£1.00	26p
S.CH.3: East Bank Lane Congregational Church, Baptisms (1824-1837)	£2.00	£2.50	50p
S.CH.4: Holy Trinity Church, Southport, Memorial Inscriptions	£5.00	£5.50	£1.00
S.CH.6: St. Maries on the Sands, Southport. Marriage records Part 1. 24 Jan 1856-10 Apr 1875 Part 2.10 Aug 1875- 8 Jun 1893	£10.50	£11.00	£2.50
S.CH.7: St. Maries on the Sands, Southport. Register of Burials Part 1. 21 Nov 1855- 25 Feb 1867 Part 2. 26 April 1867-17 Jan 1903	apply for price		
S.CH.8: St. Maries on the Sands Monumental Inscriptions.	apply for price		
S.CH.9: Leyland Road Wesleyan Chapel Marriages 1882-1939	£1.50	£2.00	50p

1841 Census returns: (One Name Extracts)

	(a)	(b)	(c)
S.CRs.1: Rimmers in North Meols	£3.00	£3.50	£0.50
S.CRs.2: Wrights in North Meols with additional info. From Registers of C.M.B. & Wills (& additional info. from 1851 Census)	£2.50	£3.00	£0.50

1851 Census returns:

	(a)	(b)	(c)
S.CRs.3: North Meols with index.	£9.50	£10.00	£2.50
S.CRs.5: Birkdale, Ainsdale, Altcar and Formby with index.	£6.50	£7.00	£1.00

One Name Extracts (from North Meols Parish Registers 1594-1837)

	(a)	(b)	(c)
S.A.1: Abram.	£2.50	£3.00	50p
S.B.1: Ball.	£3.50	£4.00	50p
S.B.2: Barton.	£1.00	£1.50	50p
S.B.3: Blundell.	£1.00	£1.50	50p
S.B.4: Brade.	£1.00	£1.50	50p
S.B.5: Brookfield.	£2.00	£2.50	50p
S.C.1: Carrs.	£1.00	£1.50	50p
S.G.1: Gregson.	£1.00	£1.50	50p
S.H.1: Halsall.	£1.50	£2.00	50p
S.H.2: Hodge.	£2.00	£2.50	50p

North Meols Family History Society (continued)

S.J.1:	Jackson.	£2.00	£2.50	50p
S.J.2:	Johnson.	£2.50	£3.00	50p
S.M.1:	Marshall.	£2.00	£2.50	50p
S.M.2:	Meadows.	£1.00	£1.50	50p
S.P.1:	Peet.	£1.00	£1.50	50p
S.R.1:	Rigby.	£1.00	£1.50	50p
S.R.2:	Robinson.	£1.00	£1.50	50p
S.S.1:	Spencer.	£1.00	£1.50	50p
S.T.1:	Threlfall.	£1.00	£1.50	50p
S.W.1:	Waring.	£1.00	£1.50	50p
S.W.2	Watkinsons.	£1.50	£2.00	50p
S.W.3:	Wrights	£4.00	£4.50	50p

Miscellaneous

	(a)	(b)	(c)
S.MIS.2: North Meols Tithe Map (in 9 sections)			
Apportionments book,	£53.00	£53.00	£2.50
or each section	£5.00	£5.00	£1.00
Apportionments book	£8.00	£8.00	£1.00

LINCOLNSHIRE

Lincolnshire Family History Society

Web Site: http://www.genuki.org.uk/big/eng/LIN/lfhs

Mr. T. A. Lamyman, 6 Godber Drive, Bracebridge Heath, Lincoln LN4 2LN
Please send your order, including postage with cheque or postal order made payable to Lincolnshire Family History Society. Overseas orders are sent surface mail. Payment in sterling only please.

Marriage Indexes

		1813-37	1754-1812	
Vol.17	Aveland & Ness	£2.00	£6.00	2 Vol
Vol.6	Beltisloe	£1.20	£3.50	
Vol.20	Bolingbroke	£2.00	£6.00	2 Vol
Vol.15a	Boston St Botolph	£2.00	£3.50	
Vol.8	Calcewaith & Candleshoe	£1.80	£6.00	2 Vol
Vol.21	Corringham	£2.00	£3.50	
Vol.14	East Elloe	£2.00	£6.00	2 Vol.
Vol.13	West Elloe	£1.80	£6.00	2 Vol
Vol.22	Gainsborough All Saints Church		£3.50	
Vol.4	Graffoe		£6.00	2 Vol
	Grantham & Loveden	£2.00		
Vol.2	Grantham St Wulfram	£1.80		
Vol.2	Grantham St Wulfram 1700-1812 & Grantham		£6.00	2 Vol
Vol.1	Grimsby & Cleethorpes		£3.50	

Lincolnshire Family History Society (continued)

Vol.9	Haverstoe		£3.50		
Vol.15	Holland East	£2.00	£3.50		
Vol.16	Holland West	£2.00	£6.00	2 Vol	
Vol.19	Horncastle	£2.00	£6.00	2 Vol	
Vol.19a	Horncastle St Mary		£2.50		
	Isle of Axholme	£2.00			
Vol.12	Lafford	£1.80	£6.00	2 Vol	
Vol.5	Lawres	£1.20	£3.50		
Vol.10	Louthesk		£6.00	2 Vol	
Vol.23	Loveden		£3.50		
Vol.18	Manlake	£2.00	£3.50		
Vol.13a	Spalding SS Mary & Nicholas		£3.00		
Vol.17a	Stamford Churches	£2.00	£3.00		
Vol.7	Westwold		£3.50		
Vol.11	Yarborough	£2.00	£6.00	2 Vol	

Census Surname Indexes

Registration District	1851	1871	1881	1891
Boston	£3.00	£2.00		£3.00
Bourne		£2.00	£1.00	£2.50
Caistor (1891 2 vol)	£3.00	£2.00		£5.00
Gainsborough & Isle of Axholme	£3.00	£2.00		£3.00
Glanford Brigg	£3.00	£2.00		£3.00
Grantham	£3.00	£2.00	£1.00	£3.00
Holbeach	£3.00	£2.00	£1.00	£3.00
Horncastle	£3.00	£2.00	£1.00	£2.50
Lincoln	£3.00	£2.00		£3.00
Louth	£3.00	£2.00		£3.00
Sleaford & parts of Newark	£3.00	£2.00		£3.00
Spalding & parts of Peterboro	£3.00	£2.00	£1.00	£3.00
Spilsby	£3.00	£2.00	£1.00	£2.50
Stamford	£3.00	£2.00	£1.00	£2.50

Miscellaneous

(a)

A Gazetteer of Historic Lincolnshire for Family and Local Historians	£3.00
Genealogical Sources (3rd ed.)	£2.00
Registration Districts of Lincolnshire in 19th c. plus Deanery map and listings.	£1.50

Poor Law Indexes

Settlement Examinations	£2.00
Kesteven QS Settlement Papers 1700 1847	£3.50
Bastardy Documents in Kesteven Q.S. 1700-1839	£3.50

Postage & packing on 1 book 40p UK, O/seas surface 90p.

NORFOLK
Norfolk Family History Society
(formerly the Norfolk & Norwich Genealogical Society)
Web Site: http://www.uea.ac.uk/~s300/genuki/NFK/organisations/nfhs
Jean Stangroom, Publications Secretary, Kirby House, 38B St. Giles St., Norwich NR2 1LL

Norfolk Parish Registers

		(a)	(c)
No.6	Frenze	£1.85	£3.00
No.7	Ryston Roxham	£1.85	£3.00
No.8	Taverham	£1.85	£3.00
No.9	Didlington with Cranwich	£1.85	£3.00
No.10	Cranwich	£1.85	£3.00
No.11	Fordham	£2.35	£3.00
No.12	Boughton	£1.85	£3.00
No.16	Santon	£1.85	£3.00
No.17	Bexwell	£1.85	£3.00
No.18	Langford	£1.85	£3.00
No.19	Ickburgh	£2.40	£4.05
No.24	Colney	£1.85	£3.00
No.27	Haveringland	£1.85	£3.00
No.28	Little Melton	£4.15	£5.80
No.29	Earlham	£1.85	£3.00
No.30	Sco Ruston	£2.40	£4.00

Non Conformist Registers:
Vol.2 Framingham Pigot pt. Bap.; Vol.3 Downham Market; Vol.4 Shelfhanger; Vol.6 Stratton St. Michael; Vol.7 Saxlingham Thorpe pt. Bap. Vol.8 Hapton Unitarian. All these books priced at U.K/Surface Mail £1.25; Air Mail £1.50.

Miscellaneous

		(a)	(c)
No.18	Rosary Cemetery Monumental Inscriptions 1819-1986 Burials 1821-1837	£13.75	£17.50
No.19	Diss Parish Registers 1551-1837	£16.75	£21.50
No.21	Norfolk & Norwich Hearth Tax Assessment Lady Day 1666	£13.75	£17.50
No.22	Norfolk Pedigrees part 5	£13.75	£17.50
No.24	The East Norfolk Poll Registers 1835	£13.75	£17.50
No.25	Norfolk Archdeaconry Marriage Licence Bonds 1813-1837	£13.75	£17.50
	Norwich Strangers 1583-1600	£2.50	£3.00

Mid Norfolk Family History Society

Mrs P Skittrall, 17 Windmill Avenue, Dereham, Norfolk, NR20 3BE

Parish Registers	(a)	(b)	(c)
Swanton Morley			
Baptisms 1784-1837	£3.25	£4.45	£6.90
Baptisms 1838-1891	£3.00	£4.20	£6.00
Marriages 1755-1837; Banns 1782-1823	£3.00	£4.20	£5.50
Marriages 1837-1891	£3.00	£4.20	£4.75
Burials 1784-1837	£3.00	£4.20	£5.50
Burials 1838-1891	£3.00	£4.20	£5.50
Burials 1892-1988	£3.00	£4.20	£5.00
Hoe			
Bapt.1733-1812; Marr.1733-1790 Banns 1754-1789; Burials 1733-1812	£4.00	£5.20	£7.00
East Bilney			
Bapt.1714-1902; Marr. 1714-1904 Banns 1757-1799; Burials 1733-1911	£4.50	£5.70	£7.00
Census Indexes			
Swanton Morley 1841-1891	£6.50	£8.30	£9.75
Shipdham 1841 only	£3.50	£4.70	£5.50
Beetley 1841-1891	£4.50	£5.70	£6.75
Westfield 1841-1891	£3.50	£4.70	£5.00
Cemetery Burial Index			
Dereham 1869 1924	£5.50	£6.70	£8.00
Monumental Inscriptions (Church and Churchyard)			
Beetley (St Mary Magdalene)	£3.75	£4.95	£5.90
Brisley (St Bartholemew)	£3.50	£4.70	£5.50
East Bradenham (St. Marys)	price on application		
East Bilney (St Mary)	£3.25	£4.45	£6.50
Gateley (St Helen)	£2.50	£3.10	£3.75
Hoe (St Andrew)	£3.25	£4.45	£5.75
Horningtoft (St Edmund)	£2.50	£3.10	£4.50
Stanfield (St. Margaret)	price on application		
Whissonsett (St Mary)	£3.50	£4.70	£5.50
Worthing (St Margaret)	£3.50	£4.70	£5.80
Yaxham (St Peter)	£5.50	£6.70	£7.75

NORTHAMPTONSHIRE

Northamptonshire Family History Society
http://ourworld.compuserve.com/homepages/NORTHAMPTONSHIRE_FHS
Mr. T.R. Cotton, 62 Nelson St, Kettering Northamptonshire NN16 8QJ

1851 Census Indexes.

	(a)	(b)	(c)
St. Sepulchres Parish, Northampton.	£3.65	£4.10	£5.50
Parishes of Barton Seagrave, Burton Latimer, Cranfords, Finedon, Isham, Orlingbury, and Warkton.	£3.50	£3.75	£4.55
Kettering Parish.	£3.55	£3.90	£5.00
Wellingborough Parish.	£3.55	£3.90	£5.00
Parishes of Brockhall, Bugbrooke, Floore, Harpole, Kislingbury & Upton, Nether Hayford. Upper Hayford, Wilton.	£3.50	£3.75	£5.00

Memorial Inscriptions.

		(a)	(b)	(c)
No. 1.	St Edmunds Church, Northampton.	£2.00	£2.25	£3.05
No. 2.	St Marys Church, Woodford, (Nr. Thrapston).	£3.75	£4.00	£4.80
No. 3.	St Botolphs Church, Stoke Albany.	£1.90	£2.10	£2.70
No. 4.	All Saints Church. Wilbarston.	£1.90	£2.10	£2.70
No. 5.	St Marys Church, Weston by Welland, with All Saints Church, Sutton Bassett	£1.90	£2.10	£2.70
No. 6.	The Church of St Mary the Virgin, Ashley.	£1.90	£2.10	£2.70
No. 7.	All Saints Church, Dingley	£1.65	£1.85	£2.45
No. 8.	The Church of St. Mary the Virgin, Whiston.	£1.55	£1.85	£2.45
No. 9.	St. Andrews Church. Arthingworth	£1.65	£1.85	£2.45
No. 10.	The Church of St. Peter and St Paul, Preston Capes.	£1.90	£2.10	£2.70
No. 11.	St Helens Church, Great Oxendon.	£1.90	£2.10	£2.70
No. 12	The Church of St Peter & St. Paul, Harrington.	£1.90	£2.10	£2.70
No. 13.	The Church of St. John the Baptist, & the Burial Ground, East Farndon.	£1.90	£2.10	£2.70
No. 14.	St Guthlacs Church, Passenham.	£1.90	£2.10	£2.70
No. 15.	The Church of St Mary Magdalene. Castle Ashby.	£1.90	£2.10	£2.70
No. 16.	St Marys Church, Brampton Ash.	£1.65	£1.85	£2.45
No. 17.	All Saints Church. Braybrooke.	£1.90	£2.10	£2.70
No. 18.	The Church of St Nicholas, Marston Trussell.	£1.90	£2.10	£2.70
No. 19.	St Marys Church, Grendon.	£2.15	£2.35	£2.95
No. 20	St. Andrews Church, Yardley Hastings Part 1. Old Churchyard & United Reform Church	£2.15	£2.35	£2.95
No. 21	St Andrews Church, Yardley Hastings, Graveyard Extension Part 2.	£2.15	£2.35	£2.95
No. 22	St. Margarets Church, Denton	£2.15	£2.35	£2.95
No. 23	St. Giles Church, Desborough	£2.40	£2.60	£3.20

Peterborough & District Family History Society

Mrs. D. Harbron, 7 Newby Close, Peterborough PE3 9PU

1851 Census Index of Surnames.	(a)	(b)
Vol.1 Peterborough R.D. (part) HO107/1747/1-678	£1.25	£2.20

British Record Society

For details of publications relating to Northamptonshire published by the British Record Society see their entry on page 200.

NORTHUMBERLAND

Northumberland and Durham Family History Society

Web Site: http://www.geocities.com/Athens/6549/

Ms. S. Senior c/o NDFHS 2nd Floor, Bolbec Hall, Westgate Rd, Newcastle upon Tyne NE1 1SE

Type A: Surname index, by family groups, giving ages and Census folio numbers.
Type B: Surname index giving names, ages, occupations, relationships, birthplaces and Census folio numbers.
Type C: Surname index giving names, ages, birthplaces and Census folio numbers.

1851 Census Indexes County Durham		(a)	(b)
South Shields, Boldon, Westoe (part), Cleadon, Harton, Whitbum and East Janow (part) (PRO piece HO 107/2399 folios 1-680)	A	£4.00	£5.25
Jarrow, South Shields St Hilda (part), Westoe (part), Holy Trinity, Monkton and Hedworth (PRO piece HO 107/2400 folios 1-417)	A	4.00	£5.25
Chester-Le-Street, Waldridge, Edmondsley, Pelton, Witton Gilbert, Ouston, Harraton, Birtley, Lamesiey, Usworth (part) andWashington (part) (PRO piece HO 107/2394 folios 1-707)	A	£4.00	£5.25
Heworth (PRO piece HO 107/2401 folios 1-278)	A	£4.00	£5.25
Bishopwearmouth Vol 1 (PRO piece HO 107/2395 folios 62-338)	B	£5.00	£6.75
Bishopwearmouth Vol 2 (PRO piece HO 107/2395 folios 339-542)	B	£4.50	£6.00
Gateshead (PRO piece HO 107/2402 folios 1-742)	A	£5.00	£6.75
Houghton le Spring (PRO piece HO107/2393 folios 1-610)	A	£4.50	£5.75
Whickham, Winlaton, Ryton (PRO piece HO107/2403 Folios. 1-450)	A	£4.00	£5.25
Stanhope, St Johns Chapel & Frosterley (PRO piece HO107/2388 folios 4-309)	C	£6.00	£7.75
Edmondbyers, Hunstanworth and Wolsingham (PRO piece HO107/2388 folios 313-492)	C	£4.50	£6.00

Northumberland and Durham Family History Society (continued)

1851 Census Indexes Northumberland

		(a)	(b)
Hartburn, Netherwitton, Longhorsley, Hebron, Mitford, Meldon (PRO piece HO107/2418 folios 1-145)	B	£4.00	£5.25
Seghill, Backworth, Burradon, Earsdon (part) (PRO piece HO107/2412 folios 1-153)	B	£4.00	£5.25
Morpeth (PRO piece HO107/2418 folios 149-289)	B	£4.00	£5.25
Bedlington, Hepscott, Netherton, Sleekburn, Choppington, Cambois (PRO piece HO107/2418 folios 293-460)	B	£4.50	£6.00
Woodhorn, Widdrington, Ugharn, Warkworth (part) Bothal, Hebron,& Felton (part) (PRO piece HO107/2418 folios 461 641)	B	£4.50	£6.00
Tynemouth, North Shields (PRO piece HO107/2410 folios 1-233)	B	£4.50	£6.00
Newcastle St Nicholas (PRO piece HO107/2406 folios 1-470)	A	£4.50	£6.00
Newcastle St Andrew (PRO piece HO107/2405 folios 1-570)	A	£4.50	£6.00
Longbenton, Walker, Killingworth, Weetslade (PRO piece HO107/2411 folios 1-288)	B	£4.00	£5.25
Newcastle West gate (PRO piece HO107/2404 folios 1-630)	A	£5.00	£6.75
Newcastle All Saints (PRO piece HO107/2407 folios 1-731)	A	£5.00	£6.75
Newcastle Byker (PRO piece HO107/2408 folios 1-367)	A	£4.00	£5.25
Wallsend, Willington & Howdon (PRO piece HO107/2409 folios 1-183)	B	£4.00	£5.25
Chirton, Preston & Murton (PRO piece HO107/2409 folios 184-304, 550-597)	B	£4.00	£5.25
North Shields (PRO piece HO107/2409 folios 305-549)	B	£5.00	£6.75
Tweedmouth (PRO piece HO107/2421 folios 146-239)	B	£3.50	£4.50
Rothbury, Elsdon (PRO piece HO107/2423)	B	£4.50	£6.00
Belford, Bamburgh (PRO piece HO107/2420 folios 1-250)	B	£4.50	£6.00
Berwick on Tweed Pt 1 (PRO piece HO107/2421 folios 243-436)	B	£4.00	£5.25
Berwick on Tweed Pt 2 (PRO piece HO107/2421 folios 440-605)	B	£4.00	£5.25
Warkworth, Felton, Shilbottle, and Lesbury (PRO piece HO107/2419 folios ?-275)	B	£4.50	£6.00
Alnwick and Eglingham (part) (PRO piece HO107/2419 folios 280-557)	B	£4.50	£6.00
Embleton, Edlington, Whittingham, Eglingham (part), Longhoughton, Howick and Ellingham (PRO piece HO107/2419 folios 564-820)	B	£4.50	£6.25
Glendale (part 1) Ford (PRO piece HO107/2422 folios 4-301)	B	£4.50	£6.00

Northumberland and Durham Family History Society (continued)

Glendale (part 2) Wooler (PRO piece HO107/2422 folios 305-557)	B	£4.50	£6.00
Tynemouth, Cullercoats, Whitley Bay (PRO piece HO107/2410 folios 237-499)	B	£4.50	£6.00
Berwick on Tweed Pt 3 and Northamshire (PRO piece HO107/2421 folios 609-809)	B	£4.50	£6.00

Miscellaneous

Personal Names in Durham Wills 1787-1791. Names, occupations, addresses, dates of wills, names of beneficiaries and witnesses to wills.	£6.50	£8.25
Personal Names in Wills Proved At Durham 1792-1794	£7.00	£8.50
Personal Names in Wills Proved At Durham 1795-1797	£6.50	£8.25
Irregular Border Marriages Lamberton Toll 1833-1849 Performed by Henry Collins, near Berwick upon Tweed	£6.50	£8.25
Personal Names in Wills Proved At Durham 1798-1800	£7.00	£8.50
Personal Names in Wills Proved At Durham 1801-1803	£7.00	£8.50

NOTTINGHAMSHIRE

Nottinghamshire Family History Society

Web Site http://www.netcomuk.co.uk/~JeffOP
Sheila Greenall, 19 Sherwin Walk, St Anns, Nottingham. NG3 1AH
email: SheilaL@netcomuk.co.uk

Miscellaneous Publications

Vol. 96 Where to find Nottinghamshire Places on Census Returns 1841-1891	£2.85	£3.15	£4.00
Vol .99 Miscellany No.3 All at Sea 1861 Census & 1881, Farnsfield Parish Book 1794-1878, The Rectors Book, Claworth, Notts 1672-1701, Edwin Lodge of the Nottingham Ancient Imperial Order of Oddfellows.	£3.60	£3.90	£4.75
Vol.100 Nottinghamshire Churches (Photographs of all pre-1900)	£7.25	£7.70	£8.50
Vol.102 Radford St Peters Church Rate Books No. 1	£3.50	£3.80	£4.65
Vol.105 Miscellany No.4 Mansfield School Census 1891, West Retford Census 1794, Extracts from Elliots Dole Minutes Book, Arnold Petition to Commons C19 Radford to Costock Removal Order 1838, Carlton upon Trent Terrier 1777 Carlton upon Trent Census 1845, Bilborough & Strelley Census 1815, Strelley Census 1818,			

Nottinghamshire Family History Society (continued)

History of Bleasby 1824, East Stoke Census 1828,
Ruddington Overseers Accounts 1698-1700,
Hucknall Torkard Census 1696, Bunny,
Removal Certificate 1700, Extracts from Constables Accounts
Radford Parish Diary 1813-1864,
Greasley Inhabitants Unemployed 1817
Basford Expenditure 1817,
Radford Bastardy Bonds 1817 & 1818,
Radford Poor House Committee Meetings,
Hucknall Torkard Petition 1817,
Radford Apprenticeship Indenture,

Norwell Census 1803	£4.20	£4.50	£5.35
Vol.106 Radford St Peters Banns Register 1853 1859	£4.40	£4.70	£5.55

Vol.107 Miscellany No.5 Nottinghamshire boys apprenticed to
Cutlers in Hallamshire 1618-1858
Stocking frames sold by auction 1772-1775,
Radford Coal Merchants Wage Books 1922-1926,
Subscribers to the Association to Prosecute Horse Stealers 1773
Nottingham & Nottinghamshire Banking Company 1845,
Cotgrave Apprenticeship Indenture 1785, 1792
Norwell Poor 1817,
Basford persons convicted of disturbances 1842,
Hawton Population 1828
Keyworth Assisted Emigration 1819,

Basford Assisted Emigration 1819,	£3.60	£3.90	£4.75
Vol.108 Jolly Bargemans Ledger	£3.35	£3.65	£4.50

Vol.109 Miscellany No.6 Wollaton Diary 1846-1854,
Trent Navigation tables 1909-1919,
Caunton Census 1846, Barnby Moor Census 1832
Laxton Parish Register Book 1836,
Walkeringham Census Questionnaire 1831
Thurgaton Absconder 1792,

Balderton Freehold List 1806	£3.60	£3.90	£4.75
Vol.110 Chesterfield Canal Boat Registers	£5.25	£5.70	£6.50

Vol.111 Miscellany No.7
Village Census of Farndon cum Balderton 1850,
The Sherwood Foresters Militia Killed & Wounded 1900,
Vicars of Balderton cum Farndon 1426-1901,
Election of Gardians of the Poor, Basford 1853,
National Patriotic Fund 1854.
Radford Poor Day Book 1811-1821,
Persons given Beef at Rufford, Xmas 1837

by Earl of Scarborough.	£4.10	£4.40	£5.25
Vol.112 Radford St Peters Church Rate Books No.2	£4.10	£4.40	£5.25

Nottinghamshire Family History Society (continued)

Vol.113 Miscellany No.8 Balderton Valuation List
1892-1896, North Wheatley Census 1861,
Absconders, Deserters and Miscreants 1772-1775
Baptisms 1830-1837, Southwell Accounts
1697-1875,West Retford Church Improvements
1824, Hawton Tithe Tental 1809,
Mounts St. Wesleyan Methodist Chapel,
New Basford, Nottingham £4.10 £4.40 £5.25

Vol.114 Methodists Ministers & Lay Officers with Notts
Connections £3.60 £3.90 £4.75

Vol.115 Miscellany No.9 Nominal Rolls of the Earl of
Scarbroughs School, Ollerton 1848-1860
Flintham Strays Marriages, Local Gravestones,
Arnold Frame-Breaking. People who paid the
Patriotic Fund at Normanton-on-Soar
Shelford Banns 1754-1808 & 1823-1894,
Rental West Bridgford Estate 1800 £4.10 £4.40 £5.25

Vol.116 List of Persons, Freemen & Non Freemen entitled
Vote in the Parish of St Mary 1853 £3.35 £3.65 £4.50

Vol.117 Miscellany No.10 Newark 1811 Census + Notes,
Beeston Executions 1832, J Charlton, Will of Kegworth 1711,
Kinoulton Census 1851,Aldermen of Newark 1549-1625
Mayors of Newark 1626-1997,
Edwalton Absence from Benifice 1861
Guardians of the Newark Union & Appointment of Overseers 1864
Hucknall Torkard Contributors for the Defence of England 1798
Mansfield Woodhouse Apprentice 1810
Edwalton Settlement Examn 1809
Edwalton Marriage Certificate 1742, Edwalton Bill 1775
& receipts 1774.
Worksop Bastardy Order 1809,1822,1823 £4.40 £4.40 £5.25

Vol.118 Southwell Minster Gravestones,
Ledger stones, Monuments, Dedications £5.55 £5.95 £7.30

Vol.119 Miscellany11, Newark Union Whouse,
Population of Oxton Blidworth 1821-1830,
Worksop Petition 1850, Caunton 1870, Pedigrees
Of Notts Families, Fansfield School 1876, Ruddington
Bastardy Warants 1806, Ruddington Bond to
maintain children 1760, Edwalton Apprenticeship
Indenture 1783, Christmas adjourned Quarter Sessions
1864, Property Tax Assesment 1863, Will of Wm.
Hancock 1794. Notts Names on Runnymede Memorial
1939-1945. £4.10 £4.40 £5.25

Vol.120 Claims to be admitted a Freeman 1850-1882
Surnames A-G £3.85 £4.15 £5.00

Vol.121 Miscellany 12 Protestant families from 1841 census
Callais; Mansfield Woodhouse Soldiers furlough
1800-1801; Notts Volunteer Regt 1914-1916;
Cromwell Churchwardens Accounts £4.10 £4.40 £5.25

OXFORDSHIRE

Oxfordshire Family History Society
Book Sales Co-Ordinator
Miss Angela Wood, 40 Kersington Crescent, Cowley, Oxford OX4 3RJ

Cheques should be made payable to OFHS. Overseas customers must send cheques in sterling drawn on a UK clearing bank.

Parish Registers

	Price
Oxfordshire Parish Registers & Bishops Transcripts, (5th ed.)	£4.50

1851 Census

Volume 1.	Henley Union	£3.50
Volume 2.	Thame Union	£3.50
Volume 3.	Wallingford Union	£3.50
Volume 4.	Headington incl. parts of Oxford City	£3.50
Volume 5.	Bicester Union	£3.50
Volume 6.	Woodstock Union	£3.50
Volume 7.	Witney Union	£3.50
Volume 8.	Chipping Norton Union	£3.50
Volume 9.	Banbury Union incl. Bloxham, Cropredy and Swalcliffe districts	£3.50
Volume 10.	Abingdon Union	£3.50
Volume 11.	Brackley, Wycombe & Bradfield Unions (pre 1974 Oxon parishes only)	£3.50
Volume 12.	Oxford City	£3.50

Miscellaneous

Index to Oxfordshire Hearth Tax	£3.50
Oxfordshire Militia Ballot 1831	£3.00
Oxfordshire Families Directory	£2.50
Oxfordshire Protestation Oath Returns	£3.00
The Return of Owners of Land 1873: Oxfordshire	£1.50

Value of Order	UK	O/seas	Airmail
Under £1.00	£0.40	£0.65	£1.30
£1.00-£1.99	£0.70	£0.85	£1.85
£2.00-£4.99	£1.00	£1.20	£2.50
£5.00-£9.99	£2.00	£2.50	£3.80
£10.00-£29.99	£3.10	£3.50	£5.25
Over £30.00	£4.00	£4.60	£7.50

British Record Society
For details of publications relating to Oxford published by the British Record Society see their entry on page 200.

SHROPSHIRE
Shropshire Family History Society
Web Site: http://www.essex.ac.uk/AMS/genuki/SAL/shrop_12.html

Items available from Mrs. Ruth Wilford, 68 Oakley Street, Belle Vue, Shrewsbury, Shropshire SY3 7JZ

Please make all cheques payable to 'Shropshire FHS' and include a self addressed adhesive label with your order. Prices do not include postage, please check with the Post Office for current charges.

Parish Registers
Place Name

				Price	Weight
Acton Burnell	St.Mary	C	1813-1840	£0.60	15g
Acton Round	n/a	M	1813-1837	£0.20	5g
	(BTs)	M	1638,1660, 1662-1713	£1.20	30g
Atcham	St.Eata	C	1813-1840	£1.20	30g
		B	1813-1840	£0.60	15g
Barrow	St.Giles	C	1813-1823	£0.60	15g
		B	1839-1930	apply	
Bettws-Y-Crwyn, MGY	Calvinistic Meth.	C	1826-1836	£0.20	5g
Bishops Castle Ind. Chapel		C	1814-1837	£0.20	5g
Bishops Castle & Clun Methodist Chapel		C	1858-1995	£2.20	55g
		M	1908-1995	£1.80	30g
Brockton, Clunton & Norbury Chapel		C	1858-1915	£0.40	10g
Bomere Heath Zions Hill Indep.		C	1827-1837	£0.60	15g
Bridgnorth Cath. & Apostolic		C	1835-1840	£0.20	5g
Stoneway Indep.		C	1769-1837	apply	
		B	1822-1837	£1.00	25g
		C	1822-1838	£0.20	5g
Brockton Methodist Chapel		C	1858-1915	apply	
Broseley Birchmeadow Chapel		C	1835-1837	£0.20	5g
	Particular Baptist	C	1817-1837	£1.60	40g
Chapel Lawn, nr. Clun St.Mary		B	1844-1987	£0.80	20g
Chirbury St.Michael		C	1828-1835	£0.20	5g
Clun St.George (extracts)		C	1661-1739	£2.10	55g
Clun Methodist Chapel		C	1858-1995	apply	
		M	1908-1995	apply	
(See also Chapel Lawn) extracts		B	1740-1798	£1.40	35g
Clunbury St.Swithin		M	1813-1837	£0.80	20g
Clunton Methodist Chapel		C	1858-1915	apply	
Dawley Magna					
	Dawley Green Meth. New Connexion	C	1829-1837 *see Madeley Wood	apply	

Shropshire Family History Society (continued)

Ditton Priors St. John the Baptist	M	1813-1837	£0.50	15g
Ellesmere Independent Chapel	C	1809-1837	£0.40	10g
	C	1812-1827	£0.20	5g
Forden, Mont. Independent Chapel	C	1827-1836	£0.10	2.5g
Gobowen Preeshenlle Indep.	C	1833-1836	£0.10	2.5g
Grimpo, nr. West Felton Independent Chapel	C	1833-1836	£0.10	2.5g
Halesowen, Worcs. Independent Chapel	C	1805-1837	£0.40	10g
Hodnet Wollerton Indep.	C	1814-1837	£0.20	5g
Holdgate Holy Trinity	CMB	1651-1701	£1.20	30g
	CMB	1701-1711	£0.40	10g
(B.Ts)	CMB	1660-1669	£0.40	10g
Hollinswood Meth. New. Connex.	C	1829-1837	apply	
*see Madeley Wood New Connex.				
Hopebendrid see Clun				
Hope Bowdler St.Andrew	CMB	1563-1837	£2.80	70g
Hopton Wafers St.Michael	M	1813-1837	£0.40	10g
Leaton Holy Trinity	C	1859-1969	£3.20	80g
Llansantffraid-Ym-Mechain, Powys	C*	1813-1838	£0.80	20g
	C*	1838-1911	£1.00	25g
	M*	1789-1837	£0.60	15g
* Extracts only	M*	1838-1911	£0.50	15g
Llanyblodwel Smyrna Independent	C	1825-1836	£0.20	5g
Ludlow Broad St Wes. Meth.	C	1815-1837	£1.40	35g
Old St., Prim. Meth.	C	1824-1837	£0.60	15g
Madeley Madeley Wood, Dawley Green & Hollins Wood Meth. New Connexion	C	1829-1837	£0.20	5g
Madeley Wood Weslyan Methodist	C	1815-1837	£0.60	15g
Marton, nr.Chirbury Independent Chapel includes list of members	C*	1829-1836	£0.20	5g
Newport Indep. Chapel	C	1814-1833	£0.30	10g
	C	1828-1837	£0.20	5g
Oldbury, Worcs. Presbyterian Chapel	C	1776-1799	£1.60	40g
	C	1800-1812	£1.00	25g
	C	1812-1837	£1.20	30g
Oswestry Nonconformist				
Castle Lane Chapel	C	1819-1837	£0.40	10g.
Old (Indep.) Chapel	C	1813-1816	£0.50	15g
Arthur St., (See also Sweeney Hall)	M	1812-1837	£0.20	5g
Primitive Methodist	C	1830-1837	£0.60	15g
Wesleyan Meth.	C	1812-1836	£0.60	15g
Pant Crickheath Indep.	C	1829-1836	£0.40	10g

Shropshire Family History Society (continued)

Penley	CB	1753-1812	£3.40	85g
	M	1753 only	with above	
	B.Ts/C	1813-1864	£3.00	75g
Pontesbury Baptist Chapel	C*	1828-1836	£0.40	10g
Pradoe, nr West Felton	B	1907-1984	£0.40	10g
Prees Green Primitive Methodist	C	1824-1837	£0.60	15g
Ratlinghope St.Margaret	B.Ts/CMB	1661-1812	£6.80	170g
Shifnal Aston St. Part. Baptist	C	1811-1836	£0.20	5g
Shrewsbury St.Giles	P.R. Index	1718-1754	£1.00	25g
Holy Cross (Abbey)	P.R. Index	1718-1754	with above	
Castle Ct. Prim.Meth.	C	1822-1837	£0.80	20g
Claremont St., Bapt.	C	1808-1825	£0.40	10g
	C	1813-1837	£0.80	20g
Ebenezer New Connex.	C	1835-1837	£0.20	5g
High St., Presbyterian	C	1813-1837		
/Unitarian	&	1842	£0.30	10g
St.Johns Hill Wes Meth	C	1812-1837	£1.00	25g
Swan Hill Independent	C	1813-1837	£0.80	15g
Wellington All Saints	C	1800-1825	apply	
Tan Bank, Indep.	C	1829-1835	£0.20	5g
	C	1835-1837	£0.20	5g
Trench Lane Wes. Meth.	C	1827-1835	£0.30	10g
Welsh Frankton Independent Chapel	C	1835-1837	£0.10	2.5g
Wem Cripple St., Bapt.		1821-1836	£0.20	5g
Noble St., Presbyt.		1822-1837	£0.20	5g
Whitchurch Dodington Indep.	C	1807-1837	£0.40	10g
Dodington, Presbyt./Unitarian	C	1814-1823	£0.20	5g
	CB	1823-1836	£0.20	5g
Weslyan Meth.		1813-1830	£0.40	10g
		1829-1837	£0.40	10g
Wombridge Hill Top, Coalpit	C	1817-1989	£1.40	35g
Bank, Wes. Meth.	C	1811-1837	£1.60	40g
Wrockwardine Wood Primitive Methodist	C	1822-1837	£1.20	30g
The Nabb, Wes Meth	C	1818-1837	£0.50	15g
Trench Wes. Meth.	C	1827-1837	£0.20p	5g

Census (photocopied material)

		Price	Weight
Abdon	1851	£0.20	5g
Acton Burnell	1851	£0.30	10g
Acton Round	1851	£0.20	5g
Acton Scott	1851	£0.20	5g
Adderley	1851 see Mkt. Drayton		
Alberbury	1851	£0.80	20g
Albrighton, nr. Shrewsbury	1851	£0.10	2.5g
Albrighton, nr. Wolverhampton	1851	£0.70	20g

Shropshire Family History Society (continued)

All Stretton	1851 see Church.Stretton		
Alveley	1851	£0.60	15g
Ashford Bowdler	1851	£0.20	5g
Ashford Carbonell	1851	£0.30	10g
Astley	1851	£0.20	5g
Aston Botterell	1851	£0.20	5g
Aston Eyre	1851 see Morville		
Atcham	1851	£0.40	10g
Badger	1851	£0.20	5g
Barrow	1851	£0.40	10g
Baschurch & Petton	1851 Full Trans inc Little Ness £5.60		140g
Battlefield	1851	£0.10	2.5g
Beckbury	1851	£0.30	10g
Bedstone	1851	£0.10	2.5g
Benthall	1851	£0.40	10g
Berrington	1851	£0.60	15g
Bishops Castle	1831	£0.60	15g
	1841	£2.40	60g
	1851	£0.80	20g
	1861	£3.40	85g
Bitterley	1851	£0.60	15g
Boningale	1851	£0.20	5g
Boscobel	1851	£0.10	2.5g
Bouldon	1851	£0.10	2.5g
Bromfield	1851	£0.40	10g
Brookhampton	1851	£0.10	2.5g
Broughton, nr. Shrewsbury	1851 includes Clive	£0.40	10g
Bucknell	1851	£0.40	10g
Buildwas	1851	£0.20	5g
Burford see Whitton			
Burwarton	1851	£0.20	5g
Cainham (Caynham)	1851	£0.50	15g
Cardeston	1851	£0.20	5g
Cardington	1851	£0.40	10g
Cheswardine	1851 see Mkt. Drayton		
	1881	£2.20	55g
Childs Ercall	1851 see Mkt. Drayton		
Chirbury	1851	£0.60	15g
Church Preen	1851	£0.10	2.5g
Church Pulverbatch	1851	£0.40	10g
Church Stretton	1851 incls. All Stretton & Little Stretton £0.80		20g
Clee St.Margaret	1851	£0.20	5g
Cleobury Mortimer	1851	£1.00	25g
Cleobury North	1851	£0.20	5g

Shropshire Family History Society (continued)

Clive	1851 see Broughton		
Clun	1851*	£0.90	25g
* includes Hopebendrid, Ediclift & Newcastle			
(See also Chapel Lawn)			
Clunbury	1851	£0.60	15g
Clungunford	1851	£0.40	10g
Cold Weston	1851 see Diddlebury		
Condover	1851 includes Sutton	£1.00	25g
Coreley	1851	£0.40	10g
Coton see Prees			
Cound	1851	£0.40	10g
Cressage	1851	£0.30	10g
Culmington	1851	£0.40	10g
Dawley Magna	1851	£0.60	15g
Diddlebury	1851 (inc Skirmage & Cold Weston)	£0.50	15g
Dinmore	1851	£0.10	2.5g
Ditton Priors	1851	£0.40	10g
Dodington see Whitchurch			
Donington	1851 includes Boscobel	£0.30	10g
Easthope	1851	£0.20	5g
Eaton	1851 see Market. Drayton		
Eaton Constantine	1851	£0.20	5g
Eaton under Heywood	1851	£0.40	10g
Edgton	1851	£0.20	5g
Ediclift see Clun			
Farlow	1851 includes Silvington	£0.20	5g
Fitz	1851 full transcript	£1.30	35g
Ford	1851	£1.40	35g
Frodesley	1851	£0.20	5g
Great Hanwood see Hanwood			
Great Ness	1851 full transcript	£2.40	60g
Greete	1851	£0.20	5g
Grindle, nr. Ryton	1851 see Ryton		
Grinshill	1851	£0.30	10g
Habberley	1851	£0.20	5g
Halford	1851 see Stokesay		
Hanwood	1851	£0.20	5g
Harley	1851	£0.20	5g
Haughmond Desmesne	1851	£0.20	5g
Heath see Abdon			
Highley	1851	£0.30	10g
Hinstock	1851 see Market. Drayton		
Hodnet	1851 see Market. Drayton	£0.40	10g
Holdgate	1851	£0.10	2.5g
Hope Bagot	1851	£0.10	2.5g

Shropshire Family History Society (continued)

Hopebendrid see Clun			
Hope Bowdler	1851	£0.20	5g
Hopesay	1851	£0.40	10g
Hopton Cangeford	1851	£0.10	2.5g
Hopton Castle	1851	£0.20	5g
Hopton Wafers	1851	£0.40	10g
	1861	£0.40	10g
	1871	£0.40	10g
	1881	£0.30	10g
Horderley Hall	1851	£0.10	2.5g
Hordley	1851	£0.20	5g
Hughley	1851	£0.20	5g
Hyssington, Mont.	1851	£0.20	5g
Kemberton	1851	£0.20	5g
Kenley	1851	£0.20	5g
Kinlet	1851	£0.30	10g
Knockin	1851	£1.00	25g
Lee Brockhurst	1851	£0.30	10g
Leebotwood	1851	£0.20	5g
Leighton	1851	£0.30	10g
Linley	1851	£0.30	10g
Little Ness	1851 full transcript see Baschurch		
Little Stretton	1851 see Church Stretton		
Little Wenlock	1851	£1.40	35g
Llanfair Waterdine	1851	£0.40	10g
Llansantffraid-Ym- Mechain, Powys	1851	£1.00	25g
	1871	£0.90	25g
	1881	£1.20	30g
Llanymynech	1851	£0.30	10g
Longnor	1851	£0.20	5g
Loppington	1851	£0.60	15g
Loughton see Wheathill			
Ludford	1851	£0.30	10g
Ludlow	1851	£2.00	50g
	1891 East Hamlet Only	£2.40	60g
Lydbury North	1851	£0.50	15g
Lydham	1851	£0.20	5g
Lyneal-cum-Colemere see Colemere			
Madeley	1851(SAE for indiv.names)	£7.70	
Mainstone	1851	£0.20	5g
Market Drayton (incls. Part of Staffs)	1851 Surname Index only R.D.354 (HO107/1996)	£1.40	35g
Melverley	1851 full transcript	£1.20	30g
Meole Brace	1851 see Shrewsbury		
Milson	1851	£0.20	5g
Mindtown	1851 see Wentnor		

Shropshire Family History Society (continued)

Minsterley	1851	£0.20	5g
Monkhopton	1851	£0.20	5g
Montford	1851 full transcript	£2.00	50g
More	1851	£0.20	5g
Moreton Corbet	1851	£0.30	10g
Moreton Say	1851see Mkt. Drayton		
Morville	1851 includes Aston Eyre	£0.40	10g
Much Wenlock	1851	£1.10	30g
Mucklewick	1851	£0.10	2.5g
Munslow	1851	£0.40	10g
Myddle	1841*	£1.20	30g
	1851	£0.40	10g
	1851 full transcript	£1.60	40g
	1861	£1.20	30g
	1871	£1.20	30g
	1881	£1.00	25g
Myndtown see Mindtown			
Neen Savage	1851	£0.40	10g
Neen Sollars	1851	£0.20	5g
Neenton	1851	£0.20	5g
Newcastle-on-Clun	1851 see Clun		
Newport	1841	£3.00	75g
	1851 Town	£3.20	80g
	1851 Outskirts	£0.60	15g
Norbury	1851	£0.30	10g
North Lydbury see Lydbury North			
Norton-in-Hales	1851 see Market. Drayton		
Ollerton	1851 see Market. Drayton		
Onibury	1851	£0.30	10g
Oswestry	1851	£1.40	35g
Petton	1851 full transcript see Baschurch		
Pitchford	1851	£0.20	5g
Pontesbury	1851	£1.50	40g
Posenhall	1851	£0.10	2.5g
Preston Gubbals	1851 full transcript	£1.00	25g
Ratlinghope	1851	£0.20	5g
Richards Castle	1851	£0.40	10g
Ruckley & Langley	1851	£0.10	2.5g
Rushbury	1851	£0.40	10g
Ryton, nr.Shifnal	1851	£0.20	5g
St Martins	1851	£1.00	25g
Selattyn	1841	£2.00	50g
	1851	£0.30	10g
Shawbury	1851	£0.40	10g
Sheinton	1851	£0.20	5g
Shelve	1851	£0.10	2.5g

Shropshire Family History Society (continued)

Sherrifhales	1851	£0.60	15g
Shifnal	1851	£2.10	55g
Shipton	1851	£0.20	5g
Shrawardine	1851 full transcript	£0.80	20g
Shrewsbury	1851	£3.60	90g
	1861	£2.60	65g
Sibdon Carwood	1851	£0.10	2.5g
Silvington	1851 includes Farlow	£0.20	5g
Skirmage	1851 see Diddlebury		
Smethcott (Smethcote)	1851	£0.20	5g
Snead	1851	£0.10	2.5g
Stanton Lacy	1851	£0.60	15g
Stanton Long	1851	£0.20	5g
Stanton-upon-Hine- Heath	1851	£0.50	15g
Stapleton	1851	£0.20	5g
Stirchley	1851	£0.80	20g
Stockton	1851	£0.40	10g
Stoke St. Milborough	1851 includes Heath.	£0.40	10g
Stokesay	1851 includes Halford	£0.40	10g
Stoke-upon-Tern	1851 see Market. Drayton		
Stottesdon	1851	£0.70	20g
Stow(e), nr. Bucknell	1851	£0.20	5g
Sutton, nr. Shrewsbury	1851 see Condover		
Sutton Maddock	1851	£0.40	10g
Tong	1851	£0.40	10g
Tugford	1851	£0.20	5g
Uffington	1851	£0.20	5g
Uppington	1851	£0.20	5g
Upton Cressett	1851	£0.10	2.5g
Upton Magna	1851	£0.40	10g
Wellington	1821	£8.20	**
	1841	£11.40	**
	1851	£14.70	**

** Individual names supplied send SSAE for quote:

Welshampton	1851	£0.40	10g
Wem	1851	£2.20	55g
	1851 Workhouse Only	£0.20	5g
Wentnor	1851	£0.40	10g
Westbury	1851	£0.20	5g
Wheathill	1851 includes Loughton	£0.30	10g
Whittington	1851	£0.40	10g
Willey	1851 see Linley		
Wistanstow	1851 see also Cwm Head	£0.50	15g
Withington	1851	£0.20	5g
Wo(o)lstaston	1851	£0.10	2.5g
Woore	1851 see Market. Drayton		

Shropshire Family History Society (continued)

Worthen	1851	£0.30	10g
Wrockwardine	1831 full Transcript inc.	£2.00	50g
Wroxeter	1851	£0.40	10g

Monumental Inscriptions (Photocopied material)

		Price	Weight
Abdon:	St. Margaret Heath Chapel	£0.10	2.5g
Acton Burnell	St.Mary	£1.00	30g
Acton Scott	St.Margaret	£2.60	65g
Adderley	St.Peter	£1.40	35g
Alberbury	St.Michael & AA Inscripts.	£3.00	75g
Biog.Notes		£1.60	40g
Press Cuts.		£5.00	125g
Albrighton, nr. Shrewsbury	St.John the Baptist	£0.40	10g
Annscroft	Christ Church	£1.70	45g
Ash	Christ Church	£2.60	65g
Ashford Carbonell	St.Mary Magdalene	£1.00	30g
Astley	St.Mary	£0.60	5g
Astley Abbots	St.Calixtus	£1.40	35g
Aston Botterell	St.Michael & AA	£0.40	10g
Aston, nr. Oswestry	Aston Hall Chapel	£0.80	20g
Atcham	St.Eata	£1.40	35g
Barrow	St.Giles	£0.80	20g
Baschurch	All Saints	£2.80	70g
Battlefield	St.Mary Magdalene	£1.20	30g
Bayston Hill	Christ Church	£0.40	10g
Bedstone	St.Mary	£1.00	25g
Benthall	St.Bartholomew	£1.40	35g
Berrington	All Saints	£1.20	30g
Bicton	Old Church	£1.00	25g
	Holy Trinity (New)	£2.40	60g
Billingsley	St.Mary	£0.20	5g
Bitterley	St.Mary	£1.40	35g
Blackford	Primitive Methodist	£0.20	5g
Bomere Heath	Methodist	£0.40	10g
	Mission Chapel	£0.20	5g
	Presbyterian	£0.20	5g
Bromfield	St. Mary the Virgin	£2.60	45g
Broseley	Birchmeadow Chapel	£0.40	10g
Broughton, nr. Bridgnorth	St.Mary	£0.40	10g
Bucknell	St.Mary	£2.30	60g
Burwarton	SS. Peter & Paul	£0.80	20g
Cainham (Caynham)	St.Mary	£1.20	30g
	Methodist Chapel	£0.20	5g
Calverhall	Holy Trinity	£1.20	30g

Shropshire Family History Society (continued)

Cardeston	St.Michael	£0.60	15g
Cefn Y Blodwel		£0.20	5g
Chapel Lawn, Nr. Clun	St.Mary	£1.00	25g
Chelmarsh	St.Peter	£1.80	45g
Chetton	St.Giles	£1.00	25g
Chetwynd	St. Michael & AA	£2.40	60g
Childs Ercall	St.Michael	£1.60	40g
Chorley	Baptist Chapel	£0.20	5g
Church Aston	St.Andrew	£1.80	45g
Church Preen	St.John the Baptist	£0.80	20g
Church Stretton	St.Lawrence	£4.80	120g
(See also All Stretton & Little Stretton)			
Clee Hill	Primitive Methodist	£0.20	10g
Clee St.Margaret	St.Margaret	£0.60	15g
Cleeton St.Mary	St.Mary	£0.60	15g
Cleobury Mortimer	St.Mary	£2.50	65g
Cleobury, North	SS.Peter & Paul	£0.90	25g
Clive	All Saints	£1.20	30g
Clunbury	St.Swithin	£1.00	25g
Coalbrookdale	Quaker (2 parts)	£1.00	25g
Cockshutt	St.Helen	£1.20	30g
Cold Weston	St.Mary	£0.20	5g
Colemere	St.John the Evang.	£1.20	30g
Condover	SS Andrew & Mary	£1.20	30g
	New Churchyard	£0.60	15g
Coreley	St.Peter	£1.20	30g
Coton see Prees			
Cound	St.Peter	£1.00	25g
Coxall	Baptist Chapel	£0.40	10g
Cressage	Christ Church	£1.40	35g
Criftins	St.Matthew	£0.60	15g
Cwm Head,	St.Michael	£0.20	5g
Diddlebury	St.Peter	£1.40	35g
Ditton Priors	St.John The Baptist	£1.10	30g
Doddington	St.John	£0.60	15g
Dodington See Whitchurch			
Dovaston	United Reform Ch.	£1.60	40g
Dowles (Worcs.)		£1.60	40g
Drayton See Market Drayton			
Dudleston	St.Mary	£0.60	15g
Dudleston Heath See Criftin			
Easthope	St.Peter	£0.20	10g
Eaton Constantine	St.Mary The Virgin	£0.80	20g
Eaton-Under-Heywood	St.Edith	£1.40	35g
Ediclift See Clun			
Edstaston	St.Mary	£2.00	50g

Shropshire Family History Society (continued)

Ellesmere	St.Mary	£1.80	45g
Farlow	St.Giles	£0.60	15g
Fauls	Holy Emmanuel	£0.40	10g
Fitz	SS.Peter & Paul	£1.40	35g
Frodesley	St.Mark	£1.40	35g
Glazeley	St.Bartholomew	£0.40	10g
Great Hanwood See Hanwood			
Great Ness	St.Andrew	£1.40	35g
Greete	St.James	£0.60	15g
Grinshill	All Saints	£1.00	25g
Habberley	St.Mary	£0.80	20g
Hadnall	St.Mary Magdalene	apply	
	Primitive Methodist	£0.20	5g
Halford	St.Thomas	£1.00	25g
Hanwood	St.Thomas	£2.00	50g
Harley	St.Mary	£0.80	20g
Harmer Hill	Chapel	£0.40	10g
Haughton, Nr.W.Felton	St.Chad	£2.00	50g
Heath see Abdon			
Hengoed	St.Barnabas	£1.00	25g
Hinstock	St.Oswald	£0.60	15g
Hodnet	St.Luke	£6.20	155g
Holdgate	Holy Trinity	£0.60	15g
Hope Bagot	St.John the Baptist	£0.60	15g
Hopebendrid See Clun			
Hope Bowdler	St.Andrew	£1.70	45g
Hopton	Methodist Chapel	£0.40	10g
Hopton Bank	Bethel Prim. Meth.	£0.20	5g
Hopton Cangeford	Chapel of Ease	£0.40	10g
Hopton Castle	St.Edward	£0.70	20g
Hopton Wafers	St.Michael	£1.20	30g
Hordley	St.Mary the Virgin	£0.80	20g
Hughley	St.John the Baptist	£0.80	20g
Ightfield	St.John the Baptist	£1.50	40g
Jackfield	St.Mary	£0.40	10g
Kemberton	St.Andrew	£0.40	10g
Kenley	St.John the Baptist	£0.80	20g
Ketley	St Mary, Red Lake	£1.90	50g
Kinlet	St.John the Baptist	£0.80	20g
Kinnerley	St.Mary the Virgin		
	W.I. Transcript	£2.80	70g
	Barclays Transcipts	£0.40	10g
Kinnersley	St.Chad	£0.60	15g
Knockin	St.Mary	£2.40	60g
	Knockin Heath Meth.	£1.20	30g

Shropshire Family History Society (continued)

Leaton	Holy Trinity	£1.40	35g
Lee Brockhurst	St.Peter	£0.80	20g
Leebotwood	St.Mary	£1.60	40g
Lilleshall	St.Michael & AA	£2.00	50g
Little Stretton	All Saints	£0.20	5g
Llandrinio, Powys		£0.40	10g
Llangedwyn, Clwyd	St.Cedwyn	£3.80	95g
Llansantffraid-Ym-Mechain, Powys		£0.80	20g
Llansilin, Clwyd	St.Silin	£3.80	95g
Llantysilio, Powys		£0.40	10g
Llanyblodwel	St.Michael	£1.00	25g
	Barclay T/S	£0.40	10g
Llanymynech	St.Agatha	£0.80	20g
Loppington	St.Michael & AA	£1.40	35g
Loughton See Wheathill			
Ludford	St.Giles	£1.80	45g
Ludlow	St.Laurence		
	Inside only	£1.20	30g
	S.E.Corner	£1.00	25g
	War Mem.	£0.40	10g
Lydbury North	St.Michael & AA	£2.00	50g
Lydham	Holy Trinity	£1.00	25g
Lyneal-cum-Colemere See Colemere			
Madeley	St.Michael	£4.80	120g
Maesbrook	St.John		
	Barclays Transcripts	£0.20	5g
	1997 Transcript	£1.00	25g
	Baptist Chapel (Demolished)	£0.20	5g
	Methodist Chapel	apply	
Market Drayton	St.Mary	£1.20	30g
	Baptist Chapel	£0.10	2.5g
	Congregational	£0.20	5g
Marton, nr.Chirbury	St.Mark	0.80	20g
Melverley	St.Peter		
	Barclays Transcripts	£0.20	5g
	W.I. Transcripts	£0.80	20g
Meole Brace	Holy Trinity	£3.00	75g
Middleton-in- Chirbury	Holy Trinity	£1.00	25g
Middleton Scriven	St.John the Baptist	£0.20	5g
Milson	St.George	£0.60	5g
Mindtown	St.John the Baptist	£0.40	10g
Minsterley	Holy Trinity	£2.00	50g
	Congregational	£0.20	5g
	Methodist	£0.20	5g

Shropshire Family History Society (continued)

Montford	St.Chad	£1.40	35g
More	St.Peter	£1.80	45g
Moreton Corbet	St.Bartholomew	£0.80	20g
Moreton Say	St.Margaret	£3.20	80g
Morton, nr. Oswestry	SS Philip & James	£0.60	15g
Morton, nr. Shawbury	Chapel	£0.10	2.5g
Morville	St.Gregory	£1.80	45g
Mossfield	Baptist Chapel	£0.20	5g
Myddle	St.Peter	£1.80	45g
Myndtown see Mindtown			
Nash	St.John the Baptist		
	Inside only	£0.20	5g
	1993 Transcript	£0.80	20g
Neen Savage	St.Mary		
	Sims Transcript	£0.20	5g
	W.I. Transcript	£1.00	25g
Neen Sollars	All Saints	£0.40	10g
Neenton	All Saints	£0.40	10g
Newcastle-on-Clun	St.John the Evangelist	£1.20	30g
Newport	St.Nicholas	£0.80	20g
Newtown, nr.Wem	King Charles	£2.20	55g
Norbury	All Saints	£0.80	20g
North Lydbury see Lydbury North			
Norton-in-Hales	St.Chad	£1.60	40g
Oakengates	Holy Trinity	£1.60	40g
Onibury	St.Michael	£1.00	25g
Oswestry	St.David Chapel of Ease (Redundant)	£1.00	25g
	St. Oswald		
	1872 Transcript	£1.70	45g
	1991 Transcript	£2.00	50g
Plealey	Methodist Church	£0.10	2.5g
Plowden	St.Francis R.C.	£0.60	15g
Pontesbury	St.George	£3.00	75g
	Baptist Chapel	£0.40	10g
	Congregational	£1.00	25g
Pradoe, nr West Felton		£0.80	20g
Prees	St.Chad	£3.20	80g
	United Reform	£0.60	15g
	Coton Meth. Chapel	£0.40	20g
Prees Green	Primitive Methodist	£0.20	5g
Preeshenlle see Gobowen			
Preston Gubbals	St.Martin	£0.80	20g
Preston upon the Weald Moors	St.Laurence	£1.00	25g
Priors Lee	St.Peter		
	Inside only	£1.40	35g

Shropshire Family History Society (continued)

Pulverbatch See Church Pulverbatch

Quatt	St.Andrew	£1.70	45g
Ratlinghope	St.Margaret	£0.60	15g
Rhydycroesau, Clwyd	Christ Church	£1.20	30g
Richards Castle	St.Bartholomew (Old)	£3.60	90g
Rowton, Ercall Magna	All Hallows	£1.20	30g
Rushbury	St.Peter	£1.80	45g
Ruyton-XI-Towns	St.John the Baptist	£1.60	40g
St.Martins	St.Martin of Tours,		
	Lloyds Transcripts	£1.40	35g
	W.I. Transcripts	£2.00	50g
	1928 Extracts	£1.40	35g
Shawbury	St.Mary	£1.80	45g
Sheinton	SS.Peter & Paul	£1.00	25g
Shelve	All Saints	£2.00	50g
Sherrifhales	St.Mary	£1.60	40g
Shifnal	St.Andrew	£6.10	apply
	Interior Only	£0.80	20g
Shipton	St.James	£0.80	20g
Shrawardine	St.Mary	£0.80	20g
SHREWSBURY	St.Alkmund	£0.80	20g
	St.Chad (Old Ch.)		
	Part 1	£1.40	35g
	Part 2	£0.60	15g
	St.George	£0.10	2.5g
	St.Giles	£0.80	20g
	Holy Cross (Abbey)	£0.80	20g
	St. Julian		
	Part 1	£0.20	2.5g
	Part 2	£0.40	10g
	Detached	£0.60	15g
	St.Mary		
	Part 1	£0.40	10g
	Part 2	£0.60	15g
	1984 Transcript	£1.20	30g
	St.Michael	£1.00	25g
SHROPSHIRE	List of Known T/s	£1.00	15g
Sidbury	Holy Trinity	£0.20	5g
Silvington	St.Nicholas	£0.30	10g
Smethcott (Smethcote)	St.Michael	£0.60	15g
Snailbeach	St.Luke	£0.20	5g
	Lordshill Baptist	£0.60	15g
Snead	St.Mary the Virgin	£0.60	15g
Stanton Lacy	St.Peter	£2.60	65g
Stanton Long	St.Michael	£0.70	20g
Stanton-Upon-Hine Heath	St.Andrew	£1.20	30g

Shropshire Family History Society (continued)

Stirchley	St.James	£0.80	20g
Stockton	St.Chad	£1.20	30g
Stoke St Milborough	St.Milburga	£1.00	25g
Stokesay	St.John the Baptist	£3.00	75g
Stoke-upon-Tern	St.Peter	£3.20	80g
Stottesdon	St.Mary	£1.00	25g
	Methodist Chapel	£0.10	2.5g
Sutton Maddock	St.Mary	£1.00	25g
Sweeney Hall, nr. Oswestry	Private N.C. Burial Ground	£0.20	5g
Tasley	SS Peter & Paul	£0.60	15g
Tibberton	All Saints	£2.00	50g
Tong	SS Mary & Barthol.	£1.80	45g
Trefonen	All Saints	£0.60	15g
Uffington	Holy Trinity	£1.00	25g
Upton Cressett	St.Michael	£0.40	10g
Upton Magna	St.Lucia	£2.20	55g
Waters Upton	Methodist Chapel	£0.10	2.5g
Weirbrook nr. West Felton	Independent Chapel (Incls. Stones removed from Grimpo)	£0.40	10g
Wellington	All Saints	£2.20	55g
	Christ Church	£1.40	35g
Welsh Frankton	St.Andrew	£0.60	50g
Wem	Aston St. Cemetery	£0.60	15g
	United Reform	£0.80	20g
Wentnor	St.Michael & AA	£1.60	40g
West Felton see Grimpo, Haughton & Weirbrook			
Weston Lullingfield	Holy Trinity	£1.20	30g
Weston Rhyn	St.John the Divine	£0.90	25g
Weston-Under-Redcastle	St.Luke	£1.40	35g
Wheathill	Holy Trinity	£0.60	15g
Whitchurch	St.Alkmund	£3.20	80g
Whittington	St.John the Baptist Williams Ts/s 1994	£4.40	110g
Whitton, nr. Burford	St.Mary	£0.60	15g
Whixall	St.Mary	£2.00	50g
	United Reform (Indp)	£0.40	10g
	Welsh End Meth.	£0.60	15g
Wilcott	Congreg. Chapel	£0.20	2.5g
Withington	St.John the Baptist	£1.20	30g
Wombridge	SS.Mary & Leonard	£3.20	80g
Woodcote	St.Peter	£0.60	15g
Wo(o)lstaston	St.Michael	£0.80	20g
Woore	St.Leonard	£3.20	80g
Worfield	St.Peter	£2.40	60g

Shropshire Family History Society (continued)

Worthen	All Saints	£3.10	80g
Wrockwardine	St.Peter	£1.20	30g
Wrockwardine Wood	Holy Trinity	£1.60	40g
Wroxeter	St.Andrew	£1.00	25g
Yockleton	Holy Trinity	£1.20	30g

Miscellaneous (photocopied material)

Baschurch
   List of all Probates from Calendar of

Wills at Lichfield J.R.O.	1472-1858	£1.40	35g
P.C.C. Wills & Administrations:	1630-1700	£0.20	5g
Cheswardine Apprentices	1729-1806	£0.60	15g
Bastardy Orders	1700-1812	£1.00	25g
Examinations	1697-1817	£1.00	25g
Settlements	1672-1817	£0.80	20g

Fitz see Baschurch
Great Ness see Baschurch
Little Ness see Baschurch
Montford see Baschurch
Shrawardine see Baschurch
Llansantffraid-Ym-Mechian, Powys

Directory 1895 Name Index		£0.10	2.5g
Some Family Trees		apply	

   Middleton-in-Chirbury Extracts from the Rev. Brewsters

Diary		£1.00	25g

Sedgeley (Staffs) Settlement Exams

(Shrops Entries)	1816-1834	£1.20	30g

Shiffnal The Indexes from Tithe Aportionment

Owners	1841	£0.50	15g
Occupiers	1841	£0.50	15g
Shrewsbury Peculiar Court Act Book	1674-1697 (St Mary)	£0.40	10g
Shrewsbury Women s Wills & Inventries 1660-1760		£4.20	105g

Poor Law Records

Removal Orders	17-19th C	apply	
Settlement Certificates 17-19th C		£1.50	40g
Settlement Examinations 17-19th C		£3.80	95g

   Settlement Strays in

Warwicks. Index 17-19th C		£1.00	25g
Society of Friends / Quakers	Extracts from		
Meeting Registers	1656-1835	£0.80	20g
	1657-1836	£0.60	15g
	1659-1837	£0.80	20g

Shropshire Family History Society (continued)

Index of all entries in Calendar of
Wills at Lichfield J.R.O.

"Jones"	1472-1860	£1.60	40g
"Low(e)"	1530-1859	£0.80	20g
Research Papers -"Swannick"		£1.70	45g
Dr. Williams Library Shropshire Extracts Baptisms	1743-1837		
Executions in England Incls Executions in Shrops.	1606-1895 1841-61.	£1.20	30g

SOMERSET (see also Bristol & Dorset)
Somerset and Dorset Family History Society

Web Site: http://ourworld.compuserve.com/homepages/Alan__J__BROWN

Murial Monk, 65 Wyke Road, WEYMOUTH, England, DT4 9QN,
e-mail: a.monk@btinternet.com

Indexes of the 1851 Census of Dorset

	(a)	(b)	(c)	(e)
Master Index of 1851 Dorset Surnames	£1.90	£2.15	£2.40	£2.90
Vol. 1 Weymouth (2nd ed., includes occupations)	£3.75	£4.00	£4.30	£5.20
Vol. 2 Portland area (2nd ed., includes occupations)	£3.75	£4.00	£4.45	£5.60
Vol. 3 Dorchester area	£2.95	£3.20	£3.80	£5.00
Vol. 4 Maiden Newton area (2nd ed. incl. occ.)	£3.75	£4.00	£4.50	£5.75
Vol.5 Poole area.	£2.95	£3.20	£3.70	£4.70
Vol 6 Bridport area (2nd ed. incl. occ)	£3.75	£4.00	£4.55	£5.75
Vol 7 Corfe & Wareham area (2nd ed. incl.occ)	£3.75	£4.00	£4.45	£5.60
Vol 8 Sherborne area	£2.95	£3.20	£3.70	£4.70
Vol 9 Bere Regis area	£2.95	£3.20	£3.70	£4.70
Vol 10 Sturminster Newton area	£2.95	£3.20	£3.70	£4.70
Vol 11 Shaftesbury area (2nd ed incl.occ)	£3.75	£4.00	£4.45	£5.60
Vol.12 Blandford area	£2.95	£3.20	£3.75	£4.75
Vol.13 Wimborne Minster area	£2.95	£3.20	£3.80	£5.00
Vol.14 Lyme Regis area	£2.95	£3.20	£3.70	£4.85
Vol.15 Beaminster area	£2.95	£3.20	£3.70	£4.85

Indexes of the 1891 Census of Dorset

Vol.1	Shaftesbury, Cann & Motcombe	£3.00	£3.25	£3.40	£4.10
Vol.2	Cranborne area	£3.00	£3.25	£3.40	£4.10
Vol.3	Wimborne area	£4.00	£4.25	£4.70	£5.85
Vol.4	Weymouth	£4 00	£4.25	£4.70	£5.85
Vol.5	Fontmell & Gillingham	£4.00	£4.25	£4.70	£5.85
Vol.6	Stalbridge & Sturminster Newton	£4.00	£4.25	£4.70	£5.85
Vol.7	Portland & Abbotsbury	£4.00	£4.25	£4.70	£5.85
Vol.8	Lyme Regis	£4.00	£4.25	£4.70	£5.85
Vol.9	Purbeck	£4.00	£4.25	£4.70	£5.85
Vol.10	Parishes around Weymouth	£4.00	£4.25	£4.70	£5.85

Somerset and Dorset Family History Society (continued)

Dorset Burial Index

Vol. 1 Lyme Regis 1813-1837	£2.40	£2.70	£2.85	£3.40

1851 Census Surname Indexes - Somerset

Master Index of 1851 Somerset Surnames	£4.00	£4.25	£4.65	£5.60
Vol.1 West Somerset	£2.00	£2.25	£2.50	£2.95
Vol.2 Taunton area	£2.00	£2.25	£2.60	£3.15
Vol.3 Bridgwater area	£2.00	£2.25	£2.50	£2.95
Vol.4 Yeovil area	£2.00	£2.25	£2.50	£2.95
Vol.5 Wincanton & Frome	£2.00	£2.25	£2.50	£2.95
Vol.6 Wells, Shepton Mallet area	£2.00	£2.25	£2.50	£2.95
Vol.7 Wedmore, Cheddar & Axbridge	£2.00	£2.25	£2.50	£2.95

Somerset Marriage Indexes

Vol.1	Taunton: St James 1610-1701	£2.15	£2.40	£2.60	£3.15
Vol.2	1702-1723	£2.15	£2.40	£2.60	£3.15
Vol.3	1724-1754	£2.15	£2.40	£2.60	£3.15
Vol.1	Taunton: St Mary Magdalene 1558-1673	£2.15	£2.40	£2.70	£3.35
Vol.2	1674-1718	£2.15	£2.40	£2.70	£3.35
Vol.3	1719-1754	£2.15	£2.40	£2.70	£3.35

Somerset Burial Index

Vol.1	Taunton: St Mary & St James 1813-1837	£2.15	£2.40	£2.60	£3.15

Miscellaneous

Dorset Volunteer Soldiers 1794-1798	£1.90	£2.15	£2.40	£2.90
Greenwood Tree Index	£2.00	£2.25	£2.75	£3.20

Cheques, made payable to S&DFHS, with orders please. Orders by Credit Card also accepted.

Postal Code for (e) is 'the rest of the world airmail.

NOTE: 1891 Indexes are joint publications with the Dorset F.H.S and can also be obtained from:
Miss S Lawrence, 179 Victoria Road, FERNDOWN, England, BH22 9HY
Cheques, made payable to Dorset F.H.S.

SUFFOLK

Felixstowe Family History Society
Mrs. S. Tod, 430 High Street, Felixstowe, Suffolk IP11 9QP
(Please add 35p P&P per book, (65p overseas)
(£1 inland & £3.00 o/seas for the Conference book)

Parish Register Transcripts

	Book Price
Walton (St. Mary) Marriages 1657-1756 (revised edition)	£2.50
Trimley St. Mary Baptisms 1655-1782	£3.00
Trimley St. Mary Marriages 1654-1785	£3.00
Trimley St. Mary Burials 1664-1785	£3.00
Trimley St Martin Baptisms, Marriages and Burials 1715-1756	£2.55
Brightwell/Foxhall Baptisms, Marriages & Burials 1653-1837	£6.75
Nacton Baptisms, Marriages and Burials 1705-1756	£2.55
Bucklesham Baptisms, Marriages and Burials 1678-1757	£3.30
Bucklesham Baptisms, Marriages & Burials 1758-1854	£6.00
Hemley Baptisms, Marnages and Burials 1698-1837	£4.65
Levington Baptisms, Marriages and Burials 1701-1812	£5.40
Levington Baptisms, Marnages and Burials 1562-1700	£4.05
Felixstowe (St. Peter and St. Paul) Marriages 1654-1840	£2.70
Felixstowe (St. Peter and St. Paul) Baptisms 1653-1812	£4.35
Felixstowe (St. Peter and St. Paul) Baptisms 1813-1874	£2.25
Felixstowe (St. Peter and St. Paul) Burials 1653-1812	£3.75
Waldringfield, Baptisms, Marriages and Burials 1695-1837	£5.85

Monumental Inscriptions

Trimley St. Mary and Trimley St. Martin	£2.50
Kirton and Falkenham	£1.50
Walton (St. Mary)	£1.75
Felixstowe (St. Peter and St Paul) pre 1925	£2.95
Felixstowe (St. Peter and St. Paul) 1925-1991	£2.95
Waldringfield, Newbourn and Hemley	£2.95

Miscellaneous

Felixstowe F.H.S. Settlers in Europe 1550-1750 Conference (a written collection of the talks given)	£7.50

Suffolk Family History Society

Web Site: http://www.genuki.org.uk/big/eng/SFK/sfhs/sfhs.htm

Suffolk 1813-1837 Marriage Index available from:
Mrs Pamela Palgrave, Crossfield House, Dale Road, Stanton, Bury St Edmunds, Suffolk IP31 2DY.

Suffolk 1851 Census Index available from: Mrs Edna Miller, Clematis, Mill Common, Westhall, Halesworth, Suffolk IP19 8RQ.

Miscellaneous
Sudden Deaths in Suffolk 1767-1858 - available from: Mrs Pamela Palgrave, as above.

Freemen of the Borough of Ipswich 1320-1996 available from: Mr R D Spilling, 7 Crofton Close, Ipswich, Suffolk IP4 4QR

King Edward VI Grammar School, Bury St Edmunds, Index of Pupils 1901-1925 available from: Mrs H E M Spencer, Bosmere, Perkins Way, Tostock, Bury St Edmunds, Suffolk IP30 9PU.

Index of Beneficiaries in Wills - Archdeaconry of Sudbury 1847-1858 - available from: Mrs M Rix, Clapstile Farm, Alpheton, Sudbury, Suffolk CO10 9BN.

Serving You Through the Years - a History of Stowmarket Business Families - available from: Mr Michael Durant, 2 Kipling Way, Stowmarket, Suffolk IP14 1TP.

British Record Society

For details of publications relating to Suffolk published by the British Record Society see their entry on page 200.

SURREY

West Surrey Family History Society

Available by post from: Mrs Rosemary Cleaver, 17 Lane End Drive, Knaphill, Woking, Surrey GU21 2QQ. Please make cheques payable to West Surrey FHS.

Research Aids Series

		(a)	(b)
2.	Suburban London - Map showing parish boundaries pre 1837 (3rd ed. 1996)	£0.85	£1.20
3.	Registration Districts in Surrey and Rural Middlesex, 1850	£0.40	£0.75
4.	A list of Surrey Parochial Poor Law Records and their location (4th ed.)	£0.65	£1.00
5.	Guide to the Surrey Censuses of 1841-1861 (5th ed.)	£0.65	£1.00

West Surrey Family History Society (continued)

6.	Guide to Genealogical Research in Victorian London (detailing all Anglican parishes outside the City created before 1870 with map showing their boundaries) (7th ed.-1998)	£2.40	£2.60
7.	Surrey Inhabitants Lists (4th ed.)	£0.65	£1.00
8.	Genealogical Gazetteer of mid-Victorian London (street index keyed to the parishes described in, and for use in conjunction with, No.6 above)	£2.40	£2.60
9.	Guide to the Surrey Censuses of 1871-1891	£0.85	£1.20
11.	Surrey Probate Records, Marriage Licences and Bishops' Transcripts (3rd ed.)	£0.65	£1.00
12	The Hundreds of Surrey	£0.50	£0.85
13.	Surrey Parishes with list of Neighbouring Parishes	£0.65	£1.00
14.	Guide to the Surrey Lay Subsidies 1500-1645	£0.50	£0.85
15.	Guide to Genealogical Research in Late Victorian Edwardian London (4th ed.) (for use in conjunction with No.6 above)	£2.40	£2.60
17.	The IGI - Parishes & periods in the 1988 edition for Surrey (2nd ed.)	£0.65	£1.00
18.	Surrey Parish Codes	£0.65	£1.00
19.	The Monumental Inscriptions of Surrey a list of copies (2nd ed.)	£1.50	£1.85
20.	Middlesex in the 1988 IGI - Parishes and periods covered	£0.50	£0.85
21.	Guide to Middlesex Lay Subsidies 1500-1645	£0.50	£0.85
22.	The Hundreds of Middlesex	£0.40	£0.75
23.	Middlesex Contiguous Parishes	£0.50	£0.85
24.	Middlesex Wills, Marriage Licences and Bishops' Transcripts (2nd ed.)	£0.65	£1.00
25.	Guide to the Middlesex Census 1801-1861(4th ed.)	£0.65	£1.00
26.	Guide to the Middlesex Census 1871-1891	£0.65	£1.00
20-26	MIDDLESEX RESEARCH AIDS (set)	£2.35	£2.60
28.	A Provisional List of City of London-Poor Law Records (2nd ed.)	£1.25	£1.60.
29.	Surrey Directories - A Finding List (2nd ed. - revised)	£2.35	£2.60
30.	Streets, Parishes and Wards of the City of London	£2.90	£3.10
31.	London, Middlesex and Surrey Workhouse Records, a guide to their nature and location	£1.75	£2.10
32.	Surrey Genealogy and Records	£2.90	£3.10
33.	A Guide to Middlesex Parish Documents	£2.35	£2.60
34.	A List of Books and Articles about Surrey Places	£2.90	£3.10
35.	A Guide to Surrey Manorial Records	£1.85	£2.10
36.	A Guide to London & Middlesex Genealogy & Records	£2.90	£3.10
37.	Middlesex Directories - A Finding List	£2.55	£2.80
38.	A Guide to London and Middlesex Manorial Records	£2.00	£2.35
39.	A List of Books and Articles about London, Middlesex and Metropolitan Surrey Places	£2.90	£3.10

West Surrey Family History Society (continued)

40.	A List of Surrey Parishes - Ancient and Modern	£1.25	£1.60
41.	Surrey map showing parish boundaries, and those parishes in other counties bounding Surrey.	£1.05	£1.60

Records Series

1.	Index to Archdeaconry Court of Surrey Wills, 1752-1858 (3rd ed.)	£3.60	£3.90
3.	Index of Wills & Administrations in Commissary and Peculiar Courts of Surrey,1752-1858 (3rd ed.)	£3.90	£4.20.
4.	Calendar of Lay Subsidies: West Surrey, 1603-1649	£2.90	£3.20
8.	Petty Sessions Minutes Copthorne and Effingham Hundreds 1784-1793	£3.15	£3.45
9.	Index to Surrey Wills Proved in the PCC 1650-1700	£3.60	£3.90
10.	The Return of Owners of Land 1873: Surrey (excluding the Metropolis)	£3.85	£4.15
11.	Index to Surrey Quaker Obituaries 1813-1892 in the "Annual Monitor"	£1.45	£1.80
12.	Calendar of Miscellaneous Elizabethan Lay Subsidies Surrey 1570-1600	£3.60	£3.90
13	The Return of Owners of Land 1873: Middlesex (excluding Metropolis)	£3.35	£3.65
14.	Surrey 1851 Census Strays	£3.30	£3.55
15.	Index to the 1775 Surrey Poll Book (with microfiche of original book)	£2.60	£2.85
16.	Index to the 1861 Census for Guildford Surrey	£3.35	£3.65
17.	Surrey Administrations in the Prerogative Court of Canterbury 1760-1781	£2.90	£3.20
18.	Worplesdon, Surrey - Index to 1891 Census	£1.75	£2.10
19.	Surrey Cases and Deponents in the Court of the Exchequer 1561-1835	£4.75	£5.10
20.	Surrey Feet of Fines 1685-1714	£3.35	£3.65
21.	Index to Archdeaconry Court of Surrey Wills 1660-1751	£6.05	£6.50
22.	Surrey Feet of Fines 1649-1684	£4.45	£4.85
23.	Index to Commissary Court of Surrey Wills, 1660-1751	£2.90	£3.20
24.	Surrey Feet of Fines 1714-1760	£5.00	£5.40
25.	Index of Surrey Wills and Admons in the Peculiar Court 1660-1751	£2.90	£3.20
26.	Surrey Feet of Fines 1603-1648	£4.45	£4.85
27.	Surrey Cases & Depositions Chancery 1714-1758 & Exchequer 1497-1603	£3.35	£3.65
28.	Surrey feet of Fines 1558-1602	£4.45	£4.85

SUSSEX

Family Roots Family History Society
(Eastbourne & District)
Publications Officer, Walcot, 1 Hindover Crescent, Seaford, East Sussex

Parish Registers
	Price
Bodle Street Green, Sussex, Baptisms 1856-1986	£5.60
Bodle Street Green Sussex, Marriages 1856-1986	£4.50

Census
Coastguards in Eastbourne Area from Censuses	£2.65
Coastguards in Eastbourne Area from Censuses (Supplement)	£1.55
Coastguards in Eastbourne Area from Parish Registers	£3.45
Railway Workers in Eastbourne Area from Census (1841-1881)	£2.65

Rolls of Honour & War Memorials in some East Sussex Villages
Vol 1. £2.65
(Alcistan, Alfriston, Arlington, Ashburnham Penhurst, Beddingham, Berwick, Bodle Street Green, Brightling Chalvington, Chiddingly, Dallington, East Dean, East Hoathly, Firle, Folkington, Friston, Glynde, Hailsham, Heathfield, Hellingly, Herstmonceux, Horam, Jevington, Laughton, Littlington, Ninfield, Pevensey, Polegate, Ringmer, Ripe, Selmeston, Stone Cross, Upper Dicker, Waldron, Warbleton, Wartling, Westham, Willingdon, Wilmington)

Vol 2. £3.75
(Barcombe, Bishopstone, Buxted Highhurstwood, Buxted St. Marys, Buxted St. Margarets, Catsfield, Chailey, Clayton. Denton, Ditchling, East Chiltington, Fletching, Framfield, Hadlow Down, Hooe, Horsted Parva (Little), Hurst, Iford, Isfield, Keymer, Kingstone - Juxta, Maresfield, Newick, Offham, Hamsey, Ovingdean, Piddinghoe, Plumpton Green, Pyecombe, Rodmell, Rottingdean, Seaford, Tarring Neville, Uckfield, West Dean, Westmeston, Streat, Wivelsfield)

Vol 3. £3.75
(Battle, Beckley, Bodiam, Brede, East Guildford, Etchingham, Ewhurst, Fairlight, Flimwell, Guestling, Hurst Green, Icklesham, Iden, Lamberhurst, Little Common, Mountfield, Netherfield, Northiam, Peasmarsh, Pett, Playden, Robertsbridge, Rye, Rye Harbour, Salehurst, Sedlescombe, Staplecross, Stonegate, Ticehurst, Udimore, Wadhurst, Westfield, Whatlington, Winchelsea)

Vol 4. £3.50
(Ashdown Forest, Bexhill, Brightling, Chalvington, Colemans Hatch, Cross-In-Hand, Crowhurst, Jarvis Brook, St. Leonards-on-Sea-Hollington, Sidley, Southeese, Telscombe, Withyham)

Family Roots Family History Society (Eastbourne & District) (continued)

Vol 5 £4.00
(Ashurstwood, Blackham, Burwash, Crowborough, Danehill, Eridge, Faiwarp, Five Ashes, Forest Row, Frant, Hartfield, Horsted Keynes, Lindfield, Mayfield, Newhaven, Nutley, Rotherfield,Tidebrook)

Vol 6 £6.00
(Alciston cum Selmeston, Ansty, Balcombe, Battle, Camber, Crawley Down Cuckfield, East Grinstead, Groombridge, Haywards Heath, High Hurstwood, Mark Cross, Newenden (Kent), Plumpton, Rye Harbour, Rye-St.Anthony's, Sandhurst (Kent), Scaynes Hill, Twineham, West Hoathly, Westmeston Cum Streat, Worth)

Vol 7 £4.00
(Albourne, Ardingly, Ashurst (Kent), Bolney, Broadwater Down (Kent), Copthorne, Cowden (Kent), Edburton, Falmer & Stanmer, Felbridge(Surrey), Hammerwood, Highbrook, Holtye, Langton Green (Kent) Newtimber, Patcham, Poynings, Rusthall (Kent), Sayers Common, Slaugham, Staplefield, Turners Hill)

Rolls of Honour & War Memorials in some East and West Sussex Villages and Towns and some border villages of Kent and Surrey.

Vol 8 £4.35
(Brighton - Egypt Campaign & Nile Expedition, Royal Sussex Boer War Memorial, Phoenix Brewery: Burgess Hill - St Andrews, St Johns, St Edwards: Burstow (Surrey) Copthorne Common: Crawley: Crowborough Golf Course: Groombridge: Hailsham - Cemetery Methodist Church: Hangleton: Ifield: Kingston Buci : Lewes - Police Station: Old Shoreham: Ore: Portslade Village: Ringmer - The Cricketers: St. Leonards-Christchurch: Shoreham by Sea - Church of the Good Shepherd-St Mary de Haura: Southwick & Fishergate: West Blatchington-St Peters: Woodmancote.)

Rolls of Honour in Lewes, Peacehaven & Piddinghoe £3.35
Rolls of Honour and War Memorials in Eastbourne £5.10
Smuggling, The Fight Against, around Eastbourne & Newhaven £5.10

Monumental Inscriptions
Wartling, Sussex, Monumental Inscriptions £3.40
Zoar Chapel, Dicker, Sussex, Monumental Inscriptions £3.60
Bodle Street Green, Sussex, Burials 1856- 1986 £4.50
Jevington, Sussex, Monumental Inscriptions £3.35
Lewes War Memorial, School Hill, Lewes, Sussex,1914-1918 £3.65
Hastings, Sussex War Memorial 1899-1902:1914-1918: 1939-1945. £4.25

Miscellaneous
Eastbourne Area Coastguard References at Kew Part I: A - J £4.00
Eastbourne Area Coastguard References at Kew Part 2: K - Z £4.00

Sussex Family History Group

Web Site: http://www.sfhs.org.uk/

Mrs P.O. Lawson, 8 Jarvis Cottages, Jarvis Lane, Steyning, West Sussex BN44 3GU
Prices include postage & packing, if more than one publication is ordered please deduct £0.10 per additional publication, airmail- £2.00 for first copy plus an additional £0.50 per copy thereafter. Cheques, sterling only please, payable to Sussex Family History Group. Credit card payment by Mastercard, Access or Visa, quoting card number and expiry date, a 15% surcharge will be made

Church Registers

	Price
Brighton Presbyterian Registers 1700-1837	£1.35
Horsham Independant, Congregational & United Reform Church 1813-1983	£1.05
St Mary, Westout, Lewes, Bishop's Transcripts 1608-1678	£5.50
Mititary Baptisms, Marriages & Burials - St Peters, Preston Village, Brighton 1793-1840	£5.50
West Sussex Catholic Baptisms 1688-1800	£4.00

Census

Kirdford 1811 Census Transcript & Index	£2.50
Rusper Census 1821 Transcript & Index	£4.50
Horsham 1841-1851 Transcript & Index	£5.00
Graffham 1837-1844 Transcript & Index	£4.50
Upper Beeding 1870-1881, Rev. Bloxham's Census Transcript & Index	£2.50

West Sussex 1851 Census Indexes

Vol.1 Stopham, Hardham, Coldwaltham, Amberley, Pulborough & West Chiltington	£2.55
Vol. 2 Storrington, Parham, Sullington, Thakeham, Ashington, Warminghurst, Wiston, Washington, Findon.	£2.55
Vol. 3 Woolavington, Tillington, Lodsworth, Selham, Cocking & Midhurst	£2.55

West Sussex 1841-1891 Census Transcript & Index

Appledram, Ashurst, Birdham, Bramber, Botolphs, Coombes, Donnington, Earnley, Edburton & Fulking, East Wittering, Ford, Greatham cum Wiggonholt, Hardham, Heyshott, Houghton, Hunston, Itchingfield, North Mundham, North Stoke, Poynings, Shermanbury, South Stoke, Steyning Union Workhouse, Tortington, Upper Beeding, West Wittering, West Itchenor, Wiston, Woodmancote.

Each parish	£4.50

Miscellaneous

Chichester War Memorials	£4.50
East Sussex Contribution to Irish Protestant Relief 1642	£2.35
Return of Owners of Land 1873: Sussex	£2.25

Sussex Family History Group (continued)

First World War Graves in Sussex	£3.50
Second World War Graves in Sussex	£4.00
Guide to West Sussex County Record Office	£6.75
Select Vestry Minutes & Surname Index, Etchingham 1819-1826	£5.50
SFHG Lewes Library Catatogue	£5.00

WARWICKSHIRE (see also Birmingham & Midlands)

Coventry Family History Society

Mrs. V.M. Morrall, 88 Howes Lane, Coventry CV3 6PJ

Census
The 1891 Census Index of Coventry and Surrounding Areas.   9 Volumes

Miscellaneous

The Poor Rate 1732-1736, Much Park St. Ward St. Michaels Parish	£0.50
Cholera Reported Deaths from The Coventry Herald During Aug. & Sept. 1849	£0.50
Foleshill Probate Wills & Inventories 1535-1599 (90p p&p)	£4.00
The Foleshill Workhouse Punishment Book 1864-1900	£1.50
The Hawksbury School Log 1860-1968 (55p p&p)	£5.00

Please add 30p per item p&p and make cheques out to The Coventry Family History Society.

WILTSHIRE

Wiltshire Family History Society

Mrs. L.Williams, Wiltshire FHS, 10 Castle Lane, Devizes, Wilts SN10 1HU

Postage & Handling on ALL Publications and Transcriptions
Orders in U.K. up to £2.00 add 60p. + 10p for each extra £1 or part;
Overseas (surface). up to £2.00 add £1 + 30p for each extra £1.00 or part

Parish Registers & Bishops Transcripts

Baverstock	CB	1559-1837	£1.80
Baydon	CB	1578-1837	£2.60
Bedwyn, Little,	CB	1591-1837	£2.80
Beechingstoke	CB	1566-1837	£2.00
Berwick Bassett	CB	1580-1837	£1.80
Bradley, North,	C	1603-1766	£3.00
Bradley, North,	C	1767-1837	£3.00
Bradley, North,	B	1603-1837	£4.50

Wiltshire Family History Society (continued)

Broad Hinton	CB	1603-1837	£5.00
Broughton Gifford	CB	1622-1837	£5.00
Bulford	CB	1608-1837	£2.00
Buttermere	CB	1605-1837	£1.30
Castle Combe	CB	1602-1837	£4.80
Charlton St Peter	CB	1611-1837	£2.00
Chiseldon	CB	1605-1837	£6.00
Cholderton	CB	1621-1837	£2.00
Clyffe Pypard	CB	1597-1837	£5.50
Dilton	C	1585-1837	£4.00
Dilton	B	1585-1837	£4.00
East Coulston	CB	1622-1837	£2.00
Eisey	CB	1574-1837	£1.60
Erlestoke	CB	1578-1837	£3.00
Fisherton Anger	C	1608-1837	£4.50
Fisherton Anger	C	1608-1837	£5.00
Great Cheverell	C	1622-1837	£2.50
Great Cheverell	B	1622-1837	£2.00
Grittleton	CB	1576-1837	£2.50
Hilperton	CB	1622-1837	£5.00
Holt	CB	1567-1837	£5.00
Horningsham	CB	1576-1837	£6.50
Imber	CMB	1623-1837	£2.50
Knoyle, West	CB	1608-1837	£2.00
Knoyle, East	CB	1538-1837	£6.50
Landford	CB	1585-1837	£2.50
Latton	CB	1576/1628-1837	£3.50
Liddington	CB	1605-1837	£3.00
Limpley Stoke	CB	1622-1837	£3.00
Manningford Abbots & Bruce,	CB	1539/1605-1837	£3.00
Marden	CB	1622-1837	£2.20
Market Lavington	C	1622-1787	£4.60
Market Lavington	C	1787-1837	£2.60
Market Lavington	B	1622-1837	£4.00
Marlborough St Mary	C	1602-1837	£6.50
Marlborough St Mary	B	1602-1837	£4.50
Marlborough St Peter	C	1607-1837	£5.00
Marlborough St Peter	B	1607-1837	£5.00
Milston	CB	1539-1837	£2.00
Milton Lilbourne	CB	1602-1837	£4.00
Monkton Farleigh	CB	1570-1837	£3.20
Newton Tony	CB	1586/1568-1837	£3.00
Patney	CB	1592-1837	£2.00
Netheravon	C	1579-1837	£2.70
Netheravon	B	1579-1837	£2.50

Wiltshire Family History (continued)

Nettleton	CB	1557-1837	£3.60
Rodbourne Cheyney	CB	1605-1837	£3.50
Sedgehill	CB	1607-1837	£2.00
Semington	C	1586-1837	£2.30
Semington	B	1588-1837	£1.50
Somerford, Great	CB	1605-1837	£2.60
Somerford, Little,	CB	1605-1837	£2.20
Southbroom (Devizes)	C	1576-1837	£5.00
Staverton	C	(1641 1837 1681-1837)-1 vol.	£2.00
Stert	B	1579-1837	£2.60
Sutton Mandeville	CB	1622-1837	£2.50
Tidecombe	CB	1646-1837	£2.50
Tilshead	CB	1603-1837	£3.00
Urchfont	CB	1538-1837	£9.00
Urchfont	C	1538-1837	£5.00
Wanborough	B	1582-1837	£4.50
Wanborough	C	1582-1837	£3.00
Whaddon	B	1582- 1837	£1.50
Winterbourne Basset	CB	1607- 1837	£2.00
Winterbourne Dauntsey, Earls & Gunner	CB	1557-1837	£6.00
Winterbourne Monkton	CB	1605-1837	£1.80
Winterbourne Stoke	CB	1726-1837	£2.20
Woodford	CB	1546-1837	£4.00
Wroughton	CB	1606-1837	£5.00
Wroughton	C	1606-1837	£3.60
Yatesbury	B	1606-1837	£2.20
	CB		

Miscellaneous

The Compleat Parish Officer — £4.00
The Handy Book of Parish Law — £4.00
The Book of Trades Volume 1, 1811 — £3.00
The Book of Trades Volume ll, 1811 — £3.00
The Book of Trades Volume III, 1818 — £3.00
Miscellany of Bastardy Records, Vol 1 — £6.00
Miscellany of Bastardy Records, Vol 2 — £5.00
Miscellany of Bastardy Records, Vol 3. — £5.50
Wootton Bassett Hiring Fair Records, Vol I — £7.00
Wootton Bassett Hiring Fair Records, Vol II. — £7.00
Wootton Bassett Hiring Fair Records, Vol. III — £7.00
Wiltshire Policemen, Vol I — £5.00
Wiltshire Protestation Returns & Taxation Records for Warminster — £5.50
First World War Tribunals in Wiltshire — £9.00
The First World War Tribunal in Swindon — £6.50
The Bell Book of St. James Church Trowbridge — £6.00

Wiltshire Family History Society (continued)

Fisherton Anger Gaol Matrons Book	£3.00
Hair Powder Tax	£5.00
Records of Highworth Congregational Church	£5.00
Formerly Of ... ,	£6.00
Wiltshire Pew Rents, Vol. 1	£5.00
Wiltshire Pew Rents, Vol. II	£5.00
Pew Rents, Vol. III	£3.00
Wiltshire Pew Rents, Vol. IV	£6.00
The Bear Club	£4.50
Salisbury Area Apprenticeships & Wilton Free School	£5.50
Wiltshire Militia Orders, 1759-70	£5.00
Wiltshire Militia Courts Martial	£6.00
Miscellany of Marlborough Records, Vol. I	£5.00
A Miscellany of Wroughton Poor Law Records	£5.00
Miscellany of Salisbury Records, Vol I	£5.00
Miscellany of Salisbury Records, Vol II	£5.00
Coroners Records of a Borough, Marlborough, Wilts 1773 to 1835	£5.00
Coroners Inquisitions for Borough of Malmesbury, Wilts 1830-54	£3.50
Wiltshire County Coroners, 1815 to 1858	£5.00
1695-1705, Tax Censuses, Part I	£5.00
1695-1705, Tax Censuses, Part II	£5.00
Miscellaneous Censuses 1695 1887, Part I	£5.00
Miscellaneous Censuses 1695 1887, Part II	£5.00
Pew Lists	£5.00
Incumbents Visiting Books, Part I	£5.00
Incumbents Visiting Books, Part II	£5.00
In A Wiltshire Valley, (Pewsey Vale mid 19c)	£3.00
In A Wiltshire Village, (Potterne 100 years ago)	£3.00
In A Wiltshire Hamlet, (Coate nr Devizes late 19c)	£3.00
Wiltshire Emigration Association	£2.00
Wiltshire Insurance Policy Holders, 1714-1731	£2.00
Wiltshire Registration Districts & Parishes	£1.00
Wiltshire Strays in Gloucester Gaol, 1815-1879	£0.60
Devizes New Baptist Church Membership, 1805-1920	£2.00
Highworth & Swindon Union Out-relief 1842-79	£3.50

YORKSHIRE

The Family History Section Yorkshire Archaeological Society
Mrs D Harris, 15 Stead Lane, Thorner, Nr Leeds LS14 3EA
(Please make cheques payable to Family History Section, Y.A.S.)

1851 Census Index
(Includes christian names, ages, and where born)

		(a)	(b)	(c)
1.	Leeds Township Vol 1 A-D, Vol 2 E-K, Vol 3 L-R, Vol 4 S-Z Price per volume	£4.30	£4.80	£6.60
2	Bramley with Stanningley	£2.90	£3.25	£4.20
3a	Pudsey (East) Part 1 Calverley, Farsley	£2.70	£2.90	£3.80
3b	Pudsey (West) Part 2 with Tyersall	£2.30	£2.50	£3.20
4	Headingley cum Burley	£1.60	£1.85	£2.40
5	Horsforth	£1.60	£1.85	£2.40
6	Rothwell	£1.80	£2.10	£2.70
7	Austhorpe, Whitkirk, Halton, Temple Newsam, Osmondthorpe, Swillington.	£1.60	£1.85	£2.40
8	Baildon, Esholt, Hawksworth	£1.60	£1.85	£2.40
9	Barwick in Elmet, Aberford,	£1.60	£1.85	£2.40
10	Guiseley with Carlton	£1.60	£1.85	£2.40
11	Kirkstall	£1.60	£1.85	£2.40
12	Potternewton, Chapel Allerton	£1.60	£1.85	£2.40
13	Rawdon	£1.60	£1.85	£2.40
14	Shadwell, Roundhay, Seacroft	£1.60	£1.85	£2.40
15	Thorner, Scarcroft, Bardsey, E. Keswick, Clifford, Boston, Collingham, etc	£1.60	£1.85	£2.40
16	Yeadon,	£1.60	£1.85	£2.40
17	Kirk & Little Fenton, Appleton Roebuck, Acaster Selby, Barkston, Sherburn, etc	£1.60	£1.85	£2.40
18	Wortley, Gildersome, Farnley, Armley (2 vols)	£4.20	£4.70	£6.50
19	Holbeck, Beeston, Churwell 2 vols	£4.20	£4.70	£6.50
20	Hunslet (2 vols)	£4.20	£4.70	£6.50
21	Morley, Batley (2 vols)	£4.20	£4.70	£6.50
22	Bramham, Thorp Arch, Newton Kyme, Ulleskelf etc	£1.60	£1.85	£2.40
23	Tadcaster, Bilbrough, Bickerton, Bilton, Tockwith, Long Marston, etc	£1.60	£1.85	£2.40
24	Garforth, Kippax, Gt & Little Preston, South Milford	£1.60	£1.85	£2.40

Miscellaneous

	(a)	(b)	(c)
List of Parish Registers held at Claremont	£2.60	£2.80	£3.45
Miscellany 2 (articles from past journals)	£2.25	£2.45	£3.10
West Riding Registry of Deeds	£0.45	£0.55	£0.85

YORKSHIRE—EAST RIDING

City of York & District Family History Society
Mrs. Carol Mennell, 4 Orchard Close, Dringhouses, York YO24 2NX

Parish Registers

	(a)	(c)
Parish Registers of St. Martin, Coney St. York 1813-1837	£2.00	£3.50
Parish Registers of Holy Trinity, Kings Court, York 1813-1837	£2.50	£4.00
Parish Registers of St. Giles, Copmanthorpe, York 1759-1837	£2.25	£3.50
Parish Registers of Holy Trinity, Goodramgate, York 1813-1837	£3.00	£4.75
Set of 4 Parish Registers	£9.00	£14.00

East Yorkshire Family History Society
The Publications Officers, 11 Euston Close, Anlaby Road, Hull, HU3 2PX

Parish Register Transcripts

				(a)	(b)	(c)
Bridlington Priory:		C	1782-1812	£2.95	£3.05	£4.00
		C	1813-1837	£2.00	£2.25	£3.10
		M	1813-1837	£1.60	£1.75	£2.40
		B	1782-1812	£1.55	£1.70	£2.40
		B	1813-1837	£1.75	£2.00	£2.60
Holmpton:		M	1739-1837	£0.55	£0.70	£0.90
Middleton on the Wolds			1678-1837	£2.45	£2.70	£3.40
Routh:		M	1750-1837	£0.65	£0.80	£1.00
Sculcoates:		C	1772-1789			
		& B	1772-1792	£1.90	£2.05	£2.70
		C	1806-1812	£2.50	£2.75	£4.40
		C	1813-1820	£1.95	£2.20	£2.85
		C	1821- June 1831	£1.95	£2.20	£2.85
		C	Jul 1831- Dec 1837	£1.35	£1.50	£2.15
		B	1813- Sept 1824	£1.70	£1.95	£2.60
		B	Sept 1824- Dec 1831	£1.40	£1.55	£2.15
		B	1832- Dec 1837	£1.35	£1.50	£3.40
		M	1804-1812	£2.55	£3.00	£4.25
		M	1813-1821	£2.30	£2.50	£3.50
		M	1821-1829	£2.75	£2.95	£3.80
		M	1830-1837	£2.75	£2.95	£3.80
Seamer		CMB	1813- 1837	£1.90	£2.15	£2.80
Skipsea:		M	1750-1837	£0.70	£0.85	£1.00
Welwick:		M	1754-1837	£0.85	£1.00	£1.20

East Yorkshire Family History Society (continued)

1851 Census
Beverley Town	£2.85	£3.25	£4.35
Beverley District, (Vol.1) (exc. Town)	£2.65	£2.75	£3.35
Bridlington & Bridlington Quay	£1.70	£1.95	£2.60
Bridlington District	£2.20	£2.45	£3.40
Cottingham, North Ferriby & Hessle	£2.95	£3.20	£4.00
Driffield & District, (Vol 1)	£3.00	£3.30	£4.55
Driffield & District, (Vol 2)	£3.00	£3.30	£4.55
Hedon & Drypool	£3.00	£3.20	£4.00
Hull Holy Trinity, (Vol.1)	£3.90	£4.35	£6.15
Hull Holy Trinity, (Vol.2)	£3.50	£3.75	£5.35
Hull Holy Trinity, (Vol 3)	£4.25	£4.65	£6.30
Howden & District	£4.70	£5.15	£6.55
Naburn, Eskrick & Dunnington	£1.90	£2.10	£2.70
Patrington & District	£2.15	£2.40	£3.45
Scarborough District (excl Town) (reprint)	£3.80	£4.30	£5.40
Scarborough (Town}	£4.00	£4.40	£6.00
East Sculcoates	£4.10	£4.50	£6.00
West Sculcoates	£4.10	£4.50	£6.00
Skirlaugh & District	£2.50	£2.65	£3.60
Sutton on Hull & District	£2.95	£3.00	£4.10

Monumental Inscriptions
Aldbrough	£2.00	£2.15	£2.60
Atwick	£0.80	£1.00	£1.60
Bainton	£1.00	£1.25	£1.85
Barmston & Harpham	£1.45	£1.65	£2.30
Beeford, Dunnington & Lissett	£1.65	£1.80	£2.40
Beswick	£0.70	£0.90	£1.50
Beverley Minster	£3.40	£3.75	£4.95
Beverley: St Mary	£2.75	£3.00	£4.00
Bilton	£1.20	£1.35	£1.80
Bishop Burton	£1.15	£1.30	£1.50
Bishop Wilton	£0.90	£1.05	£1.35
Blacktoft	£0.90	£1.05	£1.65
Brandesburton	£1.25	£1.40	£1.85
Brantingham & Ellerker	£2.05	£2.20	£2.65
Bridlington Priory	£4.90	£5.40	£7.00
Burstwick	£1.60	£1.75	£2.35
Burton Agnes & Ruston Parva	£1.30	£1.45	£2.20
Burton Pidsea	£0.90	£1.15	£1.35
Catwick	£1.05	£1.20	£1.40
Cherry Burton	£1.30	£1.45	£1.80
Cottingham	£2.65	£2.85	£3.80
Drifield	£0.75	£0.90	£1.10

East Yorkshire Family History Society (continued)

Easington	£1.60	£1.75	£2.20
Eastrington	£1.55	£ 1.75	£2.45
Ellerton	£0.85	£1.00	£1.20
Elloughton	£2.00	£2.15	£2.60
Escrick	£1.10	£1.35	£1.85
Etton & Holme-on-the-Wolds	£1.10	£1.25	£1.85
Folkton	£2.50	£2.65	£3.30
Foston on the Wolds	£1.15	£1.30	£1.90
Ganton	£2.35	£2.50	£3.15
Goodmanham	£0.70	£0.85	£1.05
Hackness	£1.60	£1.75	£2.45
Halsham	£0.90	£1.05	£1.35
Hedon: St Augustine	£1.55	£1.70	£2.15
Hessle	£1.15	£1.30	£1.70
Hollym	£1.10	£1.29	£1.65
Holmpton	£0.90	£1.05	£1.35
Hornsea & Goxhill	£1.45	£1.55	£2.25
Hotham	£0.95	£1.10	£1.30
Huggate	£2.50	£2.80	£3.45
Hull, Holy Trinity (Castle Street)	£2.70	£2.95	£3.60
Hull, Holy Trinity (churchyard only)	£3.20	£3.55	£4.85
Humbleton	£0.80	£1.05	£1.25
Keyingham & Thorngumbald	£1.00	£1.25	£1.50
Kilnwick	£0.90	£1.05	£1.65
Kirk Ella	£1.55	£1.70	£2.25
Laxton	£1.20	£1.35	£1.80
Leven St Faith (reprint) & Holy Trinity	£1.60	£1.75	£2.45
Lockington	£1.00	£1.15	£1.35
Long Riston	£1.45	£1.70	£1.95
Lowthorpe	£0.95	£1.10	£1.30
Lund	£1.00	£1.15	£1.35
Mappleton	£1.20	£1.35	£1.70
Marfleet	£1.00	£1.05	£1.45
Market Weighton	£1.25	£1.35	£1.85
Middleton on the Wolds	£1.15	£1.30	£1.50
Naburn	£0.95	£1.15	£1.75
North Cave	£2.10	£2.25	£2.90
North Dalton	£1.00	£1.20	£1.80
North Ferriby	£2.40	£2.65	£3.50
North Frodingham	£1.25	£1.40	£2.00
North Newbald	£1.60	£1.75	£2.40
Nunkeeling & Bewholme	£0.65	£0.80	£1.00
Ottringham	£1.35	£1.45	£2.10
Patrington	£2.35	£2.55	£3.40
Paull	£1.20	£1.35	£1.80
Preston	£0.85	£1.00	£1.20

East Yorkshire Family History Society (continued)

Reighton	£1.00	£1.20	£1.85
Rise	£0.95	£1.05	£1.35
Roos	£1.25	£1.40	£1.85
Routh	£0.65	£0.80	£1.00
Rowley	£0.90	£1.05	£1.35
Rudston	£1.30	£1.60	£2.20
Sancton	£1.20	£1.35	£1.80
Sculcoates: Air Street	£0.85	£0.90	£1.20
Sculcoates Lane, Hull: North Side	£3.05	£3.30	£4.60
Sculcoates Lane, Hull: South Side	£2.90	£3.30	£4.45
Sculcoates Lane, Hull: North & South Side (set)	£5.35	£5.65	£8.35
Seamer	£3.15	£3.40	£5.00
Sigglesthorne	£1.55	£1.70	£2.05
Skeffling & Kilnsea	£0.75	£0.90	£1.10
Skerne	£0.95	£1.10.	£1.30
Skidby	£1.15	£1.30	£1.50
Skipsea & Ulrome	£1.45	£1.55	£2.25
Skirlaugh	£1.55	£1.70	£2.05
Snainton	£1.60	£ 1.75	£2.45
South Cave & Broomfleet	£1.75	£1.85	£2.40
South Dalton	£1.10	£1.25	£1.50
Sproatley	£1.20	£1.40	£1.75
Sunk Island	£0.65	£0.80	£1.00
Sutton on Hull	£5.00	£5.35	£7.30
Swine	£1.55	£1.70	£2.35
Tunstall, Hilston Garton	£0.85	£1.00	£1.20
Walkington	£1.55	£1.70	£2.05
Warter	£0.70	£0.85	£1.05
Watton	£0.80	£0.85	£1.10
Wawne	£1.25	£1.40	£1.75
Welton	£1.50	£1.65	£2.10
Welwick	£1.00	£1.05	£1.45
Willerby (Staxton)	£1.10	£1.30	£1.90
Winestead	£0.80	£0.85	£1.10
Withernsea	£1.60	£1.75	£2.40
Withernwick	£1.30	£1.45	£1.80

Miscellaneous

East Riding parish map (10p each)	£0.35	£0.35	£0.50
Map of Ecclesiastical Parish Boundaries of Hull (20p each)	£0.45	£0.45	£0.60
N.B. Maps are Post Free in the U.K. if sent with other publications.			
District Register Offices in England and Wales (revised edition 1997)	£0.70	£0.85	£1.10
Transportation from Hull and the East Riding to America & Australia from Quarter Sessions Records	£1.10	£1.25	£1.45

YORKSHIRE WEST RIDING

Barnsley Family History Society
Mrs D. Poulter 10 Scarr Lane Ardsley Barnsley S. Yorks S71 5BB

1851 Census Index	UK	O/s Sur.	Air Eur.	Air Other
1. Silkston	£2.05	£2.30	£2.50	£3.00
2 Thurgoland & C. Moor	£2.05	£2.30	£2.50	£3.00
3 Penistone & Langsett	£2.05	£2.30	£2.50	£3.00
4 Cawthorne	£2.05	£2.30	£2. 50	£3.00
5 Kexborough	£2.05	£2.30	£2.50	£3.00
6 Oxspring & Hunshelf	£2.05	£2.30	£2.50	£3.00
7 Tankersley & Pilley	£2.05	£2.30	£2.50	£3.00
8 Hoylandswaine, Gunthwaite & Ingbirchworth	£2.05	£2.30	£2.50	£3.00
9 Darfield with Great & Little Houghton & Billingley	£2.05	£2.30	£2.50	£3.00
10 Wombwell & Hemingfield	£2.05	£2.30	£2.50	£3.00
11 Monk Bretton	£2.85	£3.05	£3.20	£3.60
12 Thurlstone	£2.85	£3.05	£3.20	£3.60
13 Ardsley	£2.05	£2.30	£2.50	£3.00
14 Worsborough	£4.00	£4.20	£4.20	£5.00
15 Barnsley town centre	due soon			

Miscellaneous

Hearth Tax Return 1672 Silkstone	£1.00	£1.30	£1.40	£2.00
The Reminiscences of Henry Wolston Spooner	£2.36	£2.50	£2.65	£3.00

Bradford Family History Society

Ms Pat Barrow, 37 Churchfields, Fagley, Bradford, West Yorkshire BD2 3JN

Please make all cheques payable in sterling to Bradford Family History Society

Parish Register Transcription Indexes
Name Index to Bradford Parish Church Burials, 1681-1837

    Volume 1 Surnames A - B   Volume 4 Surnames L - P
    Volume 2 Surnames C - G   Volume 5 Surnames Q - S
    Volume 3 Surnames H - K   Volume 6 Surnames T - Y (no surnames X or Z)

No. of Vols	1	6
(a)	£5.00	£30.00
(b)	£5.40	£31.00
(c)	£6.50	£37.00

Bradford Family History Society (continued)

Surname Index Series-1841 Census for Bradford

Vol. 1 District of Bradford, East End (includes Bradford Moor, Laister Dyke, New Leeds, Undercliffe, Wapping, Workhouse, Court House, Gaol & Cavalry Barracks)
Vol. 2 District of Bradford, West End (includes Black Abbey, White Abbey & Infirmary)
Vol. 3 Districts of Horton & Manningham (includes Great & Little Horton, Heaton, Shipley & part of Frizinghall)
Vol. 4 Districts of Calverley, Idle & Pudsey (includes Bagley, Bolton, Eccleshill, Fagley, Farsley, Fulneck, Greengates, Rodley, Thackley, Tyersall, Windhill, Woodhall Hills, Wrose, parts of Frizinghall and Stanningley, & Idle Workhouse)
Vol. 5 Districts of Bowling, Cleckheaton & Drighlington (includes Adwalton, Cutler Heights, Dudley Hill, East Bierley, Hartshead Moor, Hunsworth, Oakenshaw, Scholes, Toftshaw, Tong, Tyersal Gate & Wike)
Vol. 6 Districts of North Bierley, Thornton & Wilsden (includes Allerton, Buttershaw, Clayton, Cullingworth Gate, Denholme, Fairweather Green, Hallas, Hewnden, Kipping, Low Moor, Odsall, Wibsey & part of Toftshaw)

Surname Index Series-1861 Census for Bradford

Vol.1. Sub-district of Bradford, East End
Vol.2. Sub-district of Bradford, West End
Vol.3. Sub-district of Horton (Surnames A-J)
Vol.4 Sub-district of Horton (Surnames K-Z)
Vol.5. Sub-districts of Bowling, Cleckheaton & Drighlington
Vol.6. Sub-districts of North Bierley, Shipley, Thornton & Wilsden
Vol.7. Sub-districts of Calverley, Idle & Pudsey

Surname Index Series-1871 Census for Bradford

Vol. 1 Sub-district of Bradford, East End (surnames A - J)
Vol. 2 Sub-district of Bradford, East End (surnames K - Z) (includes Laisterdyke and a regiment of soldiers)
Vol. 3 Sub-district of Bradford, West End (includes Bradford Infirmary)
Vol. 4 Sub-district of Horton (surnames A - J)
Vol. 5 Sub-district of Horton (surnames K - Z) (includes Great & Little Horton, Lidget Green, Manningham & Bradford Union Workhouse)
Vol. 6 Sub-districts of Bowling & North Bierley (including Buttershaw, Dudley Hill, Odsal, Wibsey & part of Toftshaw)
Vol. 7 Sub-districts of Thornton, Wilsden & Shipley (including Allerton, Clayton, Cullingworth Gate, Denholme, Heaton, part of Frizinghall, Saltaire & North Bierley Union Workhouse)
Vol. 8 Sub-districts of Idle, Calverley & Pudsey (including Bolton, Eccleshill, Fagley, Farsley, part of Frizinghall, Fulneck, Thornbury, Tyersall, Undercliffe & Windhill)
Vol. 9 Sub-districts of Cleckheaton & Drighlington (including Adwalton, East Bierley, Hunsworth, Oakenshaw, Scholes, Tong, Wyke/Wike & part of Toftshaw)

Bradford Family History Society (continued)

Surname Index Series-1891 Census for Bradford
Vol. 1 Sub-district of Bradford, East End (surnames A - I)
Vol. 2 Sub-district of Bradford, East End (surnames J - Z) (includes Bradford Barracks, Bradford Fever Hospital & part of Heaton)
Vol. 3 Sub-district of Bradford, West End (surnames A - I)
Vol. 4 Sub-district of Bradford, West End(surnames J - Z) (includes Manningham & Bradford Infirmary)
Vol. 5 Sub-district of Horton (surnames A - I)
Vol. 6 Sub-district of Horton (surnames J - Z) (includes Listerhills & Bradford Union Workhouse)
Vol. 7 Sub-district of Bowling (including part of Bierley)
Vol. 8 Sub-districts of North Bierley, Thornton & Wilsden (including Allerton, Buttershaw, Clayton, Clayton Heights, Denholme, Low Moor, North Bierley Union Workhouse, Odsal, Wibsey & parts of Bierley & Queensbury)
Vol. 9 Sub-districts of Idle & Shipley (including Eccleshill, Saltaire, Windhill & part of Heaton including Frizinghall)
Vol.10 Sub-districts of Calverley & Pudsey (including Farsley, Fulneck, Thornbury & Tyersal)
Vol.11 Sub-districts of Cleckheaton & Drighlington (including Adwalton, East Bierley, Hunsworth, Oakenshaw, Odsal, Scholes, Toftshaw, Tong & Wyke)

Surname Index Series - Censuses for Bingley
Vol. 1 1841 and 1851 Censuses for Bingley
Vol. 2 1861 and 1871 Censuses for Bingley
Vol. 3 1891 Census for Bingley (published 1996)

Surname search facility. A check can be made for which volumes contain a particular surname before you place your order by sending an SAE or 2 IRCs with your request to Ms Pat Barrow.

Postage a = UK: b=o/seas surface: c=o/seas airmail
No. of Vols.

	1	3	5	6	9	11
(a)	£2.30	£6.60	£10.80	£13.00	£19.40	£24.00
(b)	£2.60	£7.00	£11.50	£13.70	£20.30	£25.00
(c)	£3.20	£8.40	£13.70	£16.30	£23.80	£29.50

Calderdale Family History Society

Mr. J. Sutcliffe, 12 Ewood Drive, Mytholmroyd, Hebden Bridge, West Yorks., HX7 5PQ

Halifax Parish Church Baptism Registers		(a)	(b)
1. Jan 1813/Nov 1817		£4.50	£5.00
2. Dec 1817/Dec 1821		£4.50	£5.00
3. Jan 1822/Oct 1825		£4.50	£5.00
4. July 1829/Oct 1832		£4.50	£5.00
5. Oct 1832/Nov 1835		£4.50	£5.00
6. Nov 1835/Jun 1838		£4.50	£5.00

Halifax Parish Church Marriage Registers.			
Book I	1754/1756	£3.00	£3.50
Book II	1756/1760	£3.50	£4.00
Book III	1760/1764	£3.75	£4.25
Book IV	1764/1769	£4.00	£4.50
Book V	1769/1776	£4.50	£5.00
Book VI	1776/1779	£3.50	£4.00
Book VII	1779/1784	£4.50	£5.00
Book VIII	1784/1790	£4.50	£5.00
Book IX	1790/1794	£4.40	£5.00
Book X	1794/1801	£4.50	£5.00
Book XI	1801/1805	£6.50	£7.00
Book XII	1805/1809	£4.75	£5.25
Book XIII	1809/1812	£4.50	£5.00
Vol I	1813/1814	£3.50	£4.00
Vol II	1814/1816	£3.50	£4.00
Vol III	1816/1818	£3.50	£4.00
Vol IV	1818/1820	£3.50	£4.00
Vol V	1820/1821	£3.50	£4.00
Vol VI	1821/1823	£3.50	£4.00
Vol VII	1823/1824	£3.50	£4.00
Vol VIII	1824/1826	£3.50	£4.00
Vol IX	1826/1827	£3.50	£4.00
Vol X	1827/1829	£3.50	£4.00
Vol XI	1829/1830	£3.50	£4.00
Vol XII	1830/1832	£3.50	£4.00
Vol XIII	1832/1833	£3.50	£4.00
Vol XIV	1833/1835	£3.50	£4.00
Vol XV	1835/1836	£3.50	£4.00
Vol XVI	1836/1837	£3.50	£4.00

Halifax Parish Church Burial Registers			
Jan 1813/Nov 1823		£3.50	£4.00
Nov 1823/Sept 1834		£3.50	£4.00
Sept/1834/Nov 1844		£3.50	£4.00
Nov 1844/April 1854		£3.50	£4.00

Calderdale Family History Society (continued)

Census

Pre 1841 Census	Langfield 1801 & Sowerby 1811	£2.50	£3.00
Pre 1841 Census	Midgley 1801 & 1811	£2.50	£3.00
Pre 1841 Census	Elland-cum-Greetland 1801	£2.50	£3.00
Pre 1841 Census	Elland-cum-Greetland 1811	£2.50	£3.00
Pre 1841 Census	Todmorden.& Walsden 1811	£2.50	£3.00
Pre 1841 Census	Stansfield 1821 (In 2 Vols)	£4.50	£5.00

Monumental Inscriptions

Booth U.R. Church	£3.50	£4.00
Holywell Green U.R. Church	£4.00	£4.50
Norland Prim. Meth. Chapel	£2.50	£3.00
St. George's Church, Sowerby	£2.50	£3.00
Crimsworth Meth. Chapel, Peckett Well	£2.50	£3.00
St. John's Church, Bradshaw	£2.50	£3.00
Weslyan Chapel, Mytholmroyd	£3.50	£4.00
Methodist Chapel, Boulderclough	£2.50	£3.00
Denholme U.M. Chapel, Luddenden Foot	£1.50	£2.00
Nursery Lane Meth. Chapel, Ovenden	£2.00	£2.50
Rooley Lane Wes. Chapel, Sowerby	£2.50	£3.00
Cross Lane Meth. Chapel, Hebden Bridge	£2.50	£3.00
Sowerby Green Cong. Chapel, Sowerby	£3.50	£4.00
Bolton Brow Meth. Chapel, Sowerby Bridge	£3.50	£4.00
Butts Green Bapt. Chapel, Warley	£2.50	£3.00
Methodist Chapel, Midgley	£2.50	£3.00
St. Mary's Church, Cotton Stones; Sowerby	£3.50	£4.00
St. Stephens Church, Copley	£2.50	£3.00
St. Michael's Church, Mytholmroyd	£4.40	£5.00
St. Mary's Church, Luddenden Foot	£2.50	£3.00
Society of Friends (Quakers), Halifax	£1.50	£2.00

Doncaster & District Family History Society

Mrs M Pepper, 9 Highbury Cres, Bessacarr, Doncaster, South Yorks DN4 6AL

Index to 1851 Census
1. Kirk Bramwith, Fenwick & Moss.
2. Norton & Campsall.
3. Askern, Sutton, Owston, Skellow & Carcroft.
4. Swinton.
5. Wentworth.
6. Wheatley, Long Sandall, Thorpe in Balne, Kirk Sandall & Barnby Dun.
7. Bentley with Arksey.
8. Bawtry.

Doncaster & District Family History Society (continued)

9. Armthorpe, Cantley & Loversall.
    Thorne (A - I).
    Thorne (J - Z)
    Doncaster (A - G).
    Doncaster (G - P)
    Doncaster (P - Z).
15. Burghwallis, Haywood, Skelbrooke, Hampole, Adwick le Street & Brodsworth.
16. High Melton, Barnburgh, Sprotbrough, Cadeby & Cusworth.
17. Hickleton, Hooton Pagnell, Clayton with Frickley, Marr & Pickburn.
18. Wadworth, Edlington & Rossington.
19. Pollington & Cowick.
20. Hatfield.
21. Snaith & Gowdall.
22. Balby with Hexthorpe & Warmsworth.
23. Stainforth.
24. Mexborough
25. Fishlake & Sykehouse
26. Tickhill, Wilsic, Stancil & Wellingley
27. Stapleton, Darrington, Carleton & East Hardwick
28. Glass Houghton, Whitwood, Aketon, Featherstone & Purston Jaglin
29. Pontefract (A - F)
30. Pontefract (G - O)
31. Pontefract (P - Z)
32. Adlingfleet, Eastoft, Fockerby, Garthorpe & Luddington
33. Ousefleet, Reedness & Whitgift
34. Swinefleet
35. Castleford
36. Ferrybridge, Ferry Fryston
37. Knottingley (A - I)
38. Knottingley (J - Z)
39. Goole (A - K)
40. Goole (L - Z)
41. Wath upon Dearne
42. Conisbrough
43. Hook
44. Beal, Eggborough, Kellington & Whitley Bridge
    Airmyn, Balne, Heck, Hensall & Rawcliffe
    Cridling Stubbs, Little Smeaton, Kirk Smeaton, Walden Stubbs and Womersley
    Austerfield, Auckley, Finningley & Misson
    Adwick on Dearne, Bolton on Dearne & Thurnscoe
    Stainton with Hellaby, Braithwell & Denaby
    Darfield

Nos 1-11 and 15-25 £1.25 each, nos 26-50 £1.75 each
Doncaster £2.50 each or £6.00 per set. Pontefract £4.00 per set
Please add 50p p&p for single books and £1.00 for sets, (extra for O/seas)

Doncaster & District Family History Society (continued)

Burial Indexes
Vol 1   Adlingfleet All Saints 1694-1972
Vol 2   Brampton Bierlow Christ Church 1855-1911
Vol 3   Kirk Sandall St Oswald 1679-1937
Vol 4   Barnbrough St. Peter 1558-1900
Vol 5   Burghwallis St Helen 1596-1916
Vol 6   Adwick on Dearne St. John the Baptist 1690-1980

Cost: £2.00 + UK p&p 50p

Miscellaneous
Skelbrooke Parish Register (1592-1836)	£2.00
Parish Gleanings	£2.75
Thorne Churchyard Monumental Inscriptions	£2.00
Bentley with Arksey Monumental Inscriptions	£2.00
Freemen of the Borough of Doncaster 1558-1962	
Vol 1 Surnames A-I	£2.00
Vol 2 Surnames J-Z	£2.00
Postage: 50p UK, 65p O/seas surface £1.20 airmail.	
Stainforth Cemetery Monumental Inscriptions	£5.00

Postage: £1.25 UK, £2.00 O/Seas surface, £5.00 airmail

Huddersfield & District Family History Society

Web Site: http://www.hdfhs.demon.co.uk

Please send cheque or postal order (Payable to Huddersfield & District FHS) to:
Mrs C M Starkey 28, Bishops Way, Meltham, Huddersfield, W.Yorkshire HD7 3BW
For payment by Visa/Mastercard, please write to the above

Parish Registers   Price
Almondbury, All Hallows	
bapt 1783-1788	£2.00
bapt 1788-1793	£2.00
bapt 1793-1799	£2.00
bapt 1799-1806	£2.00
bapt 1807-1812	£2.00
bapt 1813-1822	£2.00
Batley bapt 1777-1790	£2.00
bapt 1791-1812	£2.00
bapt 1813-1826	£2.00
Dewsbury	
bapt 1813-1819	£2.00
Golcar (all) 1828-1865	£2.00

Huddersfield & District Family History Society (continued)

Honley bapt 1813-1837	£2.00
Huddersfield High St Meth.	
bapt 1794-1815	£2.00
Huddersfield St. Peter's	
bapt 1750-1759	£2.00
bapt 1760-1770	£2.00
bapt 1771-1778	£2.00
bapt 1779-1786	£2.00
bapt 1787-1792	£2.00
bapt 1793-1798	£2.00
bapt 1799-1805	£2.00
bapt 1806-1812	£2.00
bapt 1813-1819	£2.00
marr 1690-1724	£2.00
marr 1724-1756	£2.00
Kirkburton	
bapt 1711-1733	£2.00
bapt 1781-1789	£2.00
bapt 1789-1796	£2.00
bapt 1795-1812	£2.00
bapt 1813-1825	£2.00
bapt 1825-1837	£2.00
Kirkheaton	
bapt 1750-1772	£2.00
bapt 1800-1812	£2.00
bapt 1813-1822	£2.00
Linthwaite Parish Church	
all 1828-1860	£2.00
Marsden	
bapt 1734-1782	£2.00
bapt 1783-1812	£2.00
Mirfield Parish Church	
bapt 1776-1795	£2.00
bapt 1796-1812	£2.00
bapt 1813-1826	£2.00
Paddock	
all 1830-1870	£2.00
Salendine Nook	
Dedications 1783-1822	£2.00
Slaithwaite	
bapt 1685-1726	£2.00
bapt 1727-1760	£2.00
South Crosland	
all 1829-1855	£2.00

Huddersfield & District Family History Society (continued)

1841 Census Indexes

Location	Volume	Price
Almondbury	A-C, D-J, K-R, S-Z	£2.00 each
	All 4 volumes	£7.00
Batley	A-G, H-P, R-Z	£2.00
	(All 3 volumes)	£5.50
Golcar	A-N, O-Z	£2.00
	(Both volumes)	£3.70
Heckmondwike	A-K, L-Z	£1.75
	(Both volumes)	£3.00
Huddersfield (All 10 volumes)		£15.00
	A-Bl, Bo-Ci, Cl-D, E-G, Ha-Hz	£2.00
	I-Me, Mi-Re, Rh-Sp, Sq-V, W-Z	£2.00
Kirkheaton	A-Z	£2.00
Meltham	A-L, M-Z	£1.75
	(Both volumes)	£3.00
Mirfield	A-G, H-N, O-Z	£2.00
	(All 3 volumes)	£7.00
Soothill	A-L, M-Z	£1.75
	(Both Volumes)	£3.00
Thornhill	A-Z	£2.00

Please note that the discounted prices for sets only apply to complete sets as stated in this price list. There is no discount for combinations of individual volumes.

1851 Census Indexes

Almondbury (4 Volumes)		£7.00
Vol 1	A-C	£2.00
Vol 2	D-I	£2.00
Vol 3	J-Q	£2.00
Vol 4	R-Z	£2.00
Austonley	A-Z	£2.00
Batley (4 Volumes)		£7.00
Vol 1	A-E	£2.00
Vol 2	F-J	£2.00
Vol 3	K-R	£2.00
Vol 4	S-Z	£2.00
Cartworth	A-Z	£2.00
Clayton West & High Hoyland	A-Z	£2.00
Cleckheaton (Both Volumes)		£3.70
Vol 1	A-H	£2.00
Vol 2	I-Z	£2.00
Cumberworth (Both Volumes)		£3.70

Huddersfield & District Family History Society (continued)

Cumberworth Half			
	Vol 1	A-K	£2.00
	Vol 2	L-Z	£2.00
Dalton (Both Volumes)			£3.70
	Vol 1	A-J	£2.00
	Vol 2	K-Z	£2.00
Denby		A-Z	£2.00
Dewsbury (5 Volumes)			£8.75
	Vol 1	A-C	£2.00
	Vol 2	D-Ha	£2.00
	Vol 3	He-M	£2.00
	Vol 4	N-Sm	£2.00
	Vol 5	Sn-Z	£2.00
Emley		A-Z	£2.00
Farnley Tyas		A-Z	£1.25
Fixby		A-Z	£1.25
Flockton		A-Z	£1.25
Fulstone		A-Z	£2.00
Golcar (Both Volumes)			£3.70
	Vol 1	A-N	£2.00
	Vol 2	O-Z	£2.00
Gomersal (4 Volumes)			£7.00
	Vol 1	A-D	£2.00
	Vol 2	E-J	£2.00
	Vol 3	K-R	£2.00
	Vol 4	S-Z	£2.00
Hartshead	A-Z		£2.00
Heckmondwike (Both Volumes)			£3.70
	Vol 1	A-K	£2.00
	Vol 2	L-Z	£2.00
Hepworth		A-Z	£2.00
Holme		A-Z	£1.25
Honley (Both Volumes)			£3.70
	Vol 1	A-J	£2.00
	Vol 2	K-Z	£2.00
Huddersfield A (Both Volumes)			£3.70
(Enum Dist 1-6)			
	Vol 1	A-I	£2.00
	Vol 2	J-Z	£2.00
Huddersfield B (Both Volumes)			£3.70
(Enum Dist 7-12)			
	Vol 1	A-H	£2.00
	Vol 2	I-Z	£2.00

Huddersfield & District Family History Society (continued)

Huddersfield C (Both Volumes)			£3.70
(Enum Dist 13-18)			
	Vol 1	A-H	£2.00
	Vol 2	I-Z	£2.00
Huddersfield D (Both Volumes)			£3.70
	Vol 1	A-I	£2.00
	Vol 2	J-Z	£2.00
Huddersfield E (3 Volumes)			£5.50
	Vol 1	A-G	£2.00
	Vol 2	H-O	£2.00
	Vol 3	P-Z	£2.00
Huddersfield F (Both Volumes)			£3.70
	Vol 1	A-H	£2.00
	Vol 2	I-Z	£2.00
Hunsworth		A-Z	£1.25
Kirkburton (Both Volumes)			£3.70
	Vol 1	A-J	£2.00
	Vol 2	K-Z	£2.00
Kirkheaton		A-Z	£2.00
Lepton (Both Volumes)			£3.70
	Vol 1	A-K	£2.00
	Vol 2	L-Z	£2.00
Lindley cum Quarmby			
	(Both Volumes)		£3.70
	Vol 1	A-I	£2.00
	Vol 2	J-Z	£2.00
Lingards		A-Z	£1.25
Linthwaite (Both Volumes)			£3.70
	Vol 1	A-K	£2.00
	Vol 2	L-Z	£2.00
Liversedge (3 Volumes)			£5.50
	Vol 1	A-F	£2.00
	Vol 2	G-O	£2.00
	Vol 3	P-Z	£2.00
Lockwood (Both Volumes)			£3.70
	Vol 1	A-H	£2.00
	Vol 2	I-Z	£2.00
Longwood		A-Z	£2.00
Marsden		A-Z	£2.00
Meltham (Both Volumes)			£3.70
	Vol 1	A-K	£2.00
	Vol 2	L-Z	£2.00
Mirfield (3 Volumes)			£5.50
	Vol 1	A-G	£2.00
	Vol 2	H-O	£2.00
	Vol 3	P-Z	£2.00

Huddersfield & District Family History Society (continued)

Netherthong	A-Z	£1.25
Scammonden	A-Z	£1.25
Shelley	A-Z	£2.00
Shepley	A-Z	£1.25
Slaithwaite	A-Z	£2.00
Soothill (Both Volumes)		£3.70
Vol 1	A-I	£2.00
Vol 2	J-Z	£2.00
South Crosland	A-Z	£2.00
Thornhill	A-Z	£2.00
Thurstonland	A-Z	£1.25
Upper and Lower Whitley	A-Z	£2.00
Upperthong	A-Z	£2.00
Wooldale (Both Volumes)		£3.70
Vol 1	A-H	£2.00
Vol 2	I-Z	£2.00

Please note that the discounted prices for sets only apply to complete sets as stated in this price list. There is no discount for combinations of individual volumes.

Monumental Inscriptions

Huddersfield St Peter's	£2.00
Milnsbridge Baptist Graveyard	£1.25
Salendine Nook Graveyard	
(Both Volumes)	£3.70
Vol 1	£2.00
Vol 2	£2.00

Postage & Packing :- UK 25p per volume; Overseas surface mail 50p per volume; Overseas air mail £1.00 per volume.

Keighley & District Family History Society

Mrs. Julia Wood, High Wheathead Farm, Exley Head, Keighley, West Yorks., BD22 6NB
(Sterling Cheques only please, made out to: Keighley & District F.H.S.)

Monumental Inscriptions

Utley Cemetery Vols 1-6	£2.50 U.K., £3.20 O/seas surface
Utley Cemetery Vols 7-9	£2.85 U.K., £3.55 O/seas surface

Miscellaneous

		O/s
Keighley News Indexes (Marriages)	U.K.	Sur.
Vol.1. 1862-1870	£2.25	£2.50
Vol.2. 1871-1876	£2.25	£2.50
Vol.3. 1877-1880	£2.25	£2.50

Keighley & District Family History Society (continued)

Vol.4. 1881-1885	£2.25	£2.50
Vol.5. 1886-1890	£2.75	£3.25
Vol.6. 1891-1895	£2.75	£3.25
Vol.7. 1896-1901 (Deaths)	£5.50	£6.00
Vol.1. 1862-1870	£2.75	£3.50
Vol.2. 1871-1876	£2.75	£3.50
Vol.3. 1877-1880	£2.75	£3.50
Vol.4. 1881-1885	£3.25	£3.75
Vol.5. 1886-1890	£3.75	£4.50
Vol.6. 1891-1895	£3.75	£4.50
Lothersdale 'A Brief Look Back' condensed history of a small Pennine Village	£2.35	£2.70

Ripon Historical Society & Ripon Harrogate & District Family History Group

Web site: http://www.users.globalnet.co.uk/~gdl/index.htm

J.R. Hebden, Aldergarth, Galphay, Ripon, North Yorkshire HG4 3NJ

Please make out cheques to Ripon Historical Society.

Yorkshire Hearth Tax Lists
North Riding: Michaelmas 1673
1. Gilling West & Hang West Wapentakes (Richmond, Middleham, Upper Wensleydale, Upper Swaledale south side of Upper Teesdale)
2. Allerton, Gilling East, Halikeld & Hang East Wapentakes (Vale of Mowbray, northern part of Vale of York, including Northallerton, Bedale & Masham)
3. Birdforth & Bulmer Wapentakes (Thirsk, Easingwold, almost reaches Helmsley & Malton & includes some townships now part of York City)
4. Ryedale, Pickering Lyth & Scarborough Wapentakes (Helmsley, Malton, Pickering, Scarborough & southern. part of the North York Moors)
5. Langbarugh West, Langbarugh East & Whitby Strand Wapentakes (stretches west of Stokesley through Guisborough to Whitby & includes northern part of North York Moors).

West Riding, Lady Day 1672
1. Claro Wapentake (Ripon, Harrogate, Knaresborough., Wetherby etc)
2. Staincliffe & Ewcross Wapentakes (all the north west of the West Riding from Keighley in the south to Sedbergh in the north and west to the Lancashire border)
3. Agbrigg & Morley Wapentakes (much of later industrial area: Bradford, Halifax, Huddersfield, suburbs of Leeds, Wakefield etc)
4. Barston (sic) Ash & Osgoldcross Wapentakes (Goole, part of Tadcaster, Selby, Pontefract and Castleford)

Ripon Historical Society & Ripon Harrogate & District Family History Group (continued)

East Riding, Lady Day 1672
1   Howden, Harthill. Holme, Ouse & Darwant, Harthill Wilton, and Buckrose wapentakes (the Western side bordering the Ouse and the Derwent including Pocklington, Market Weighton and Norton opposite Malton)
2. The Town and County of Hull and the East Riding wapentakes of Harthill. Hunsley and Harthill and Bainton (the central portion including Beverley and north to Great Driffield).
3. Dickering, North, Mid and South Holderness (the eastern side from Filey to Spurn Head including Bridlington, Hornsea and Patrington).

York City & Ainsty Wapentake, Lady Day 1672
All except C1 contain a delineated map of the Ridings and all are indexed to townships thus giving some idea of the distribution of surnames.

North & East Riding each part; West Riding parts 1, 2, & 4 £3 + 40p UK postage, overseas £1 surface mail & £1.50 airmail. West Riding part 3 is £4.50 + 65p UK postage, 40p postage UK, overseas £1 surface, £1.30 airmail.

Index of Wills & Administrations
Masham Peculier: Masham Parish North Riding, Kirkby, Malzeard Parish West Riding
Lists all the original documents and probate copies for this Peculier held by Leeds District Archives at Sheepscar, Leeds. It includes four indexes: Testators Occupations, Places outside the Peculier, all surnames in the documents other than that of the testator, the naming of field names is noted and a map of the townships with O.S. references of some of the less well known residences is included.

£4.50 + 65p UK postage, overseas £1.10 surface, airmail £2.25 to North America, £2.65 to Australasia.

A Guide to Historical Sources for Ripon and District
Ed T. R. Hebden published on behalf of the Ripon Records Project. It covers the ancient parishes of Ripon, Masham and Kirkby Malzeard thus including Fountains Abbey and Upper Nidderdale. A5

Price £3.00 + 40p UK postage, overseas £1 surface mail, £1.50 airmail.

1851 Census Index
Includes surname, Christian name, age, place of birth, piece and folio number.
1. Parishes Of Aldbrough (incl. Boroughbridge) Marton Cum Grafton, Staveley, Copgrove & Ripley.
2. Parishes Of Hampsthwaite (Incl. Birstwith & Felliscliffe) & Pannal (Incl Low Harrogate & Beckwithshaw) and the Townships of Kirkby Overblow & Follifoot (Par Spofforth)
3. Townships of Bilton with Harrogate (Part of Knaresborough)
4. & 5. Knaresborough & Scotton

Ripon Historical Society & Ripon Harrogate & District Family History Group (continued)

6. Townships of Farnham, Goldsbrough, Great Ouseburn, Kirk Hammerton, Nidd, Nun Monkton & Whixley with parts of Hunsingore, Knaresborough & Spofforth
7. Parishes Of Allerton, Mauleverer, Cowthorpe, Hunsingore, Kirkby Overblow (part), Kirk Deighton & Spofforth (incl. Wetherby)

Nos 1,2,3 & 7 £2.00, No. 6 £3.00 all plus 40p UK postage, overseas surface £1, airmail £1.50. Nos 4 & 5 £4 + post as Masham wills.

Miscellaneous
The Thirlway Journal: A Record of Life in Early Victorian Ripon. 17 illustrations with maps of Ripon.
Kith & Kin: Nidderdale Families 1500-1750. 24 illustrations & 4 maps.

Both books priced at £7.50 each + 85p UK post, O/seas Surface £1.50, air Europe £1.80, Zone 1 £3.00, Zone 2 £3.50.

Wharfedale Family History Group

S.R. Merridew, 206 Moseley Wood Gardens, Cookridge, Leeds, LS16 7JE

Parish Registers

		Price
Addingham St Peter Marr & Bur	1813-1837	£2.50
Addingham St Peter Baptisms	1813-1837	£2.50
Bolton Abbey	1813-1837	£2.50
Bolton Abbey	pre 1689	£1.00
Horsforth St. James Woodside Marrs	1848-1904	£2.50
Kettlewell St Mary Index	1698-1760	£2.50

Non Conformist Registers

Addingham & Draughton Wesleyan Baptisms	1840-1899	£1.50
Addingham Wes. Methodist Marrs	1843-1899	£1.00
Addingham Wes.Methodist Burials	1844-1995	£4.00
Draughton Wes Meth. Bur & M.I.s	1847-1956	£1.00
Rawdon Greenhill Wes. Methodist Burials	1905-1961	
M.I.s	1836-1961	£1.50
Rawdon Society of Friends Burials	1695-1976	
& MIs	1830-1993	£2.00
Yeadon Town Hall Square Primative Methodist Bur. & M.I.s	1844, 1852-1944	£1.00

Wharfdale Family History Group (continued)

1851 Census Indexes
1. Askwith, Burley in Wharfedale, Denton, Ilkley, Middleton & Weston.
2. Bramhope, Farnley, Leathley, Lindley, Menston, Newall with Clifton, Pool in Wharfedale & Stainburn.
3. Adel, Alwoodley, Arthington, Bardsey, Castley, Blubberhouses, Clifton with Norwood, Duneswick, Eccup, Fewston, Great Timble, Harewood, Havarrah Park, Little Timble, North Rigton, Weardley, Wigton & Wike.
4. & 5. Otley (in 2 parts, Surnames A-K & L-Z).
6. Addingham, Barden, Beamsley, Bolton Abbey, Drebley, Rylstone, Halton East, Hazelwood/ Storiths, Nesfield/Langbar.
7. Appletreewick, Arncliffe, Beckermonds, Bordley, Buckden, Burnsall, Conistone, Cracoe, Foxup, Grassington, Halton, Gill, Hartlington, Hawkswick, Hebden, Hetton, Hubberholme, Kettlewell, Kilnsey, Linton, Litton, Oughtershaw, Starbottom, Thorpe, Threshfield, Yockenthwaite.

Each of the above volumes priced at £2.50.

1861 Census Horsforth	£2.50
1871 Census - Horsforth	£2.50
Ilkley	£2.50
Rawdon	£2.50
Adel, Alwoodley, Arthington, Bramhope, Dunkeswick, Eccup, North Rigton, Pool & Weeton	£2.50
Blubberhouses, Fewston, Lindley, Norwood & Timble	£1.50
Otley (part 1) A-K	£2.50
Otley (part 2) L-Z	£2.50
1891 Census Guiseley & Hawksworth	£2.50

Memorial Inscriptions

Addingham, St Peter	£4.00
Addingham, Wesleyan Methodist	£1.50
Adel, St John the Baptist	£4.00
Arthington, St Peter	£1.00
Bolton Priory	£4.00
Burley in Wharfedale, St Mary	£1.00
Burley in Wharfedale, God's Acre Cemetery	£2.00
Conistone, St Mary	£1.00
Denton, St Helen	£1.00
Farnley, All Saints	£1.00
Fewston, Meagill Lane Cemetery	£1.00
Guiseley, Providence PM Otley Rd	£1.00
Guiseley, St Oswald	£5.00
Hawksworth Methodist	£1.00
Horsforth, Cragg Hill Baptist	£1.50
Horsforth, St James Woodside	£1.00

Wharfdale Family History Group (continued)

Hubberholme, St Michael & All Angels	£1.50
Ilkley, All Saints	£2.00
Leathley, St Oswald	£1.00
Menston, St John	£1.50
Pool, St Wilfrid	£1.50
Rawdon, Cragg Baptist	£1.50
Rylstone, St Peter	£1.50
Weeton, St Barnabas	£1.50
Weston, All Saints	£1.50
Yeadon, St John	£1.50
Yeadon, Chapel Hill P.M.	£2.00

Miscellaneous

Cloggers Daybook (Henry Gill of Addingham) 1894	£1.50
Whereabouts of Wharfedale Records	£2.50

Postage Extra:
Orders under £4.00 U.K. 50p Airmail £1.35;
Orders under £7.00 U.K. 75p Airmail £2.00;
Orders under £10.00 U.K. £1.50 Airmail £3.00;
Orders under £15.00 U.K. £2.50 Airmail £4.50;
Orders £15.00 & over post free U.K & Airmail.

WALES

ANGLESEY

Cymdeithas Hanes Teuluoedd Gwynedd Family History Society

G.F.H.S. 36 Y Wern, Y Felinheli, Port Dinorwic, Gwynedd, Wales LL56 4TX

Memorial Inscriptions are A4 size, and these contain all of the inscriptions as well as a full index and notes to assist the non-Welsh reader. All other publications are also A4 size. The price quoted include post & packing UK only. The same publications are offered on micro-fiche to overseas customers, write for costs.

Ynys Mon / Anglesey
Monumental Inscriptions

	Order Number	Cost
Amlwch. Capel Salem (B)	M147	£2.50
Amlwch. St Eleth	M006	£6.00
Beaumaris. St Mair & St Nicolas	M129	£5.50
Bodedern. St Edern	M178	£4.50
Bodewryd. St Mair	M184	£3.50
Ceirchiog. Betws y Grog	M189	£2.00
Coedana. St Anna	M082	£2.50
Holyhead. Capel Bethel (B)	M194	£3.00

Cymdeithas Hanes Teuluoedd
Gwynedd Family History Society (continued)

Holyhead, St Cybi	M215	£4.50
Llan-faes. St Catrin	M170	£4.00
Llanallgo. St Gallgo	M070	£5.00
Llanbabo. St Pabo	M046	£2.50
Llanbadrig. Cemaes, Capel Bethesda (C.M.)	M065	£4.00
Llanbadrig. St Padrig	M094	£6.00
Llanbedr-goch. St Pedr	M135	£4.50
Llanbeulan. St Peulan	M234	£2.00
Llanddaniel Fab. St Deiniol Fab	M117	£3.50
Llanddona. St Dona	M091	£4.00
Llanddyfnan. St Dyfnan	M191	£6.00
Llandegfan. St Tegfan	M067	£2.50
Llandyfrydog. St Tyfrydog	M021	£3.50
Llandysilio. St Tysilio	M077	£14.00
Llanedwen. St Edwen	M118	£5.00
Llaneilian. St Eilian	M022	£7.50
Llaneilian. Penysarn. Capel Carmel (B)	M010	£3.50
Llaneugrad. St Eugrad	M131	£4.00
Llanfair Mathafarn Eithaf. St Mair	M069	£4.50
Llanfair Pwllgwyngyll. St Mair	M107	£8.50
Llanfair-yng-Nghornwy, St Mair	M209	£4.00
Llanfair Yn Neubwll. St Mair	M071	£4.00
Llanfair Yn Neubwll. Capel Seilo (B)	M230	£2.50
Llanfechell. Capel Jerusalem (C.M.)	M149	£2.00
Llanfechell. St Mechell	M181	£4.00
Llanfihangel Din Sylwy. St Mihangel	M086	£2.50
Llanfihangel Ysgeifiog. Capel Moriah (B)	M026	£2.50
Llanfihangel Ysgeifiog. St Mihangel (Old)	M025	£2.50
Llanfihangel Yn Nhowyn. St Mihangel	M031	£2.50
Llanffinan, St Ffinan	M078	£3.50
Llangefni, Rhosmeirch. Capel Ebenezer (C)	M002	£4.50
Llangefni. Capel Cildwrn (B)	M182	£3.00
Llangefni. St Cyngar	M247	£3.50
Llangeinwen. Capel Dwyran (C.M.)	M124	£4.00
Llangoed. St Cawrda	M102	£5.50
Llanidan. St Nidan (Old)	M140	£2.50
Llanidan. St Nidan, Brynsiencyn (New)	M176	£9.50
Llaniestyn. St Iestyn	M088	£4.00
Llanrhwydrys. St Rhwydrys	M126	£2.50
Llanrhyddlad. St Rhyddlad	M083	£3.00
Llansadwrn. St Sadwrn	M087	£4.00
Llantrisant. Capel Ainon (B)	M028	£2.00
Llantrisant (Old). St Afran	M217	£3.00
Llanwenllwyfo. Capel Sardis (B)	M011	£2.50
Llanwenllwyfo. St Gwenllwyfo	M054	£6.50

Cymdeithas Hanes Teuluoedd
Gwynedd Family History Society (continued)

Llanynghenedl. St Cenedl	M201	£3.00
Llanynghenedl. St Mihangel	M109	£2.50
Llechylched (Old)	M188	£2.00
Llechylched. Capel Gwyn (B)	M229	£2.50
Memorials Inside Anglesey Churches	M137	£3.50
Penmon. St Seiriol	M175	£4.00
Penmynydd. Capel Pencarneddi (B)	M186	£3.00
Penmynydd. St Gredifaol	M072	£4.50
Penrhollugwy. St Mihangel	M005	£4.50
Pentraeth. St Mair	M169	£8.00
Rhodogeidio. St Ceidio	M084	£2.50
Rhosbeirio. St Mair	M027	£2.00
Rhoscolyn. Capel Sardis (B)	M044	32.00
Rhoscolyn. Capel Wesla (W)	M052	£3.00
Rhosybol. Eglwys Grist / Christ Church	M029	£2.50
Tregaean. St Caean	M122	£3.00

Arfon (Central Caernarfonshire)

Betws Garmon. St Garmon	M123	£4.50
Llanbeblig. Capel Moriah (C).Waunfawr	M163	£2.00
Llanbeblig. Christ Church.Caernarfon	M050	£2.00
Llanbeblig. St Peblig (8 parts)	M064 Pt1	£7.50
	M064 Pt2	£6.00
	M064 Pt3	£5.00
	M064 Pt4	£8.00
	M064 Pt5	£9.50
	M064 Pt6	£9.50
	M064 Pt7	£8.00
	M064 Pt8	£3.00
Llanberis, St Peris, Nant Peris	M190 Pt1	£10.50
Llanberis, St Peris, Nant Peris	M190 Pt2	£7.50
Llanberis, St Peris, Nant Peris	M190 Pt3	£5.50
Llandygai. St Tegai (Pt)	M038	£4.00
Llanddeiniolen. Capel Bethel (C)	M203	£3.00
Llanddeiniolen. Capel Ebenezer (C)	M216	£2.50
Llanddeiniolen. St Deiniol. Pt 1	M214 Pt1	£10.50
Llanddeiniolen. St Deiniol. Pt 2	M214 Pt2	£11.00
Llanfaglan. St Baglan.	M007	£4.00
Llanfair-Is-gaer. St Mair	M128	£12.00
Llanrug. Capel Caeathro (C.M.)	M033	£6.50
Llanrug. Capel Mawr (C.M.)	M200	£2.50
Llanwnda. Capel Horeb (C.M.),Rhostryfan	M142	£3.00

Cymdeithas Hanes Teuluoedd
Gwynedd Family History Society (continued)

Aberconwy (Eastern Caernarfonshire)

Betws y Coed. St Mihangel	M223	£9.00
Caerhun. Capel Talybont (C.M.)	M187	£4.50
Caerhun. Capel Ty'n-y-Groes. (C.M.)	M199	£3.00
Caerhun. St Mair	M198	£5.50
Conwy. St Agnes	M040	£8.00
Conwy. St Mair	M085	£4.50
Dolwyddelan. St Gwyddelan	M139	£4.00
Eglwys Bach. Capel Pwllterfyn.(C.M.)	M114	£2.00
Llan-rhos (Eglwys Rhos). St Ilar	M106	£15.00
Llandudno. St George	M101	£2.50
Llandudno. St Tudno	M041	£11.50
Llanfairfechan. St Mair	M243	£6.50
Llanfairfechan. Erw Feiriol Nondenominational	M238	£9.50
Llangelynnin. St Celynnin (New)	M160	£4.50
Llangelynnin. St Celynnin (Old)	M068	£2.50
Llangystennin. Capel Einion (B)	M089	£3.00
Llangystennin. St Cwstennin	M174	£7.00
Llanrhychwyn. Capel Ardda (C.M.)	M138	£2.00
Llanrhychwyn St. Rhychwyn	M157	£2.50
Penmachno. Capel Salem (C.M.)	M197	£6.50
Penmachno. Capel Tabor (B)	M127	£2.00
Penmachno St Tudclud	M196	£6.50
Trefriw. St Mair	M158	£4.00
Ysbyty Ifan. St Ioan	M225	£5.50

Dwyfor (Western Caernarfonshire)

Aber-erch. Capel Peniel (B), (Tyddyn Sion)	M039	£2.50
Aberdaron. Capel Bethesda (B),Rhoshirwaun	M185	£2.50
Aberdaron. St Hywyn (Old)	M165	£9.00
Aberdaron. St Hywyn (New)	M204	£3.50
Aberdaron. Ynys Enlli	M205	£2.00
Beddgelert. St Mair	M219	£10.00
Bodfean. St Buan	M161	£6.00
Botwnnog. Capel Nanhoron (C)	M079	£2.00
Botwnnog. Capel Ty'n Donnen	M103	£1.50
Botwnnog. St Beuno	M132	£3.50
Bryncroes. St Mair	M133	£6.50
Carnguwch. St Cuwch	M018	£3.50
Ceidio, Capel Peniel (C)	M051	£2.00
Clynnog Fawr. Capel Tai Duon (C.M.)	M024	£2.50
Cricieth. St Catrin	M095	£3.50
Cricieth.Nondenominational	M100	£9.00
Deneio. St Beuno Section A	M159 Pt1	£6.00

Cymdeithas Hanes Teuluoedd
Gwynedd Family History Society (continued)

Deneio. St BeunoSection B	M159 Pt2	£4.50
Deneio. St Beuno Section C	M159 Pt3	£4.00
Deneio. St Beuno Section D	M159 Pt4	£8.00
Deneio. Capel Pen Lan (C) Pwllheli	M080	£2.00
Dolbenmaen. Capel Horeb (B), Garndolbenmaen	M098	£2.00
Dolbenmaen. Capel Tabor (C), Pentre'rfelin	M004	£4.00
Dolbenmaen. Prenteg Nondenomination Cty;	M045	£3.50
Dolbenmaen. St Mair	M096	£8.50
Edern. Capel Edeyrn (C.M.)	M036	£6.00
Edern. St Edern	M092	£4.00
Llanaelhaearn. St Aelhaearn	M167	£9.50
Llanarmon. St Garmon	M008	£4.50
Llandegwnning. St Gwyninin	M121	£6.00
Llandudwen. Capel Dinas.(C.M.)	M113	£4.00
Llandudwen. St Tudwen	M042	£2.00
Llanengan. Capel Bwlch (C.M), Abersoch	M090	£12.00
Llanengan. St Engan	M111	£6.00
Llanfaelrhys. St Maelrhys	M154	£3.00
Llanfihangel Bachellaeth. St Buan	M152	£2.50
Llanfihangel y Pennant. St Mihangel	M009	£5.50
Llangian. St Cian	M001	£6.00
Llangynnadl. Capel Hebron (C)	M108	£5.00
Llangwnnadl. St Gwynhoedl	M120	£4.50
Llangybi. Capel Helyg (C)	M037	£6.00
Llangybi. St Cybi	M032	£3.50
Llaniestyn. Capel Rehoboth (C)	M150	£2.50
Llaniestyn. St Iestyn	M143	£3.50
Llanystumdwy. Capel Pencaenewydd (C.M.)	M141	£1.50
Llanystumdwy. Capel Rhos-lan (C)	M097	£2.00
Llanystumdwy. St Ioan Fedyddiwr	M066	£6.00
Llanystumdwy.Chwilog Nondenom; Cty	M171	£8.00
Mellteyrn. Capel Brynmawr (C.M.)	M168	£2.50
Mellteyrn. St Pedr	M134	£5.00
Nefyn, Morfa Nefyn St Mair	M239	£4.50
Nefyn, Capel Y Fron (B)	M035	£2.50
Nefyn. Nondemoninational Cemetery	M145	£7.00
Penllech.,St Mair	M125	£2.50
Penmorfa. St Beuno	M034	£7.00
Penrhos, St Cynfil	M162	£2.50
Pistyll, St Beuno	M156	£3.00
Rhiw, Y. Capel Pisga (W)	M115	£2.00
Rhiw, Y. St Aelrhiw	M153	£3.00
Rhiw, Y. Capel Nebo (C)	M220	£4.50
Treflys. St Mihangel	M047	£6.00
Tudweiliog. St Cwyfan	MI66	£6.00

Cymdeithas Hanes Teuluoedd
Gwynedd Family History Society (continued)

Ynyscynhaearn, Capel Garth, (C.M.), Porthmadog	M074	£2.50
Ynyscynhaearn. Capel Salem (B) Porthmadog	M053	£2.50
Ynyscynhaearn. St Cynhaearn	M023	£5.50
Ynyscynhaearn. Moel y Gest,Nondenominational	M081 Pt1	£6.50
Ynyscynhaearn, Moel y Gest.Nondenominational	M081 Pt2	£7.50
Ynyscynhaearn. St Mair, Tremadog	M207	£2.00
Ynyscynhaearn. St John, Porthmadog	M208	£2.00

Meirionnydd

Dolgellau, Capel Brithdir (C)	M253	£4.50
Dolgellau. Capel Bryn Celyn, Brithdir (C.M.)	M226	£2.50
Dolgellau. Capel Islaw- r Dref (C.M.)	M105	£2.50
Dolgellau. Capel Judah. (B)	M057	£2.50
Dolgellau. St Marc, Brithdir	M244	£2.00
Dolgellau. Capel Salem. (C.M)	M073	£3.50
Dolgellau. Capel Tabor (C)	M003	£3.00
Dolgellau. St Mair	M043	£10.00
Dolgellau. St Mair. Marian Mawr. Dafydd Ionawr	M056	£6.50
Dolgellau. St Paul, Bryncoedifor	M058	£2.50
Ffestiniog. Bl Festiniog.(Nondenom;) Section A1-A3	M148 Pt1	£6.50
Section A4-A6	M148 Pt2	£5.50
Section D1-D2	M148 Pt3	£5.50
Section E	M148 Pt4	£5.00
Section F	M148 Pt5	£4.00
Section G	M148 Pt6	£4.00
Section H	M148 Pt7	£6.00
Section K	M148 Pt8	£4.50
Section M & N	M148 Pt9	£3.50
Section P,S,T.	M148 Pt10	£6.00
Festiniog, Bl; Festiniog.(Capel Bethesda C.M)	M202	£4.50
Ffestiniog. St Mihangel	M155	£15.00
Ffestiniog. Nondenominational Cemetery	M211	£13.00
Ffestiniog. Dewi Sant, Bl; Ffestiniog	M144	£3.50
Llanaber. Capel Cutiau (C)	M173	£2.00
Llanaber. St Mair. Abermaw. Pt 1	M227 Pt1	£9.00
Llandanwg. Capel Moreia (C.M). Harlech	M183	£3.00
Llandanwg. St Tanwg (Old)	M048	£2.00
Llandecwyn. St Tecwyn	M249	£4.00
Llandderfel. Capel Bethel (C)	M212	£2.00
LlaneLltud. Capel Libanus (C)	M076	£3.00
Llanfachreth Capel Bethel (C.M.)	M013	£3.00
Llanfachreth. Capel Hermon (C.M.)	M012	£2.00
Llanfachreth. Capel Rhydymain (C)	M112	£4.00
Llanfachreth. Capel Siloh (C.M.).Rhydymain	M015	£2.50
Llanfachreth. Capel Siloh. (C)	M014	£2.50

Cymdeithas Hanes Teuluoedd
Gwynedd Family History Society (continued)

Llanfachreth. St Machreth	M016	£7.00
Llanfihangel y Pennant. St Mihangel	M119	£4.50
Llanfor. St Marc, Frongoch	M242	£2.00
Llanfor, Eglwys y Drindod, Rhosgwalia	M245	£2.00
Llanfrothen. St Brothen	M232	£5.50
Llanfrothen, Capel Ramoth (B)	M241	£5.50
Llanuwchllyn. Capel Einion (B)	M104	£2.00
Llanuwchllyn. Capel Rhosyfedwen (C)	M017	£2.50
Maentwrog. St Twrog	M222	£8.00
Maentwrog. Capel Utica (C)	M248	£3.00
Pennal. St Pedr	M019	£4.00
Tal y Llyn. Capel Rehoboth (C) Corris	M116	£6.50
Tal y Llyn. St Mair	M110	£6.50
Trawsfynydd. Capel Penstryd (C)	M130	£3.00
Trawsfynydd. Capel Salem (B)	M075	£2.50
Trawsfynydd. St Madryn	M151	£6.00
Tywyn. Capel Maothlon. (C.M)	M049	£2.00
Tywyn. St Pedr, Aberdyfi	M020	£2.50
Tywyn. St Cadfan	M213	£7.50

Dinbych/ Denbighshire

Eglwys Bach. Capel Pwllterfyn (C.M.)	M114	£2.00
Ysbyty Ifan. St Ioan	M225	£5.50

Tramor / Overseas

Bangor. St John. Pennsylvania. USA	M164	£2.00
Iowa, Cambrian Cemetery, Cotter. USA	M059	£2.50
Iowa. Foreston Cemetery. Howard County.USA	M055	£2.00
Kansas-Evergreen Cemetery	M063	£2.00
Kansas. Greenwood Cometery, Emporia. USA	M062	£3.00
Mafiken.Bophuthatswana (Bechuanaland), Africa	M136	£3.00
Wisconsin, Rock Hill, Green Lake, USA	M061	£2.00

Mynegai Priodas/ Marriage Index
Ynys Mon / Anglesey

Ynys Mon / Anglesey 1754-1812	P07	£28.00
Ynys Mon / Anglesey 1813-1837	P02	£18.00

Aberconwy (Eastern Caernarfonshire)

Aberconwy (All) 1813-1837	P03	£7.50

Arfon (Central Caernarfonshire)

Llanbeblig. 1754-1837	P01	£4.50
Arfon (All) 1813-1837	P04	£10.50

Cymdeithas Hanes Teuluoedd
Gwynedd Family History Society (continued)

Dwyfor (Western Caernarfonshire)

Dwyfor (All) 1813-1837		P05	£11.00

Meirionnydd

Meirionnydd (All) 1754-1812		P08	£23.50
Meirionnydd (All) 1813-1837		P06	£12.50

Mynegai Cyfrifiad / Census Index
Ynys Mon / Anglesey

Amlwch & District	1801	C22	£2.50

Aberconwy (Eastern Caernarfonshire)

Betws Y Coed, Dolwyddelan, Capel Curig Llanrhychwyn & Trefriw	1851	C08	£9.00
Caerhun, Llanbedr y Cennin & Llangelynnin	1851	C11	£7.00
Conwy & Gyffin	1851	C02	£7.50
Dwygyfylchi & Llanfairfechan	1851	C03	£6.50
Llandudno, Llan-rhos & Llangystennin	1851	C01	£8.50
Llandudno	1861	C05	£8.00
Penmachno	1851	C07	£9.50

Arfon (Central Caernarfonshire)

Abergwyngregyn	1851	C29	£3.00
Bangor & Pentir	1851	C25	£23.50
Betws Garmon	1851	C33	£2.00
Llanbeblig (Caernarfon) All parts	1851	C12	£27.00
Llanbeblig (Caernarfon) Part 1 Caernarfon Town, West Ward			£10.50
Llanbeblig (Caernarfon) Part 2. Caernarfon Town, East Ward			£12.00
Llanbeblig (Caernarfon) Part 3. Bontnewydd & Waunfawr			£4.50
Llanberis	1851	C35	£4.00
Llandygai & pt Capel Curig	1851	C27	£9.50
Llanfaglan	1851	C24	£3.00
Llanfair Isgaer	1851	C34	£4.00
Llanllechid	1851	C28	£14.50
Llanrug	1851	C36	£5.50
Llanwnda	1851	C31	£5.00

Dwyfor (Western Caernarfonshire)

Aber-erch (& pt Pwllheli)	1851	C13	£6.50
Boduan	1851	C23	£3.00
Criciesth	1851	C18	£4.00
Deneio (Pwllheli)	1851	C14	£8.00
Edern	1851	C26	£3.50
Llannor	1851	C15	£5.00

Cymdeithas Hanes Teuluoedd
Gwynedd Family History Society (continued)

Llanystumdwy	1851	C17	£5.50
Penllech	1851	C19	£3.00
Penrhos	1851	C16	£2.50
Tudweiliog	1851	C20	£3.00
Meirionnnydd Ffestiniog	1851	C06	£10.50
Llanfair	1851	C40	£2.50
Llandanwg	1851	C38	£4.00
Llanfrothen	1851	C39	£4.50
Trawsfynydd	1851	C37	£5.00

Sir Ddinbych / Denbighshire

Capel Garmon, Llanrwst, Eglwys Bach & Llanddoged	1851	C04	£11.00
Llansanffraid Glan Conwy	1851	C09	£8.00
Llandrillo yn Rhos & Llysfaen	1851	C10	£7.50
Ysbyty Ifan, Pentrefoelas	1851	C07	£9.50

Mynegai Bedyddiadau / Index to Baptisms

Pre 1837. Calvinistic Methodist & Congregational Chapels of Aberconwy (Eastern area of Caernarfonshire)	B01	£10.00
Pre 1837 Calvinistic Methodist Chapels, Anglesey	B02	£8.00
Pre 1837 Calvinistic Meth; Chapels Anglesey (By Chapel)	B03	£9.50
Pre 1837 Baptist, Congregationalists & Wesleyan. Anglesey	B04	£6.50

Cofrestri Plwyf / Parish Registers

Llanbadrig, Ynys Mon / Anglesey 1754-1812	PR02	£5.00

Amrywiol / Miscellaneous

Cofebion / Memorials, Plwyfi / Parishes of Ffestiniog Trawsfynydd and Maentwrog, Meirionnydd	A03	£5.00
Ymfudo / EmigrationEmigrants from Gwynedd to USA, 1795- 1932. A Selected List	A01	£17.50
Anglesey only	pt1	£5.00
Caernarfonshire only	pt2	£6.50
Meirionnydd only	pt3	£6.00

Arfon / Caernarfonshire

M214 St. Deiniol, Llanddeiniolen,	pt1	£10.50
C31 Llanwnda Census 1851		£5.00

Meirionnydd

M248 Maentwrog. Capel Utica (C)	£3.00
M249 Llandecwyn. St Tecwyn.	£4.00
C37 Trawsfynydd. Census 1851	£5.00
C38 Llandanwg Census 1851	£4.00
C39 Llanfrothen Census 1851	£4.50

DENBIGHSHIRE

Cymdeithas Hanes Teuluoedd Clwyd
Clwyd Family History Society

Dafydd Hayes, Pen y Cae, Ffordd Hendy, Gwernymynydd, Sir Fflint, CH7 5JP

Parish Registers

	(a)	(c)
Abergele		
Vol. 1 C1647-1708	£5.60	£7.20
Vol. 2 M1647-1708, B1647-1708	£5.70	£7.40
Vol. 3 B1709-1761	£5.70	£7.40
Vol. 4 M1709-1753, B1709-1761	£5.70	£7.50
Vol. 5 C1761-1781, B1761-1781	£5.60	£7.20
Vol. 6 C1782-1812, B1782-1812	£5.70	£7.50
Vol. 7 M1754-1812	£5.50	£6.80
Bangor On Dee		
Vol. 1 (pt1) C1675-1734.	£6.60	£820
Vol. 1 (pt2) M1675-1734, B1675-1734	£6.70	£8.50
Vol. 2 (pt1) C1735-1796.	£6.70	£8.70
Vol. 2 (pt2) M1735-1754, B1735-1812	£6.70	£8.50
Vol. 3 M1754-1812.	£5.50	£6.60
Vol. 4 C1797-1812.	£4.40	£5.20
Betws Gwerful Goch		
Vol. 1 C1670-1812.	£6.50	£7.40
Vol. 2 M1755-1812.	£5.50	£6.40
Vol. 3 M1671-1754, B1670-1812.	£6.70	£8.70
Betws Yn Rhos		
Vol. 1 C1663-1759, M1663-1703, B1663-1703	£5.60	£7.00
Vol. 2 M1705-1754, B1705-1812.	£5.60	£7.00
Vol. 3 C1760-1812, M1754-1812.	£5.60	£7.00
Bodfari		
Vol.1 C1571-1620.	£5.60	£6.80
Vol. 2 M1571-1620, B1571-1620.	£5.60	£7.00
Vol. 3 C1756-1791, B1755-1791	£5.50	£6.80
Vol. 4 C1792-1812, B1792-1812	£5.50	£6.60
Vol. 5 C1621-1643, M1621-1643, B1621-1643.	£5.50	£6.80
Vol. 6 C1648-1720, M1670-1720, B1655-1720	£5.70	£7.40
Vol. 7 C1721-1754, M1721-1754, B1721-1754	£5.60	£6.80
Vol. 8 M1754-1812.	£5.40	£6.20
Bryneglwys		
Vol. 1 C1661-1812.	£5.60	£7.00
Vol. 2 M1662-1812, B1663-1812.	£5.70	£7.40
Caerwys		
Vol. 1 (pt1) C1673-1728.	£5.70	£7.40
Vol.1 (pt2) M1673-1727, B1673-1728	£5.50	£6.60
Vol. 2 C1728-1789, M1728-1754, B1728-1789	£5.70	£7.50
Vol. 3 C1790-1812, M1754-1812, B1790-1812	£5.60	£7.00

Cymdeithas Hanes Teuluoedd Clwyd
Clwyd Family History Society (continued)

Capel Garmon
    Vol. 1 C1696-1769, M1696-1752, B1696-1768   £5.70   £7.40
    Vol. 2 C1769-1842   £5.50   £6.40
    Vol. 3 M1754-1812, B1769-1841   £5.50   £6.80
Cerrigydrudion
    Vol. 1 (pt1) C1590-1735   £6.80   £9.10
    Vol. 1 (pt2) M1591-1734, B1590-1734   £6.80   £9.10
    Vol. 2 C1805-1812, M1735-1760, B1735-1812   £6.70   £8.40
    Vol. 3 M1754-1812   £5.50   £6.40
    Vol. 4 C1735-1804   £6.70   £8.50
    Vol. 5 C1813-1846   £5.50   £6.40
Chirk
    Vol. 1 C1666-1706, M1612-1706, B1611-1706   £5.60   £6.80
    Vol. 2 C1705-1758, M1719-1754, B1708-1757   £6.80   £9.10
    Vol. 3 C1759-1803, M1754-1803, 1758-1803   £6.80   £9.10
    Vol. 4 C1803-1812, M1804-1812, B1803-1812   £5.60   £6.80
Cilcain
    Vol.1   C1577-1723, M1583-1723, B1576-1722   £10.30   £14.00
    Vol. 2   C1723-1742, M1723-1742, B1723-1742   £5.50   £6.80
    Vol. 3   C1743-1787, M1743-1743, B1743-1787   £5.70   £7.40
    Vol. 4   C1788-1812, B1788-1812   £5.60   £6.80
    Vol. 5   M1754-1843   £5.60   £7.00
Clocaenog
    Vol. 1 C1672-1812   £5.60   £7.20
    Vol. 2   M1676-1812, B1672-1812   £6.70   £8.70
Corwen
    Vol. 1 C1667-1719, M1667-1721, B1667-1720   £5.70   £7.40
    Vol. 2 C1719-1740, M1722-1740, B1720-1740   £5.50   £6.60
    Vol. 3 C1741-1812,   £5.50   £6.80
    Vol. 4   M1741-1754, B1741-1812   £5.60   £7.00
    Vol. 5   M1754-1812,   £5.60   £7.00
Cwm
    C1727-1812, M1727-1837, B1727-1812   £6.70   £8.70
Denbigh
    Vol. 1 (pt1) C1683-1706   £6.60   £8.20
    Vol. 1 (pt2) M1683-1706, B1683-1706   £5.60   £7.20
    Vol. 2 (pt1) C1703-1739   £5.60   £6.80
    Vol. 2 (pt2) M1703-1739, B1703-1739   £6.80   £8.90
    Vol. 3 C1739-1773   £5.70   £7.40
    Vol. 4   M1739-1753, B1739-1773   £5.80   £8.10
    Vol. 5   C1774-1790   £5.60   £6.80
    Vol. 6   C1800-1812, B1800-1812   £5.60   £7.20
    Vol. 7   M1754-1812   £8.00   £10.30
    Vol. 8   C1790-1800, B1790-1800   £5.60   £7.00
    Vol. 9   B1774-1790   £5.50   £6.60

Cymdeithas Hanes Teuluoedd Clwyd
Clwyd Family History Society (continued)

Derwen
    Vol. 1 C1632-1812   £7.00   £9.50
    Vol. 2 M1632-1812, B1632-1812   £7.00   £9.30

Dyserth
    Vol. 1 C1602-1701, M1602-1701, B1602-1702   £5.50   £6.60
    Vol. 2 C1704-1759, M1706-1754, B1705-1759   £5.60   £7.00
    Vol. 3 C1759-1812, M1755-1812, B1759-1812   £5.70   £7.50

Efenechtyd
    C1693-1812, M1693-1811, B1694-1812   £5.70   £7.40

Eglwysbach
    Vol. 1 C1601-1552, M1601-1662, B1601-1662   £6.80   £8.90
    Vol. 2 C1666-1729 M1668-1729 B1666-1729   £5.70   £7.70
    Vol. 3 C1760-1812   £5.70   £7.50
    Vol. 4 M1730-1753, B1730-1812.   £5.60   £7.00
    Vol. 5 M1754-1812   £5.50   £6.80

Erbistock
    Vol. 1 C1679-1760, M1679-1754, B1679-1760   £5.60   £6.80
    Vol. 2 C1761-1812, M1754-1812, B1761-1812   £5.50   £6.60

Flint
    Vol. 1 (pt1) C1598-1685, M1598-1687   £6.70   £8.50
    Vol. 1 (pt2) C1685-1709, M1684-1708, B1598-1709   £6.80   £8.70
    Vol. 2 C1707-1730, M1707-1720, B1707-1723.   £5.60   £7.00
    Vol. 3 C1737-1764, M1727-1754, B1727-1764.   £6.80   £8.70
    Vol. 4 C1765-1786, B1765-1786.   £5.60   £6.80
    Vol. 5 M1754-1837.   £6.60   £8.20
    Vol. 6 C1787-1812, B1787-1812   £5.60   £7.00

Gresford
    Vol. 1 C1660-1713, M1670-1713, B1660-1713   £9.00   £11.70
    Vol. 2 C1714-1740, M1714-1739, B1714-1740   £7.80   £9.70
    Vol. 3 C1740-1772, M1740-1754, B1740-1772   £7.80   £10.10
    Vol. 4 C1773-1810, B1773-1811   £11.20   £13.20
    Vol. 5 M1754-1812   £6.80   £8.90

Gwaenysgor C1538-1812, M1540-1812, B1539-1812   £6.80   £9.10

Gwyddelwern
    Vol. 1 C1662-1770, M1662-1754, B1662-1770   £7.00   £9.50
    Vol. 2 C1769-1812.   £5.50   £6.40
    Vol. 3 B1771-1812.   £5.40   £6.20
    Vol. 4 M1754-1812.   £5.50   £6.60

Gwytherin
    Vol. 1 C1667-1812   £5.70   £7.40
    Vol. 2 M1672-1812, B1667-1812   £5.60   £7.00

Gyffylliog
    Vol. 1 C1617-1716   £6.60   £8.20
    Vol. 2 M1617-1754, B1617-1715   £6.70   £8.50
    Vol. 3 C1717-1812   £6.70   £8.50
    Vol. 4 M1755-1812, B1716-1812   £6.70   £8.50

Cymdeithas Hanes Teuluoedd Clwyd
Clwyd Family History Society (continued)

Halkyn
Vol. 1 C1595-1698, M1595-1698, B1594-1698	£5.60	£7.00
Vol. 2 C1699-1706 & C1719-1764	£5.60	£7.00
Vol. 3 C1706-1719, M1698-1754, B1698-1764	£5.60	£7.00
Vol. 4 C1765-1803, B1764-1803	£5.70	£7.50
Vol. 5 M1754-1812	£5.50	£6.60
Vol. 6 C1803-1812, B1803-1812	£6.60	£8.00
Vol. 7 M1813-1837	£5.50	£6.60
Vol. 8 C1813-1840, B1812-1840	£6.80	£8.90

Hanmer
Vol 1 (pt1) C1563-1600	£6.60	£8.00
Vol. 1 (pt2) M1563-1600, B1563-1600	£6.60	£8.20
Vol. 1 (pt3) C1601-1658	£6.70	£8.40
Vol. 1 (pt4) M1601-1641, B1601-1648	£6.70	£8.50
Vol. 2 (pt1) C1653-1708, M1655-1708	£7.00	£9.70
Vol. 2 (pt2) B1653-1748	£8.20	£11.20
Vol. 2 (pt3) C1709-1748, M1709-1748	£6.80	£9.10
Vol. 3 (pt1) C1749-1781	£6.70	£8.70
Vol. 3 (pt2) B1749-1781	£5.60	£7.00
Vol. 3 (pt3) M1749-1787, B1782	£5.50	£6.80
Vol. 4 C1782-1812	£6.80	£8.70
Vol. 5 B1784-1812	£5.50	£6.60

Hawarden
Vol. 1 (pt1) C1585-1624	£5.60	£6.80
Vol. 1 (pt2) C1585-1631, B1585-1624	£6.70	£8.40
Vol. 2 C1625-1665	£5.60	£7.20
Vol. 3 M1632-1665, B1625-1665.	£5.60	£7.00
Vol. 4 (pt1) C1666-1682	£5.50	£6.60
Vol. 4 (pt2) C1683-1697	£5.50	£6.60
Vol. 5 M1668-1696, B1666-1698,	£6.80	£9.10
Vol. 6 (pt1) C1697-1717	£5.60	£6.80
Vol. 6 (pt2) M1697-1717, B1699-1716	£6.60	£8.00
Vol. 7 C1718-1726, M1718-1726, B1717-1726	£6.70	£8.50
Vol. 8 C1727-1741, M1727-1741, B1726-1741	£6.80	£8.90
Vol. 9 C1742-1754, M1742-1754, B1742-1754	£6.70	£8.50
Vol. 10 M1755-1770	£5.50	£6.60
Vol. 11 C1755-1770, B1755-1770	£6.70	£8.50
Vol. 12 C1771-1790	£6.70	£8.50
Vol. 13 M1771-1790, B1771-1790.	£6.80	£8.70
Vol. 14 (pt1) C1791-1800	£5.60	£7.00
Vol. 14 (pt2) M1791-1800, B1791-1800.	£5.60	£7.00
Vol. 15 C1801-1810	£5.60	£7.20
Vol. 16 M1801-1810, B1801-1810	£5.60	£7.00

Cymdeithas Hanes Teuluoedd Clwyd
Clwyd Family History Society (continued)

Vol. 17 C1811-1820	£5.80	£7.70
Vol. 18 M1811-1820, B1811-1820	£5.60	£7.00
Vol. 19 C1821-1830	£5.70	£7.50
Vol. 20 M1821-1830, B1821-1830	£5.60	£7.00
Vol. 21 C1831-1840	£5.60	£7.00
Vol. 22 M1831-1837, B1831-1840	£5.50	£6.60
Vol. 23 C1841-1850	£5.60	£6.80

Henllan

Vol.1 C1684-1746	£6.70	£8.50
Vol. 2 B1684-1746	£5.50	£6.80
Vol. 3 M1684-1799	£6.70	£8.40
Vol. 4 C1746-1787	£5.50	£6.80
Vol. 5 B1746-1800	£5.60	£6.80
Vol. 6 C1788-1812, M1799-1812, B1801-1812	£6.80	£8.90

Holt

Vol. 1 C1661-1700, B1661-1700	£5.50	£6.80
Vol. 2 C1701-1739, B1701-1739	£5.60	£7.00
Vol. 3 M1661-1754	£5.50	£6.40
Vol. 4 C1740-1772, B1740-1772	£5.50	£6.60
Vol. 5 C1772-1812, B1772-1812	£5.60	£6.80
Vol. 6 M1754-1837	£5.60	£7.00

Holywell

Vol. 1 (pt1) C1677-1719	£5.60	£6.80
Vol. 1 (pt2) M1677-1713, B1677-1714	£5.60	£7.00
Vol. 2 (pt1) C1714-1741	£5.60	£7.00
Vol. 2 (pt2) M1714-1740	£5.60	£7.00
Vol. 2 (pt3) B1714-1741	£5.60	£7.00
Vol. 3 (pt1) C1741-1772	£7.80	£9.90
Vol. 3 (pt2) M1741-1754, B1741-1772	£7.80	£10.10
Vol. 3 (pt3) M1754-1771	£5.60	£6.80
Vol. 4 (pt1) C1773-1793	£7.70	£9.70
Vol. 4 (pt2) M1772-1787	£5.60	£7.00
Vol. 4 (pt3) M1787-1800	£6.70	£8.50
Vol. 4 (pt4) B1772-1792	£5.60	£7.20
Vol. 5 (pt1) C1793-1812	£8.00	£10.50
Vol. 5 (pt2) B1793-1812	£5.60	£7.00
Vol. 6 C1813-1825	£6.70	£8.50
Vol. 7 M1801-1812	£6.60	£8.20
Vol. 8 B1813-1828	£5.60	£7.00
Vol. 9 C1826-1831	£5.50	£6.40
Vol. 10 C1832-1840	£5.50	£6.60
Vol. 11 B1829-1841	£5.60	£7.20

Hope

Vol. 1 (pt1) C1668-1731	£5.70	£7.40
Vol. 1 (pt2) M1668-1731, B1668-1731	£5.70	£7.70

Cymdeithas Hanes Teuluoedd Clwyd
Clwyd Family History Society (continued)

Vol. 2 (pt1) C1732-1754	£5.50	£6.60
Vol. 2 (pt2) M1732-1754, B1732-1754	£5.50	£6.60
Vol. 2 (pt3) C1755-1770, B1755-1770	£5.60	£6.80
Vol. 2 (pt4) C1771-1781, B1771-1781	£5.50	£6.60
Vol. 3 M1754-1812	£5.70	£7.70
Vol. 4 C1781-1812, B1781-1812	£10.10	£12.90
Isycoed C1749-1813, M1750-1837, B1750-1813	£5.50	£6.80
Llanarmon Dyffryn Ceiriog		
Vol. 1 C1625-1768, M1624-1769, B1624-1769	£5.70	£7.70
Vol. 2 C1769-1815, M1769-1813, B1769-1813	£5.60	£7.00
Llanarmon Mynydd Mawr		
C1681-1812, M1683-1812, B1681-1812	£5.60	£7.00
Llanarmon Yn Ial		
Vol. 1 C1683-1746, M1767-1743, B1683-1743	£5.70	£7.70
Vol. 2 C1744-1812, M1744-1812, B1744-1812	£10.00	£12.30
Llanasa		
Vol. 1 C1619-1663, M1629-1707, B1629-1663	£8.80	£10.90
Vol. 2 C1664-1707, B1664-1707	£9.10	£11.70
Vol. 3 C1708-1760, M1808-1753, B1708-1760	£9.10	£12.10
Vol. 4 C1761-1794, B1761-1794	£6.80	£8.90
Vol. 5 C1795-1812, M1754-1812, B1795-1812	£6.80	£9.10
Llanbedr Dyffryn Clwyd		
Vol. 1 C1605-1812	£5.70	£7.40
Vol. 2 M1654-1812	£5.50	£6.40
Vol. 3 B1632-1812	£5.50	£6.60
Llanddoget		
Vol. 1 C1600-1812	£5.70	£7.50
Vol. 2 M1600-1837, B1601-1812	£6.70	£8.50
Llanddulas C1665-1812, M1665-1812, B1665-1812	£5.70	£7.40
Llandegla		
Vol.1 C1710-1743, M1710-1738, B1710-1741	£5.50	£6.80
Vol. 2 C1744-1776, B1741-1776	£5.50	£6.40
Vol. 3 C1777-1812, M1744-1812, B1777-1812	£5.50	£6.60
Llandrillo Yn Edeirnion		
Vol. 1 C1662-1720, M1662-1720, B1662-1720	£5.70	£7.70
Vol. 2 C1720-1760, B1720-1770	£5.60	£7.20
Vol. 3 C1761-1812, B1770-1812	£5.60	£7.20
Vol. 4 M1720-1825	£5.60	£6.80
Llandrillo Yn Rhos		
Vol. 1 C1663-1774	£5.50	£6.60
Vol. 2 M1665-1754, B1663-1774	£5.60	£6.80
Vol. 3 C1775-1837	£5.60	£7.00
Vol. 4 M1754-1837, B1775-1837	£5.70	£7.40
Llanelian Yn Rhos		
Vol. 1 (pt1) C1589-1722	£5.60	£7.00
Vol. 1 (pt2) M1591-1721, B1589-1722	£5.50	£6.80

Cymdeithas Hanes Teuluoedd Clwyd
Clwyd Family History Society (continued)

Vol. 2 C1722-1812	£5.60	£7.00
Vol. 3 M1722-1812, B1722-1812	£5.60	£7.00
Llanelidan		
Vol. 1 C1686-1754, B1695-1754	£5.70	£7.40
Vol. 2 C1755-1812, M1696-1812, B1755-1811	£6.80	£9.10
Llanfair Dyffryn Clwyd		
Vol. 1 C1680-1782, M1691-1754, B1680-1782	£10.30	£13.60
Vol. 2 C1782-1812, M1755-1812, B1782-1812	£6.80	£8.90
Llanfair Talhaearn		
Vol. 1 C1652-1739, M1671-1739, B1667-1739	£5.60	£7.20
Vol. 2 C1740-1812, B1740-1812	£5.70	£7.40
Vol. 3 M1740-1812	£5.50	£6.60
Llanfawr		
Vol. 1 C1722-1754, M1722-1754, B1722-1754	£5.60	£7.20
Vol. 2 C1754-1796, B1754-1796	£5.60	£7.00
Llanferres		
Vol. 1 C1587-1730, M1588-1730, B1587-1730	£6.70	£8.70
Vol. 2 C1731-1790, M1733-1754, B1731-1790	£5.60	£7.20
Vol. 3 C1791-1810, M1754-1837, B1791-1810	£5.50	£6.60
Llanfihangel Glyn Myfyr		
Vol. 1 C1662-1728, M1663-1728, B1662-1728	£5.60	£7.20
Llanfihangel Glyn Myfyr		
Vol. 1 C1662-1728, M1663-1728, B1662-1728	£5.60	£7.20
Vol. 2 C1729-1812, M1729-1812, B1729-1812	£6.67	£8.70
Llanfwrog		
Vol. 1 C1638-1755	£6.80	£8.90
Vol. 2 M1638-1753, B1638-1755	£6.80	£9.10
Vol. 3 C1756-1780, B1756-1780	£5.60	£7.00
Vol. 4 C1780-1812, B1780-1812	£5.60	£7.20
Vol. 5 M1754-1837	£5.60	£7.20
Llangadwaladr		
C1736-1813, M1739-1813, B1736-1813	£5.50	£6.80
Llangar		
Vol. 1 C1614-1719, M1615-1715, B1614-1720	£5.60	£7.20
Vol. 2 C1720-1762, M1723-1812, B1720-1762	£5.60	£7.20
Vol. 3 C1762-1812, B1762-1806	£5.60	£7.00
Vol. 4 C1813-1849, £5.50	£6.40	
Vol. 5 C1672-1813, M1697-1812, B1675-1812	£6.80	£8.90
Llangernyw		
Vol. 1 C1569-1671, M1570-1667, B1570-1667	£5.70	£7.40
Vol. 2 C1672-1730, M1672-1730, B1672-1730	£6.80	£8.90
Vol. 3 C1730-1779, B1730-1779	£5.70	£7.50
Vol. 4 C1779-1812, B1779-1812	£5.60	£7.20
Vol. 5 M1730-1812	£5.50	£6.80

Cymdeithas Hanes Teuluoedd Clwyd
Clwyd Family History Society (continued)

Llangollen
Vol. 2 C1670-1706, M1670-1705, B1670-1706	£6.70	£8.40
Vol. 3 C1707-1738, M1708-1737, B1707-1738	£9.10	£11.90
Vol. 4 C1738-1769, M1738-1754, B1738-1769	£9.10	£11.90
Vol. 5 C1770-1782, B1770-1791	£5.70	£7.50
Vol. 6 C1782-1791	£5.50	£6.40
Vol. 7 C1791-1812	£5.70	£7.50

Llangwm
Vol. 2 C1738-1775, M1738-1754, B1738-1775	£5.50	£6.60
Vol. 3 M1754-1812	£5.50	£6.40
Vol. 4 C1776-1812, B1776-1812	£5.60	£6.80

Llangwyfan
C1676-1812, M1683-1837, B1676-1812	£5.60	£7.00

Llangynhafal
Vol. 1 C1676-1812	£5.50	£6.80
Vol. 2 M1677-1812	£5.50	£6.40
Vol. 3 B1676-1812	£5.50	£6.60

Llannefydd
Vol. 1 M1754-1812	£5.40	£6.20
Vol. 2 C1754-1812	£5.60	£6.80
Note 1 3 B1754-1812	£5.60	£6.80
Note 1 4 C1665-1753	£5.50	£6.60
Note 1 5 M1666-1754, B1665-1753	£5.60	£7.00

Llanrhaeadr Ym Mochnant
Vol. 1 C1678-1692, M1678-1691, B1678-1692	£5.60	£7.00
Vol. 2 (pt1) C1759-1812	£11.20	£14.60
Vol. 2 (pt2) M1754-1812	£5.60	£7.00
Vol. 2 (pt3) B1759-1812	£8.00	£10.50
Vol. 3 C1695-1713, M1696-1713, B1695-1713	£5.60	£7.20
Vol. 4 (pt1) C1713-1758	£7.80	£10.10

Llanrhaeadr Yng Nghinmeirch
Vol. 1 C1676-1735	£5.70	£7.40
Vol. 2 M1676-1735, B1676-1735	£5.70	£7.70
Vol. 3 (pt1) C1736-1777	£5.60	£7.20
Vol. 3 (pt2) M1736-1755, B1736-1777	£5.60	£7.00
Vol. 4 M1754-1812	£5.60	£7.00
Vol. 5 C1778-1812, B1778-1812	£5.70	£7.70

Llanrhydd
Vol. 1 C1608-1756, B1610-1756	£6.80	£8.70
Vol. 2 M1610-1812	£5.60	£7.00
Vol. 3 C1757-1812, B1757-1812	£5.60	£6.80

Llanrwst
Vol. 1 C1613-1691, M1614-1691, B1615-1690	£5.60	£7.20
Vol. 2 C1691-1736	£5.60	£7.20
Vol. 3 M1692-1737, B1691-1736	£6.70	£8.70
Vol. 4 M1738-1812	£6.70	£8.70
Vol. 6 B1737-1812	£5.70	£7.40

Cymdeithas Hanes Teuluoedd Clwyd
Clwyd Family History Society (continued)

Llansanffraid Glan Conwy		
Vol. 1 C1660-1744, M1662-1744, B1662-1744	£5.70	£7.50
Vol. 2 C1744-1784, M1745-1753, B1744-1794	£5.60	£7.00
Vol. 3 C1784-1812, M1754-1812, B1784-1812	£5.70	£7.50
Llansanffraid Glyn Ceiriog		
C1768-1814, M1754-1814, B1768-1814	£5.60	£7.20
Llansannan		
Vol.1 C1666-1726, M1667-1726, B1666-1725	£5.70	£7.40
Vol. 2 C1727-1781	£5.70	£7.40
Vol. 3 M1727-1754, B1727-1781	£5.60	£7.00
Vol. 4 M1754-1812	£5.50	£6.60
Vol. 5 C1782-1812, B1782-1812	£5.70	£7.40
Llansilin		
Vol. 1 C1666-1714, M1666-1714, B1666-1714	£6.70	£8.50
Vol. 2 C1715-1764, M1715-1754, B1715-1764	£8.00	£10.30
Vol. 3 C1765-1812, M1754-1812, B1765-1812	£9.10	£12.10
Llantysilio		
Vol. 1 C1671-1717, M1671-1717, B1671-1717	£5.70	£7.70
Vol. 2 C1721-1755, M1721-1812, B1721-1755	£5.70	£7.50
Vol. 3 C1759-1812, B1759-1812	£5.60	£7.00
Llanychan		
C1677-1813, M1677-1812, B1676-1812	£5.60	£6.80
Llanynys		
Vol. 1 C1626-1733, M1626-1733, B1626-1731	£8.00	£10.50
Vol. 2 C1739-1812, M1739-1812, B1739-1812	£6.80	£9.10
Llysfaen		
Vol. 1 C1661-1760, M1662-1752, B1661-1760	£5.60	£6.80
Vol. 2 C1760-1812, M1755-1812, B1760-1812	£5.60	£7.20
Marchwiel		
Vol. 1 C1652-1700, M1665-1700, B1662-1700	£5.50	£6.60
Vol. 2 C1701-1750, M1701-1750, B1701-1750	£5.50	£6.60
Vol. 3 C1751-1812, M1751-1812, B1751-1812	£5.60	£7.20
Meliden		
Vol. 1 C1602-1718, M1603-1718, B1602-1718	£5.60	£7.00
Vol. 2 C1716-1783, M1718-1812, B1716-1783	£5.70	£7.40
Vol. 3 C1783-1812, B1783-1812	£5.40	£6.20
Minera C1772-1820	£6.70	£8.40
Mold		
Vol. 1 C1612-1623, M1604-1623, B1617-1623	£5.60	£7.00
Vol. 2 C1624-1659, M1624-1644, B1624-1647	£5.80	£7.90
Vol. 3 C1650-1675, M1653-1673, B1652-1675	£5.80	£7.90
Vol. 4 C1674-1721	£5.70	£7.50
Vol. 5 M1674-1721, B1674-1721	£5.70	£7.40
Vol. 6 C1722-1772,	£9.10	£11.90
Vol. 7 M1722-1754	£5.60	£6.80
Vol. 8 M1754-1812	£10.20	£13.40

Cymdeithas Hanes Teuluoedd Clwyd
Clwyd Family History Society (continued)

Vol. 9 C1773-1797	£5.70	£7.40
Vol. 10 B1722-1772	£5.70	£7.50
Vol. 11 B1773-1812	£7.80	£10.10
Vol. 12 C1798-1812	£7.80	£10.10
Nannerch		
Vol. 1 C1664-1770, M1664-1754, B1664-1770	£6.80	£8.70
Vol. 2 C1771-1812, M1755-1812, B1771-1812	£5.60	£7.00
Nantglyn		
Vol. 1 C1663-1812	£5.70	£7.40
Vol. 2 M1664-1812, B1663-1812	£5.60	£7.20
Nercwys		
Vol. 1 C1665-1731, M1669-1754, B1669-1731	£5.70	£7.40
Vol. 2 C1732-1812, M1755-1812, B1732-1812	£6.80	£8.90
Northop		
Vol. 1 (pt1) C1590-1626.	£5.60	£6.80
Vol. 1 (pt2) C1627-1656	£5.60	£7.20
Vol.1 (pt3) M1590-1626, B1590-1625	£5.60	£7.20
Vol. 1 (pt4) M1627-1656, B1627-1656	£5.60	£6.80
Vol. 2 (pt1) C1656-1698	£5.60	£7.20
Vol. 2 (pt2) M1656-1698, B1656-1698	£5.70	£7.70
Vol. 3 C1698-1749	£5.70	£7.40
Vol. 4 M1698-1754, B1698-1749	£5.70	£7.40
Vol. 5 C1750-1812	£8.00	£10.70
Vol. 6 M1754-1812, B1750-1812	£6.80	£9.10
Overton		
Vol. 1 C1602-1639, M1602-1644, B1602-1650	£5.60	£7.00
Vol. 2 (pt1) C1654-1690, M1654-1681, B1654-1690	£5.50	£6.80
Vol. 2 (pt2) C1691-1724, M1692-1724, B1691-1724	£5.60	£7.20
Vol. 3 (pt1) C1727-1754, M1727-1754, B1730-1754	£5.60	£7.00
Vol. 3 (pt2) C1755-1782, B1755-1782	£5.60	£7.00
Vol. 4 M1754-1837	£5.50	£6.80
Vol. 5 C1783-1812, B1783-1812	£6.70	£8.50
Penley		
Vol. 1 C1657-1812, M1753, B1753-1812	£5.70	£7.50
Vol. 2 C1813-1864	£5.70	£7.40
Pentrefoelas C1782-1812, M1772-1837, B1773-1812	£5.60	£7.20
Rhuddlan		
Vol. 1 C1681-1734	£6.70	£8.70
Vol. 2 M1681-1734, B1681-1734	£6.60	£8.20
Vol. 3 C1734-1772, M1734-1772, B1734-1772	£6.80	£8.90
Vol. 4 C1773-1797	£5.50	£6.60
Vol. 5 M1773-1795, B1773-1796	£5.50	£6.60
Vol. 6 C1798-1812, M1796-1837, B1797-1812	£6.70	£8.40
Ruabon		
Vol. 1 C1559-1680, M1599-1680, B1599-1680	£15.30	£20.80
Vol. 2 C1681-1731, M1681-1731, B1681-1731	£9.30	£13.00

Cymdeithas Hanes Teuluoedd Clwyd
Clwyd Family History Society (continued)

Vol. 3 C1732-1772, M1732-1754, B1732-1777	£12.30	£16.00
Vol. 4 C1773-1802	£11.20	£14.40
Vol. 5 B1778-1802	£7.80	£9.90
Vol. 6 M1754-1812	£8.00	£10.30
Vol. 7 C1803-1812, B1803-1812	£6.80	£9.10
Vol. 8 C1813-1828	£6.80	£9.10
Vol. 9 B1813-1832	£5.70	£7.50
Vol. 10 M1813-1827	£5.60	£7.20
Vol. 11 C1828-1853	£6.70	£8.70
Vol. 12 M1827-1837	£5.60	£6.80
Vol. 13 M1837-1843	£5.50	£6.60
Vol. 14 B1832-1847	£5.70	£7.50

Ruthin

Vol. 1 C1592-1744	£8.20	£11.60
Vol. 2 M1593-1744, B1592-1744	£8.30	£11.80
Vol. 3 C1744-1812, M1745-1812, B1745-1812	£9.10	£11.90

St. Asaph

Vol. 1 C1593-1669, M1606-1689, B1594-1669	£8.00	£10.70
Vol. 2 C1677-1707, M1671-1706, B1671-1707	£6.80	£9.10
Note 2 3 C1704-1727, M1704-1726, B1704-1727	£5.50	£6.40
Note 3 4 C1704-1726, M1704-1726, B1704-1750	£5.70	£7.40
Note 4 5 C1704-1750, M1704-1715, B1704-1726	£6.80	£9.10
Note 5 6 C1704-1726, M1704-1750, B1704-1725	£5.70	£7.40
Vol. 7 (1) C1750-1779	£5.60	£6.80
Vol. 7 (2) M1750-1780, B1750-1780	£6.70	£8.50
Vol. 8 C1780-1812	£5.60	£7.20
Vol. 9 M1781-1812	£5.60	£6.80
Vol.10 B1781-1812	£5.60	£6.80

St. George

Vol. 1 C1694-1742, M1695-1741, B1694-1741	£5.50	£6.60
Vol. 2 C1741-1812, M1741-1812, B1741-1812	£6.70	£8.40

Trelawnyd

Vol. 1 C1700-1812	£5.70	£7.40
Vol. 2 M1700-1836, B1699-1812	£6.80	£8.70

Tremeirchion

Vol. 1 C1599-1694, M1600-1689, B1599-1692	£6.80	£8.90
Vol .2 C1695-1812, M1695-1812, B1695-1812	£6.80	£9.10

Treuddyn

Vol. 1 C1611-1694, M1618-1683, B1613-1695	£5.60	£7.20
Vol. 2 C1695-1812	£5.60	£7.20
Vol. 3 M1696-1812, B1695-1812	£5.60	£7.20

Whitford

Vol. 1 C1643-1742	£9.10	£11.90
Vol. 2 M1643-1742	£5.60	£6.80
Vol. 3 B1662-1741	£5.70	£7.70
Vol. 4 C1742-1778	£5.70	£7.70

Cymdeithas Hanes Teuluoedd Clwyd
Clwyd Family History Society (continued)

Vol. 5 B1742-1778	£5.60	£7.20
Vol. 6 M1742-1778	£5.50	£6.80
Vol. 7 C1779-1812	£5.70	£7.50
Vol. 8 M1779-1812	£5.60	£6.80
Vol. 9 B1779-1812	£5.60	£7.00
Worthenbury		
Vol. 1 C1597-1692	£5.60	£6.80
Vol. 2 M1597-1690, B1597-1692	£5.60	£7.20
Vol. 3 C1685-1745	£5.60	£7.00
Vol. 4 M1683-1745, B1683-1745	£5.60	£7.20
Vol. 5 M1745-1820	£5.50	£6.60
Vol. 6 C1745-1813	£6.80	£8.70
Vol. 7 B1746-1812	£5.60	£7.00
Wrexham		
Vol. 1&2 C1618-1666, M1632-1666, B1620-1666	£11.60	£15.40
Vol. 3&4 C1661-1682, M1667-1682, B1668-1686	£10.60	£14.20
Vol. 5 C1682-1702, M1682-1702, B1682-1702	£14.00	£18.90
Vol. 6 C1703-1729, M1703-1729, B1703-1729	£14.60	£20.60
Vol. 7 C1730-1756, M1730-1754, B1730-1756	£16.60	£22.20
Vol. 8 C1757-1776	£10.60	£14.40
Vol. 9 C1776-1789	£10.20	£13.40
Vol. 10 C1789-1800, B1788-1800	£9.10	£12.10
Vol.11 C1800-1812, B1800-1812	£13.60	£17.80
Vol. 12 B1757-1788	£9.10	£12.10
Vol. 13 (1) M1754-1780	£5.50	£6.80
Vol. 13 (2) M1781-1813	£5.50	£6.80
Vol. 14 (1) M1754-1768	£5.50	£6.80
Vol. 14 (2) M1769-1800	£6.80	£9.10
Ysbyty Ifan		
Vol. 1 C1677-1731, B1677-1812	£5.60	£7.20
Vol. 2 C1732-1812	£5.70	£7.70
Vol.3 M1677-1812	£5.60	£7.00
Ysceifiog		
Vol. 1 C1662-1710	£5.50	£6.80
Vol. 2 M1662-1710, B1662-1709	£5.50	£6.80
Vol. 3 C1711-1741, B1710-1741	£5.60	£7.20
Vol. 4 M1711-1812	£5.70	£7.40
Vol. 5 C1742-1784, B1742-1784	£5.70	£7.50
Vol. 6 C1785-1800, B1785-1800	£5.60	£7.00
Vol. 7 C1801-1812 B1801-1812	£5.50	£6.60

Notes On Parish Register Transcript List:

C=Baptism, M= Marriage, B=Burial.
Note 1: Reconstituted from Bishops Transcripts.
Note 2: 1704-1726 Baptisms, Marriages and Burials for Brynpolyn, Cyrchynan and Gwernglefryd townships.

Cymdeithas Hanes Teuluoedd Clwyd
Clwyd Family History Society (continued)

Note 3: 1704-1726 Baptisms, Marriages and Burials for Bodeugan, Cilowen, Gwerneigron, Rhyllon and Talar townships; 1727-1750 Marriages For all townships.
Note 4: 1704-1726 Marriages and Burials for alll townships; 1727-1750 Baptisms for all townships.
Note 5: 1704-1726 Bodelwyddan, Pengwern and Faenol townships; 1727-1750 burials for all townships.

P.R Transcripts Indexes

Burials Trefynant Acrefair Vol 1	£6.80	£9.10
Burials Trefynant Acrefair Vol 2	£5.60	£7.20
M.I.Cefn Bychan Baptist	£5.60	£7.00
M.I.Cefn Mawr Baptist	£5.60	£7.20
M.I.Maes Hyfryd (Church Cemetery) Rhyl	£13.60	£17.80
M.I.Morley Road Rhyl	£8.00	£10.30
Welsh Wills Proved At Chester	£5.50	£6.40
Marriage Strays Vol.1	£5.60	£7.00
Marriage Strays Vol 2	£5.60	£7.00

Census

1841 Census - Wrexham Town	£9.10	£11.90
Notitiae of St Asaph Diocese Vol. 1 (Census of Denbighshire Parishes C1680)	£15.00	£19.30

GLAMORGAN

Glamorgan Family History Society

Mrs. R. Knight 6 St. Margarets Crescent, Roath, Cardiff CF2 5AU Glamorgan

Parish Registers
Baptisms; Burials; Marriages. (in this order)

	(a)	(b)
Aberdare, St John the Baptist 1734-1900; 1734-1924; 1717-1837	£11.00	£11.70
Barry, St. Nicholas 1724-1900; 1724-1900; 1724-1837.	£2.25	£2.50
Bishopston, St. Teilo 1677-1891; 1677-1890; 1678-1838	£3.40	£4.00
Bonvilston. St. Mary1696-1900; 1696-1901; 1696-1837	£2.25	£2.50
Cadoxton J. Barry, St. Cadog 1724-1889; 1724-1901; 1724-1837	£3.40	£4.00
Cadoxton J. Neath, St. Catwg 17211899; 1721-1889; 1721-1837	£16.50	£17.50
Caerau, St. Mary 1725-1903; 1725-1902; 1727-1836 and Michaelston Super-Ely, St. Michael, 1721-1905; 1724-1909; 1724-1835	£3.40	£4.00
Cardiff, St. John 1669-1840; 1669-1841; 1669-1837	£14.70	£15.70
Cogan, St. Peter 1724-1857; 1724-1823; 1728-1821 and Lavernock, St. Lawrence 1724-1904; 1724-1902; 1725-1836	£2.25	£2.50
Colwinston St. Michacl 1696-1951; 1696-1992; 1725-1836	£3.40	£4.00
Cowbridge, The Holy Cross 1718-1887; 1735-1873; 1721 -1837	£5.50	£6.00

Glamorgan Family History Society (continued)

Coychurch, St. Crallo 1733 1900; 1736-1900; 1723-1837	£5.50	£6.00
Eglwys Brewis, St. Brewis (See Gilston)		
Eglwysilan, St.Llan 1679-1900; 1694-1891; 1695-1838	£11.00	£11.50
Flemingston. St. Michael 1576-1900; 1576-1900; 1678-1839	£2.25	£2.50
Gileston, St. Giles 1701-1940; 1702 1946; 1701-1836 and Eglwys Brewis. St. Brewis.1750-1939; 1755-1935; 1724-1860	£2.25	£2.50
Glyncorrwg St John 1702-1905; 1702-1908; 1724-1837	£3.40	£4.00
Laleston, St. David 1721-1899; 1721-1900; 1721-1837	£3.40	£4.00
Lavernock, St. Lawrence (see Cogan)		
Leckwith, St. James 1724-1880; 1724-1880; 1725-1838 and Michaelston Le Pit, St. Michael 1724-1900; 1724-1900; 1724-1837	£2.25	£2.50
Lisvane, St. Denys 1724-1902; 1724-1902; 1724-1838	£2.25	£2.50
Llanblethian, St. Blethian 1673-1893; 1661-1893; 1664-1837	£3.40	£4.00
Llancarfan, St Cadoc 1696-1900; 1696-1899; 1619-1838	£4.40	£5.00
Llandaff, The Cathedral 1724-1844; 1724-1845; 1724-1838	£6.50	£7.00
Llandough-J-Cowbridge, St. Dochd.1583-1943; 1583-1986; 1585-1839	£2.25	£2.50
Llandough-J-Penarth, St. Dochau 1724-1880; 1725-1883; 1724-1839	£2.25	£2.50
Llanederyn, St. Ederyn 1701-1900; 1701-1998; 1701-1837	£3.40	£4.00
Llangan St.Canna 1689-1978; 1705-1984; 1724-1838	£2.25	£2.50
Llangyfelach, SS. David & Cyfelach 1686-1905; 1686-1863; 1693-1837	£14.70	£15.70
Llanharan, Parish of SS. Julius & Aar.1615-1900; 1641-1900; 1721-1838	£2.25	£2.50
Llanharry, St. Illtud 1725-1901; 1725-1901; 1725-1837	£2.25	£2.50
Llanilid, SS. Illid & Curig 1696-1922; 1696-1924; 1730-1834	£2.25	£2.50
Llanishen, St. Isan 1717-1901; 1717-1900; 1725-1837	£3.40	£4.00
Llanrhidian, SS Rhidian & Illtyd, 1671-1885; 1671-1908; 1671-1928	£8.00	£8.70
Llansannor, St. Senwyr 1726-1900; 1727-1900; 1724-1845	£2.25	£2.50
Llantrisant, SS. Illtyd, Gwynno, Dyfod.1717-1871; 1728-1870; 1717-1837	£8.00	£8.70
Llantwit Fardre, St. Illtyd 1632-1850; 1632-1850; 1625-1837	£5.50	£6.00
Llantwit Major, St. Illtud 1721-1900; 1721-1901; 1696-1837	£6.50	£7.00
Marcross, Holy Trinity, 1690-1987; 1696-1986; 1728-1836	£2.25	£2.50
Margan, St. Mary 1672-1901; 1672-1900; 1675-1837	£11.00	£12.00
Merthyr Dyfan, St. Dyfan 1724-1886; 1724-1900; 1728-1836	£2.25	£2.50
Merthyr Mawr, St. Teilo, 1696-1899; 1696-1900; 1727-1836	£2.25	£2.50
Merthyr Tydfil, St.Tydfil 1704-1837; 1704-1837; 1717-1837	£20.00	£22.00
Michaelston Le Pit, see Leckwith		
Michaelston-Super-Ely, see Caerau		
Monknash St. Mary Magdalene1721-1987; 1721-1901; 1721-1837	£2.25	£2.50
Newton Nottage, St. John 1715-1900; 1715- 1898; 1716-1837	£5.50	£6.00
Penarth, St. Augustine 1724- 1900; 1724-1900; 1725-1837	£6.50	£7.00
Pendoylan St Cadoc 1569-1901; 1569- 1902; 1569-1840	f3.40	£4.00
Penllyn. St. Brynach 1721 1902; 1721-1902; 1631 -1845	£2.25	£2.50
Penmark, St. Mary 1696- 1893; 1696-1898; 1696-1837	£3.40	£4.00
Pentyrch, St Catwg 1678- 1868; 1695-1868; 1695-1845	£3.40	£4.00
Peterson super Ely, St. Peter 1724-1900; 1724-1900; 1724-1839	£2.25	£2.50

Glamorgan Family History Society (continued)

Peterstons Montem, St. Peter, 1745-1900, 1745-1900; 1721-1837 and Bethlehem Welsh Congreg. Chapel 1777-1814; 1830-1837 (no marrs)	£2.25	£2.50
Port Eynon, St. Cattwg 1672-1921; 1672-1939; 1681-1837	£3.40	£4.00
Porthkerry, St. Curig 1724-1899; 1724-1902; 1724-1836	£2.25	£2.50
Pyle & Kenfig, St. James 1695-1876; 1695-1898; 1688-1837	£6.50	£7.00
Radyr, St. John 1725-1900; 1725-1900; 1717- 1836	£2.25	£3.00
Roath, St. Margaret 1724- 1879; 1724-1876; 1724-1837	£4.40	£5.00
Rudry, St. James, 1637-1900; 1637-1900; 1640-1835	£3.40	£4.00
St. Andrews Major, St. Andrew 1696-1905; 1696-1901; 1696-1837	£4.40	£5.00
St. Athan, St. Tathan 1677-1891; 1663-1899; 1683-1838	£3.40	£4.00
St Brides Major St. Bridget 1721-1901; 1721-1901; 1721-1837	£5.50	£6.00
St. Brides Minor, St. Bride 1723-1899; 1723- 1901; 1696-1837	£4.40	£5.00
St. Brides Super-Ely, St. Bride 1717-1901; 1717-1902; 1724-1837	£2.25	£2.50
St. Donats, St. Donat 1572-1900; 1571-1900; 1570-1837	£3.40	£4.00
St. Fagans, St. Mary 1689-1882; 1689-1884; 1689-1837	£3.40	£4.00
St. Georges Super Ely, St. George 1693-1900; 1695-1900; 1697-1837	£2.25	£2.50
St. Lythans, St. Lythan, 1724-1901; 1724-1901; 1724- 1838	£2.25	£2.50
St. Mary Church, The Annunciation 1584-1912; 1605- 1985; 1577-1839	£2.25	£2.50
St. Mary Hill, St. Mary 1696-1985; 1696-1985, 1696-1837	£2.25	£2.50
St. Nicholas, St. Nicholas 1724-1900; 1724-1902; 1724-1837	£3.40	£4.00
Sully, St John 1725-1901; 1725-1900; 1717-1836	£2.25	f2.50
Tythegston, St. Tydwg 1721-1901; 1721-1901; 1723-1837	£2.25	£2.50
Wenvoe, St. Mary 1585-1891; 1587-1900; 1586-1837	£5.50	£6.00
Whitchurch, St. Mary 1717-1837; 1717- 1837; 1732-1837	£5.50	£6.00
Wick. St James 1721-1915; 1721-1987; 1721-1837	£3.40	£4.00
Ystradowen, St.Owain 1696-1904; 1696-1927; 1697-1837	£2.25	£2.50
Ystradyfodwg, St. John Baptist 1717- 1883; 1629-1987; 1717-1837	£5.50	£6.00

Monumental Inscriptions
a Aberbargoed, (Mon.) Caersalem Baptist;
a Aberdare: Aberaman Saron Congregational, Cwmbach Abernant y Groes Unitarian Chapel & Trecynon Hen Dy Cwrdd Unitarian
a Aberdare Calvaria Welsh Baptist
c Aberdare. St. Johns
b Aberdare Trecynon, St Fagans
a Barry, St. Nicholas & Merthyr Dyfan SS Dyfan & Teilo
c Bedwas (Mon.) Hephzibah Welsh Baptist
c Bedwellty (Mon) St. Sennan;
d Bishopston St Teilo & Murton Methodist;
a Bonvilston, Carmel United Reformed;
a Bonvilston, St. Mary;
a Bonvilston ,Zoar Presbyterian;
b .Bridgend Newcastle Hill Unitarian ;
a Bridgend, Ruhamah Welsh Baptist;
a Bridgend, Tabernacle Independent;
a Bridgend Penyfai, All Saints;

Glamorgan Family History Society (continued)
b Bridgend Penyfai, Smyrna Welsh Baptist;
a Brynmenyn, Betharan Independent;
b Cadoxton-juxta-Barry, St. Cadoc & Philiadelphia Bapt.
a Caerau (with Ely), St. Mary & Michaelston S Ely St Michael
c Caerphilly, Ton-y-Felin
b Caerphilly, Watford Independent
a Capel Llanilterne, St. Ellteyrn
b Cardiff Adamsdown Cemetery
b Cardiff; St. John
b Cardiff, The Hayes Tabernacle Welsh Baptist
a Cefn Cribbwr, Nebo Welsh Baptist
a Cefn-Coed-y-Cymmer, Carmel C.M.
a Cefn-Coed-y-Cymmer, Ebenezer
c Cefn-Coed-y-Cymmer, Hen-dy-Cwrdd Unitarian
a Cheriton, St. Cadoc
a Church Village, Salem Welsh Baptist
a Cogan St. Peter & Lavernock St. Lawrence
b Colwinston St. Michael
b Cowbridge, Holy Cross
a Cowbridge, Ramoth Baptist
a Craig Penllyn Presbyterian
a Cwm Taff, Llwyn-On, Brecon St. Mary
a Efail Isaf Tabernacle Welsh Independent
a Eglwysbrewis, Bethesda Fro
a Eglwys Brewis, St.Brewis & Gileston St Giles
b Eglwysilan, St. Illan
b Ewenny St. Michael
a Flemingston, St. Michael
a Gileston see Eglwys Brewis
b Gower - Calvinistic Methodist Chapels
a Groesfaen, Babell Presbyterian
a Groesfaen, St. David
a Hopkinstown, Capel Rhondda
b Hopkinstown, St. David
b Kenfig Hill, Pisgah Welsh Baptist
b Killay Siloam Baptist & Knelston & Providence Baptist
a Laleston, Bethel Welsh Baptist
b Laleston, St. David
a Lavernock see Cogan
a Leckwith, St. James & Michaelston Le Pit St Michael
a Lisvane, Baptist Chapel
a Lisvane, St. Denys
a Llanblethian Maendy Congregationalist
b Llanblethian St. John
b Llancarfan, St. Cadoc & Bethel Baptist
b Llandaff Cathedral, (interior)

Glamorgan Family History Society (continued)
b Llandaff Cathedral, old burial ground
b Llandaff Cathedral, Victorian burial ground
a Llandewi, (Gower) St. David
a Llandough juxta-Cowbridge, St. Dochau
b Llandough juxta-Penarth, St. Dochdwy
a Llandow, Holy Trinity
a Llanederyn, St. Ederyn
a Llanfrynach, St. Brynach
b Llangennith, St. Cennydd
a Llangyfelach Baran Welsh Ind.
d Llangyfelach, SS. David & Cyfelach
b Llanharan, Bethlehem Congregational
b Llanharan, St. Julius & St. Aaron
a Llanharry, Peniel Chapel
a Llanharry, St. Illtud
a Llanilid St. Illid & St.Curig
b Llanishen St. Isan
a Llanmadoc St. Madoc
a Llanmaes. St. Cattwg & Llanmihangel St Michael & All Saints
b Llanrhidian St. Rhidian, St. Illtyd
b Llansamlet, Ebenezer
b Llansannor, St. Senwyr
b Llantrisant, Castellau Independent & Penuel Calvinistic Methodist
a Llantrithyd, St. Illtud
b Llantwit Fardre, Bryntirion C.M.
b Llantwit Fardre, St. Illtyd
b Llantwit Major, Cemetery
b Llantwit Major, St. Illtud
a Llantwit Major, Tabernacle C.M., Bethel Baptist & Ebenezer Congregational
a Llysworney. St.Tydfil
b Maesteg, Bethania
a Maesycymmer, All Saints and Old Zoar Methodist
a Marcross, Holy Trinity
a Merthyr Dyfan see Barry
a Merthyr Mawr St Teilo
b Merthyr Tydfil St. Tydfil
b Merthyr Tydfil Cae-pant-tywyll, Capel Bethlehem
b Merthyr Tydfil Thomastown Cemetery
a Michaelston Le Pit see Leckwith
a Michaelston-super-Ely, see Caerau
b Michaelston-y-Fedw, St. Michael
b Monknash, St. Mary Magdalene
a Morganstown, Bethel C.M.
b Nantyffyllon, Salem Welsh Baptist & Saron Independent
a Nelson, Ebenezer
d Newton Nottage St. John Baptist

Glamorgan Family History Society (continued)

a Nicholston St. Nicholas
b Oxwich, St. Illtyd
b Oystermouth All Saints
b Pencoed, Salem C.M.
a Pendoylan, Bethania C.M.
b Pendoylan, St. Cadoc
a Penmaen St. John the Baptist
b Penmark St. Mary
a Pennard (Gower) St. Mary
b Penrice, St. Andrew
b Pentyrch, Penuel Welsh Bapt, Bronllwyn Ind.& Horeb Preb.
b Pentyrch, St. Cattwg
b Penygraig, Zoar Baptist
b Peterston-super-Ely, Croes-y-Parc Baptist
b Peterston-super-Ely, St. Peter
b Pontypridd, Sardis Independent, with history
b Port Eynon, St. Cattwg
b Porth, Cymmer Independent
b Porthkerry, St. Curig
b Pyle, Capel-y-Pit C.M.
b Radyr, St. John
b Reynoldston St.George
a Rhiwceiliog, Zoar
a Rhossili, St. Mary the Virgin
a Rhydyfelin, Bethlehem Baptist, with history
c Rhymney Valley, St. David
b Rhymney Valley, Soar y Graig Congregational
a Rhymney Valley, Twyn Carno Ebenezer Calvinistic Meth.
b Roath, St. Margaret
c Rudry St. James
c Rumney, St Augustines
b St. Andrews Major, St. Andrew
b St. Athan, St.Tathan
c St Brides Major, St Bridget
a St. Brides-super-Ely, St. Bride & Ebenezer Congregation
a St. Donats, St. Dunwyd
b St. Fagans, St. Mary
a St. George's-super-Ely, St. George
a St. Hilary, St. Hilary
a St. Lythans, St. Bleddian
a St. Mary Church, St. Mary
a St. Mary Hill, St. Mary
b St. Mellons, Bethania Calvinistic Methodist
a St. Mellons, Caersalem Baptist
c St. Mellons, St Mellon
a St. Nicholas, St. Nicholas

Glamorgan Family History Society (continued)

b Sully, St. John
b Swansea, Crug Glas Calvinistic Methodist
c Swansea Cwmbwrla, Babel Calvinistic Methodist
a Taffs Well, Glyndwr Taf Independent
a Taffs Well, Tabor C.M.
a Tongwynlais, Ainon Baptist
a Tonyrefail, Ainon Welsh Baptist
b Tonyrefail, Capel-y-Ton C.M.
b Trecynon, see Aberdare
b Treforest, Saron C.M. with history
a Trehafod, Siloam Welsh Chapel
a Treherbert, Carmel Ind.& Libanus Welsh Baptist
a Tythegston, St. Tydwg
a Welsh St. Donats St Donat
b Wenvoe, Chapels & Cemetery
a Wenvoe, St. Mary
a Whitchurch, Ararat Baptist & Rhiwbina, Beulah
b Whitchurch, St. Mary (old burial ground)
a Wick, Baptist
a Wick, St. James
b Ystrad Mynach, Bethania Congregational
a Ystradowen, St.Owain
a Ystrad Rhondda, Nebo Baptist
b Ystradyfodwg St. John

PRICES
Price Code (a) inc.UK POSTAGE £1.80 inc. SURFACE MAIL £2.00
Price Code (b) inc.UK POSTAGE £3.00 inc. SURFACE MAIL £3.50
Price Code (c) inc.UK POSTAGE £4.00.inc. SURFACE MAIL £4.50
Price Code (d) inc.UK POSTAGE £6.20 inc. SURFACE MAIL £6.70

Chapel Registers and Members Lists

	(a)	(b)
Aberdare Chapels; One Booklet containing the following 7 Chapels	£2.25	£2.50
Aberdare, Wesleyan Chapel Christenings 1857 1916		
Carmel Baptist, Births 1806 1837, Deaths 1824 -1836		
Robertstown, Salem Congregationalists Births 1792 -1837		
Trecynon, Ebenezer Congregationalists Burials 1811-1835		
Hirwaun, Nebo Congregationalists Burials, 1824 -1835		
St. David's Presbyterian C of E Christenings 1890-1951,		
Trecynon, Hen-dy-Cwrdd, Presbyterian Christenings 1788 1793		
Llangyfelach Congregationalists, Mynyddbach Register 1688-1792	£3.40	£4.00
Merthyr Tydfil Penyslvannia Methodist Baptisms 1807-1907	£2.25	£2.50
Porth, Cymmer Independent Chapel, C1813-1844, B 1813-1817	£2.25	£2.50
Senghenydd, Noddfa Chapel Members Register 1894-1904	£1.75	£2.00

Glamorgan Family History Society (continued)

Miscellaneous	(a)	(c)
Dowlais Iron Company Leases, 1818-1877	£2.25	£2.75
Glamorgan Parish with Map Pre 1813,126 Parishes	£3.00	£3.50
Pontypridd Congregational History1881-1981	£3.40	£4.00
Welsh Words & Phrases, Gravestone Welsh	£1.75	£2.00
Barry, Merchant Navy Roll of Honour, WW1 1914-1918	£2.25	£2.50
Barry, Merchant Navy Roll of Honour, WW2 1939-1945	£2.25	£2.50
South African War Memorial,Welsh Casualty List 1899-1902	£2.25	£2.50
Waterloo, 1815 Battle Memorial Chapel Name Index	£2.25	£2.50
Welsh Guards Died in Service 1915-1918	£2.25	£2.50

MONMOUTHSHIRE

Cymdeithas Hanes Teuluoedd Gwent
Gwent Family History Society

Mrs G Seal, 13 Glasllwch Crescent, Newport, NP9 3SF

	(a)	(b)
"and they work us to death" vol 1 by B Fieldhouse & J Dunn	£3.50	£4.50
"and they work us to death" vol 2 by B Fieldhouse & J Dunn	£3.50	£4.50
Both of these books contain details of casualties in the mines.		
"Family History Research in Gwent", The Gwent Starter Pack.	£3.00	£4.00

MONTGOMERYSHIRE

Cymdeithas Hanes Teuluoedd
POWYS Family History Society

M.E. MacSorley 112 Holbein Close BASINGSTOKE Hants RG21 3EX

Census Transcriptions
Radnorshire 1841   Census full indexes: Completed
Hundred of Cefnllys: Parishes of Bleddfa, Cefnllys, Llanbadarn Fawr, Llandegley,

Hundred of Colwyn: Parishes of Aberedw, Bettws Diserth, Llanbadarn Garreg, Cregrina, Diserth, Llansanffraid-in-Elfael, Glascwm, Llanfaredd, Llanelwedd & Rhiwlen.

Hundred of Knighton: Parishes Abbey Cwmhir, Beguildy, Heyop, Knighton (inc Farringdon), Llananno, Llanbadarn Fynydd, Llanbister & Llanddewi Ystradenni.

Hundred of Llanbedr Painscastle: Parishes of Bochrwd, Bryngwyn, Clyro, Glasbury, Llanbedr Painscastle, Llanddewi Fach, Llandeilo Graban, Llansteffan, Llowes, Michaelchurch-on-Arrow & Newchurch.

Cymdeithas Hanes Teluoedd Gwent
Powys Family History Society (continued)

Hundred of Radnor: Parishes of Casgob, Colfa, Gladestry, Llanfihangel Nant Melan, Norton, New Radnor, Old Radnor & Presteigne.

Hundred of Rhaeadr: Parishes of Llanfihangel Helygen, Llansanffraid Cwmddeuddwr, Llanyre, Nantmel, Rhaeadr & St. Harmon.
Each Book £3.60

Radnorshire 1851 Census Short Indexes: Complete.

Rhaeadr	Volume 1	Llansanfraid Cwmteuddwr, Rhaeadr, St.Harmon.
Rhaeadr	Volume 2	Llanfihangel Helygen, Llanyre, Nantmel.
Knighton	Volume 3	Abbey Cwm-hir, Llanbister, Llanddewi Ystradenni.
Knighton	Volume 4	Beguildy, Llananno, Llanbadarn Fynydd.
Knighton	Volume 5	Heyop, Knighton, The Lordship of Stanage.
Cefnllys	Volume 6	Cefnllys, Llanbadarn Fawr, Llandrindod
Cefnllys	Volume 7	Bleddfa, Llandegley, Llanfihangel Rhydieithon
Cefnllys	Volume 8	Llangynllo, Pilleth & Whitton
Radnor	Volume 9	Casgob, New Radnor & Old Radnor
Radnor	Volume 10	Disgoed, Norton & Presteigne
Radnor	Volume 11	Colfa, Llanfihangel Nant Melan, Gladestry
Colwyn	Volume 12	Aberedw, Llanfaredd, Llansanffraed-Yn-Elfael
Colwyn	Volume 13	Cregina, Glasgwm, Llanbadarn Garreg & Rhiwlen
Colwyn	Volume 14	Betws Diserth, Diserth, Llanelwedd
Painscastle	Volume 15	Llanbedr Painscastle, Llanddewi Fach, Llandeilo Graban & Llansteffan
Painscastle	Volume 16	Bryn-gwyn, Clyro, Michaelchurch-on-Arrow & Newchurch
Painscastle	Volume 17	Bochrwd, Glasbury & Llowes

£2.50 each plus 40p p & p (£1.00 overseas)

1861 Census
Colwyn sub-district: Parishes of Diserth, Tre-coed, Llandrindod, Bettws Diserth, Cregrina, Llansanffraed-yn-Elfael, Rhiwlen, Llanbadarn-y-garreg, Aberedw, Llanfaredd. Full surname Index: A5 booklet: £3.00. plus 40p p & p (£1.00 overseas)

Breconshire Monumental Inscriptions

Breconshire	MIs from The 16th & 17th Centuries. D.Leitch.	£2.50
Builth Wells	St. Mary's Parish Church In Wales, (Index Only)	£3.00
Crucadarn	St. Mary's Parish Church	£3.00
Glasbury	Index.	£3.00
Llanigon	St. Eigon Parish Church In Wales	£3.00
Llanwrtyd	Congregational Chapel & Gel-Y-Nos Burial Ground,	£2.50
Llanynys	St David's Church In Wales,	£1.80
Talgarth	Volume 1: St Gwendoline's Church: Churchyard.	£2.50

Cymdeithas Hanes Teluoedd Gwent
Powys Family History Society (continued)

Talgarth	Volume 2: St Gwendoline's Church: M.I.s & Index.	£2.50
Talgarth	Volume 3: Bethania United Reform Church & Tredustan Ind. Chapel.	£2.50
Talgarth	Volume 4: Bethlehem Presbyterian Chapel: Coleg Trefecca Chapel: Mid-Wales Hospital Chapel: Moriah Prebyterian Chapel & Tabernacle Baptist Chapel.	£2.50

Census Transcriptions
Full Transcription Surname Index
1861 Census Northwest Breconshire (RG9/4205): Parishes of Llanafanfawr, Llangamarch, Llanddewi Abergwesyn, Llanfihangel Abergwesyn, Llanfihangel Bryn Pabuan, Llanlleonfel, Llanfechan.
1861 Census Builth, Breconshire (RG9:4207): Parishes of Llanelwedd(RAD), Builth, Crickadarn, Erwood, Gwenddwr, Alltmawr, Llanddewir Cwm, Llanganten, Llangynog, Llysdinam, Maesmynis & Rhosferig.
1861 Census Brecon: Volume 1, Merthyr Cynog: (RG9 4208): Parishes of Merthyr Cynog, Garthbrengi, Llanfihangel Nant Bran, Llanfihangel Fechan.

A5 booklets: £3.00 each plus 40p postage (£1.00 overseas)

Register of Successful Vaccinations

Breconshire	Vol 1:	1853-1859.	£3.00
Breconshire	Vol 2:	1859-1864.	£3.00
Breconshire	Vol 3:	1864-1869.	£3.25
Breconshire	Vol 4:	1869-1873	£3.25
Breconshire	Vol 5:	1873-1878	£3.00

A register of vaccination of 500 children with details taken from the Register of Births of Llangamarch, Llanlleonfel, Llanafan Fawr, Llanfechan, Llanddewi Abergwesyn, Llanfihangel Abergwesyn, Llanfihangel Bryn Pabuan, giving date of birth, place of birth, fathers name and occupation (or mothers if illegitimate), date registered and date vaccinated. Sometimes with minor details such as the death of the child (date not entered) or if the family moved away.

1841 Census.
Parish of KERRY: Full transcript with Surname Index. £3.00 (plus 40p postage, £1 overseas)

Monumental Inscriptions

Trefeglwys	Parish Church	£5.00
Mochdre	Parish Church	£3.50
Mochdre	Baptist Church	£1.50
Llanllwchaiarn	Parish Church	£5.00
Hyssington	Parish Churchyard.	£2.75

Cymdeithas Hanes Teluoedd Gwent
Powys Family History Society (continued)

Llanbrynmair	Llan Churchyard & Bont Dolgadfan Chapel.	£3.00
Llanfair Caereinion	Capel Horeb Calvalnistic Methodist Chapel.	£2.50
Llanfair Caereinion	Old Baptist Chapel Burial Ground & Zion Baptist Chapel.	£1.80
Llanfair Caereinion	Penarth Independent Chapel.	£2.50
Llangurig	Cefn Burial Ground.	£2.50
Llanllugan	St. Mary's Church In Wales.	£2.50
Llanwyddelan	Adfa Calvanistic Methodist Chapel	£2.50
Sarn	Baptist Church & Village Hall.	£2.50
Sarn	Holy Trinity Church & New Burial Ground.	£2.50

IRELAND

North of Ireland Family History Society

C/o School of Education, 69 University Street, Belfast, Northern Ireland.
(please make cheques out to 'North of Ireland FHS)
For o/seas purchasers an easy inexpensive way to obtain U.K. sterling cheques is from RUESH INTERNATIONAL BANK 700 Eleventh Street, NW, Washington DC. Freephone 1-800-424-2923. For a small fee they will post a sterling cheque made out to the Society.

	UK/Eur	US/Aust
Carved in Stone Carnmoney Parish Gravestones	£3.00	£5.00
Tombstones of the Ormey, Wm McGrew, Omargh	£9.00	£11.00
Mallusk Memorials, South Antrim Cemetery	£6.00	£9.00

Cumann Geinealais Dhun Laoghaire
Dun Laoghaire Genealogical Society

Hon. Secretary, 11, Desmond Avenue, Dun Laoghaire, Co. Dublin, Ireland

Please note that prices quoted are in **Irish Pounds**

Deansgrange Memorial Inscriptions

Memorial Inscriptions of Deansgrange Cemetery, Blackrock, Co. Dublin, Ireland Vol 1. South West Section, price IRP6.00 (postage IRP 1.00 Ireland & IRP2.00 overseas). Publication aimed at the genealogist, social historian and local historian contains transcriptions of the memorials in a predominately non-Catholic section of this cemetery, the largest in South. Co. Dublin. Co-ordinator: Barry OConnor

Memorial Inscriptions of Deansgrange Cemetery, Blackrock, Co. Dublin, Ireland Vol. 2 Lower North Section.
Memorial Inscriptions of Deansgrange Cemetery, Blackrock, Co. Dublin, Ireland Vol.3 Upper North Section, price each volume IRP7.00 (postage IRP1.00 Ireland and IRP2.00 overseas). Publication aimed at the genealogist, social and local historian contains transcriptions of the memorials in the Catholic sections of south County Dublins largest cemetery opened in 1864. Co-ordinator: Barry OConnor

Cumann Geinealais Dhun Laoghaire
Dun Laoghaire Genealogical Society (continued)

Irish Genealogical Sources Series
Irish Genealogical Sources No. 1. Shillelagh & Ballinacor South, Co. Wicklow 1837 - A Memorial, price IRP5.00 (postage IRP1.00 - Ireland & IRP2.00 overseas). This memorial of 1837, contains details of 1,500 people from south west County Wicklow. The date of this memorial is intermediate between the Tithe Applotment Survey and the Primary Valuation Survey (Griffiths Valuation) and covers an area which includes the vast Coolatin Estate of the Earl FitzWilliam which witnessed large scale assisted emigration between 1847 and 1856. Compiled & edited by Sean Magee.

Irish Genealogical Sources No. 2. Corn Growers, Carriers & Traders, County Wicklow 1788, 1789 & 1790, price IRP3.00 (postage IRP1.00 - Ireland & IRP2.00 overseas). Document extracts covering the period before The Great Rebellion of 1798 provide a valuable census substitute almost fifty years before the Tithe Applotment Books.

Irish Genealogical Sources No. 3. Newcastle, County Wicklow - School Register 1864-1947, price IRP5.00 (postage IRP1.00 - Ireland & IRP2.00 overseas). George H. OReilly has compiled and edited this valuable genealogical source as a census substitute for this area of north County Wicklow.

Irish Genealogical Sources No. 4. Croasdailes History of Rosenallis, Co. Laois, Ireland, price IRP5.00 (postage IRP1.00 - Ireland & IRP2.00 overseas) is an account of the turbulent history of the Civil Parish of Rosenallis in North County Laois (Queens County) by Fr. L. H. Craosdaile. The publication includes an index to the Primary Valuation Survey for the Parish, including the Town of Mountmellick, and sources for the genealogist & local historian.

Irish Genealogical Sources No. 5. Dublin City 1901- Census Index to the North Strand, Clonliffe Road & Summerhill District, price IRP5.00 (postage IRP1.00 - Ireland & IRP2.00 overseas). Extracted and indexed by Marie Keogh, this provides the names, surnames and addresses of each householder and visitor in the district.

Irish Genealogical Sources No. 6 - Booterstown, Co. Dublin, Ireland - School Registers 1861-1872 & 1891-1939, price IRP7.00 (postage IRP1.00 Ireland & IRP2.50 overseas). Compiled by Frieda Carroll, Archivist of Dun Laoghaire Genealogical Society, this publication contains circa 1,700 names of the boys who attended this National Primary School situated on the road from Dublin City to Dun Laoghaire. School Registers are a source for social historians as they provide an insight into the socio-economic situation for the area during the period from the mid-nineteenth century to the outbreak of World War II.

Miscellaneous
Weavers & Related Trades, Dublin 1826 - A Genealogical Source price IRP5.00 (postage IRP1.00 Ireland & IRP2.00 overseas). Sean Magee has skilfully researched the OP 726 & OP 727 series of records in the National Archives in Dublin and extracted the names, addresses, family details and trades of the persons applying for relief of distress due to the collapse of the Irish Textile Industry in 1826. This is not only a Genealogical source, but a very valuable publication for the social historian.

Cumann Geinealais Dhun Laoghaire
Dun Laoghaire Genealogical Society (continued)

A Guide to the Articles and Sources Published by the Dun Laoghaire Genealogical Society 19921996, price IRP2.00 (postage IRP1.00). The essential reference source for the genealogist and social historian researching aspects of County Dublins history and genealogical heritage. Compiled & Edited by Brian Smith.

AUSTRALIA

Prices quoted in this section are in Australian Dollars

Australian Institute of Genealogical Studies Inc.
P.O. Box 339, Blackburn, Victoria 3130

AIGS English Resources Guides:
Holdings of the AIGS Library for every English County. Prices on application as they vary according to quantity of resources held but range between $1.00 and $6.00 + postage.

Holdings of AIGS Library for Scotland General, Scottish Counties, Ireland General, Irish Counties and Wales. Prices vary between $4.00 and $6.00 + postage.

AIGS Australian Resources Guides:
Holdings of the AIGS Library for Australia General, New South Wales & Australian Capital Territory, Queensland, Northern Territory, South Australia, Tasmania, Victoria General, Victoria Cemeteries, Victorian Schools & Local Histories, Victorian Shipping & Immigration, Western Australia. Prices on application but vary between $1.00 and $5.00 + postage.

Birth, Death & Marriage Certs. & Information contained	$3.50 + p& p.
British India Resources held in the AIGS Library	$2.00 + p& p.
Cornwall: a bibliography of resources in the State Library of Victoria	$4.50 + p& p.
Family Search on CD-Rom Getting Started	$1.50 + p& p.
How to Use the Griffiths Valuation	$1.00 + p& p.
Index to Volume VIII of 'The Genealogist	$10.00 +p&p.
Land Records in Victoria & their Locations	$6.00 + p&p
Londoners Occupations-Bibliography of resources held at State Library of Victoria	$5.50 + p&p
South Australian Family History Research for Victorians	$12.00 + p&p
Sussex A bibliography of resources at the State Library of Victoria	$8.00 + p&p

CAPITAL TERRITORY

Heraldry & Genealogical Society of Canberra
G.P.O. Box 585, Canberra ACT 2601
Web Site: http://www.netspeed.com.au/hagsoc

Monumental Inscriptions	Cost	Local	O/s Air	O/s Econ. Air	Sur. Mail
Goulburn N.S.W.	$10.00	$2.20	$6.50	$5.00	$4.00
Yass N.S.W.	$15.00	$2.20	$12.00	$9.00	$7.00
Gundagai North & South N.S.W.	Apply	$2.20	$6.50	$5.00	$4.00
Braidwood N.S.W.	Apply	$2.20	$6.50	$5.00	$4.00
Miscellaneous					
Family History for Beginners & Beyond (10th ed)	$10.00	$2.20	$12.00	$9.00	$7.00
Family History Research Manager (4th ed)	$10.00	$2.20	$12.00	$9.00	$7.00
Biographical Register of the Australian Capital Territory 1820-1911	$27.50	$4.50	$17.50	$13.00	$10.00

NEW SOUTH WALES

Bega Valley Genealogy Society Inc.
P.O.Box 19 Pambula, New South Wales 2548

Monumental Inscriptions in the Bega Valley Shire
Book 1. Bega, Corridgeree, Tarranganda, Angledale & some private burials.
Book 2. Eden, Boydtown, Kiah, Greencape, Wonboyn, Timbillica, Towamba, Rocky Hall, Wyndham, Lochiel, Nungatta, Wangarabell.
Book 3. Pambula, Candelo, Wolumla South, Kameruka, Tantawanglo & some small burial sites.
Book 4. Bermagui, Cobargo, Quaama, Bemboka & some isolated graves in Bemboka and Brogo.

Each book $20.00 + postage & handling

	Cost.
Index to Ratepayers 1885 1939 Municipality of Bega	$15.00 + p&p
Index to Ratepayers 1907 1958 Imlay Shire	$15.00 + p&p
Index to Ratepayers 1907 1953 Mumbulla Shire	$15.00 + p&p
Index to Death registers 1871-1918 held at Bega Courthouse.	$8.00 + p&p
Index to Death registers 1856-1918 held at Eden Courthouse	$8.00 + p&p
From Cardboard Box to Courthouse 1987 1997. The First 10 years of the Bega Valley Genealogy Society by Leslie Sullivan	$10.00 + p&p
Subject Index of the Library Holdings in the Bega Valley Genealogy Societys Library	$6.00 + p&p

Botany Bay Family History Society

P.O.Box 1006, Sutherland, New South Wales 1499, Australia

Sterling cheque service: The exchange rate applicable will be the prevailing rate on the day of issue plus a service fee of $2.00 for each $20 exchanged.

Property Names in NSW 1837-1850 & 1885.

An amalgamated index of place names compiled from 2 indexes i.e. Index & Guide to Landholders with Livestock in NSW in 1885 and Index to Squatters Licensed in NSW 1837-1850. (These indexes available on disk). Many birth, death and marriage certificates of the 1880s have a town or place name recorded on them. If you are unable to find them on the gazetteer, it may be the name of a property or leasehold. The index lists the Landholders Districts & a map showing the Squatters Districts.

$5.00 + p&p

Cape Banks Family History Society Inc

Web Site: http://www.ozemail.com.au/~hazelb/capebank

Publications Officer, PO Box 67, Maroubra, New South Wales 2035 Australia

Overseas organisations should write for cost of postage by airmail or surface mail. All prices below are quoted in Australian dollars. Payment to be made in Australian currency or cheques made out to Cape Banks Family History Society Inc.

Botany Cemetery Monumental Inscriptions:

	Cost	Local Post
Pioneer Memorial Park (746 headstones transferred from Sandhills Cemetery in 1901)	$10.00	$3.00 p&p
Botany Pioneer Memorial Park	$10.00	$3.00 p&p
Botany Church of England (10,000 inscriptions 1893-1987)	$16.00	$3.00 p&p
Botany Roman Catholic (26,000 inscriptions 1893-mid 1990)	$28.00	$6.00 p&p
Botany Congregational, Presbyterian, Methodist, Children, Jewish. (3,700 inscriptions)	$10.00	$3.00 p&p
Botany General 13,200 inscriptions 1893-1995)	$18.00	$3.00 p&p

Miscellaneous

Prince Henry (Coast) Hospital Cemetery Headstones	$5.00	$2.50 p&p
Randwick General	$28.00	$6.00 p&p
St. Mary's Cathedral Chapel School 1820, 1830, 1833 Registers	$5.00	$2.00 p&p
Randwick Destitute Children's Asylum Deaths and Burials 1853-1916	$5.00	$2.00 p&p
Walter Carter Funeral Directors Index Volume II 1896-1912	$5.00	$1.50 p&p
A Genealogical Potpourri (Lighter Side of Family History)	$5.00	$2.50 p&p

Dubbo & District Family History Society Inc.

P.O Box 868, Dubbo N.S.W 2830 AUSTRALIA

Web Site: http://www.ozemail.com.au/~plantale/ddfhs/

Cemetery and Burial Records

		Cost
Vol 1	Baldry, Cumnock, Curra Creek, Tomingley	$5.00
Vol 2	Binnaway, Cobbora, Elong, Ballimore, Spicer's Creek, Yeoval, Obley, Leadville, Merriwa	$8.00
Vol 3	Coonabarabran, Baradine, Binnaway, Nandi, Belar Creek	$12.00
Vol 4	Warren Shire	$6.00
Vol 5	Old Dubbo and Pioneer Cemetery	$10.00
Vol 6	Coolah & Shire (out of print - photocopy only)	$3.00
Vol 7	Peak Hill	$8.00
Vol 8	Gilgandra & Shire	$17.00
Vol 9	Cobar Shire Cemetery & Burial Records	$25.00

Miscellaneous

Vol 1	Pioneer Register, Dubbo & Western Region of NSW	$25.00
Vol 2	Pioneer Register, Dubbo & Western Region of NSW	$25.00
Vol 1	Settlers Register, Dubbo & Western Region of NSW 1881-1920	$25.00
The History of Bourke Surname Index Volumes 1 - 6		$12.50
The History of Bourke Surname Index Volumes 7 12		$12.50
Cobar Public School Centenary 1878-1978		$2.00
Narromine News and Trangie Advocate BDMs 1924-1929		$22.50
Ecclesiastical Courts, Their Officials & Their Records, C. Chapman		$10.50
The Growth of British Education And Its Records, Colin Chapman		$10.50
Tracing Your British Ancestors, Colin Chapman		$8.50
Pre-1841 Censuses & Population Listings (British Isles), C. Chapman		$10.50
The Irish Australians, Reid and Johnson		$6.95
Oversees Research from Australia, Janet Reakes		£10.00
How to Trace Your English Ancestors, Janet Reakes		$14.95
Back Issues of Western Connections		$3.00

Prices are plus postage & handling. Overseas orders pay on invoice.

Lithgow & District Family History Society Inc

PO Box 516, Lithgow NSW 2790, Australia

Cemetery Transcripts

	Cost
Vol. 1 Lithgow	$20
Vol. 2 South Bowenfels RC, Pres/Wes; Glenroy & J.Drews Property; Lowther RC, General & Lowther Park Mem.; Isolated graves Lithgow (Wolgan Valley, Cooerwull & Vale of Clwydd); Hartley RC & Pres; Mt.York	$10
Vol. 3 Portland; Pipers Flat RC, CE, Meth, Pres; Barton Park Wallerawang; Cullen Bullen & roadside graves; Ben Bullen; Blackmans Flat	$15
Vol. 4 Dark Corner; Sunny Corner; Yetholme; Meadow Flat; Kirkconnell	$10
Vol. 5 Oberon; Hazelgrove; OConnell RC, General, CE; Macquarie Plains	$15
Vol. 6 Rockley; Burraga Old & New; Porters Retreat; Isabella	$ 8
Vol 7 Sofala; Wattle Flat	$10
Vol 8 Rydal / Sodwalls; Muttons Falls; Isolated graves Fish River; Mt.Lambie	$10
Vol. 9 Round Swamp; Running Stream; Crudine; Cudgegong & district	$10
Vol.10 Hill End general & RC; Sallys Flat	$10

Registers

Lithgow & District Pre 1856 Spouse Supplement Vol. 1	$5.00
Lithgow & District Pre 1856 Pioneer Register Vol. 2	$12.50

Miscellaneous

100 Years of Education - Sodwalls by Yvonne Jenkins, Suzanne Graves & Jean Perry	$12.50
A Short History of Rydal by Eunice Murray & Helen Baber	$6.00
Black Springs: Edward & Anne Hughes Family compiled by Lorraine Legge	$15.00
Edward & Anne Hughes re-union	$5.00
Finding the Foundation of my Griffiths Family by Tony Griffiths	$17.50
A History of William & Sarah ONeill of Off Flats & Hampton NSW by Brian Johnston	$5.00
Cecily Cosgrove – A Bush Pioneer by Brian Johnston	$10.00
Victoria Pass Opened 1832 by Susan Williams	$1.00
A Hundred Years of St. Thomas Church Hampton 1897 - 1997 by Stuart Braga	$7.00
Mount Victoria The Toll Bar Cottage	$1.00
Biographical Sketches from Aldine Centennial History of New South Wales incl. postage	$ 6.00

Sketchbooks

Hartley Village by Yvonne Jenkins	$10.00
Hartley Village by Neville Morgan & Yvonne Jenkins A4	$5.00
Collits Inn – pen sketches by Yvonne Jenkins	$1.00

Please contact the Society for current postage rates.

Shoalhaven Family History Society Inc.

The Secretary, Shoalhaven FHS Inc, P.O. Box 591, Nowra, New South Wales, Australia 2541

	Cost	Surface Mail	Air Mail
Glimpses of Shoalhaven	$2.00	$1.40	$2.20
Index to Nowra Births 1856 1859	$5.00	$2.00	$3.50
Index to Nowra Births 1860 1869	$10.00	$2.00	$3.30
Index to Nowra Births 1870 1879	$10.00	$2.00	$3.30
Index to Nowra Births 1880 1889	$10.00	$3.00	$5.80
Index to Nowra Births 1890 1899	$10.00	$3.00	$5.80
Index to Nowra Births 1900 1905	$10.00	$2.00	$3.50
Index to Nowra Births 1906 1918	$5.00	$2.00	$3.50
Index to Nowra Births 1906 1918	$10.00	$2.00	$3.50
Index to Berry & Kangaroo Valley			
Births 1886 1905	$10.00	$2.00	$3.50
Births 1906 1918	$10.00	$2.00	$3.50
Complete Set of Index to Births	$80.00	$14.00	$24.00
Index to Births, Deaths, Marriages & Obituaries from the Shoalhaven News 1867-1873.	$9.00	$3.40	$6.30
Index to Land Sales & Auctions from the Shoalhaven News 1867-1873.	$15.00	$4.50	$11.00
Shoalhaven Residents pre 1871 Index	$19.50	$4.50	$11.00

QUEENSLAND

Genealogical Society of Queensland Inc.
Cemetery Sub-Committee, PO Box 8423, Woolloongabba, Qld 4102

(Postage rates not included in this entry, please send the amount charged for the publication/s and you will be invoiced for postage). Allow 4-6 weeks for delivery.

Queensland Cemetery Record Series
No.1: $5.00   Part A: Surat Burial Register Index
               Part B: Surat Monumental Inscriptions
No.2. $5.00   Part A: Boulia/Urandange Burial Records Index
               Part B: Aramac Burial Register Index
               Part C: Muttaburra Burial Register Index
               Part D: Tambo Burial Register Index
No.3 $5.00   Part A: Byrnestown/Gayndah Burial Register Index
               Part B: Mundubbera Burial Register Index
               Part C: Eidsvold/Grosvenor Burial Register Index
No.4 $4.00   Part A: Amby Burial Register Index
               Part B: Mungallala Burial Register Index
               Part C: Quilpie Burial Register Index

Genealogical Society of Queensland Inc. (continued)

No.5 $6.50 Part A: Murphys Creek Burial Records Index
Part B: Caffey Burial Register Index
Part C: Gatton Burial Register Index
No.6 $12.00 Part A: Hodgson Burial Register Index
Part B: Injune Burial Register Index
Part C: Roma Burial Register Index
No.7. $8.50 Part A: Howard Garden of Rest Burial Index
Part B: Howard Monumental Section Burial Index
Part C: Polson Columbarium Wall Burial Index
Part D: Polson Garden of Rest Burial Index
Part E: Polson Monumental Section Burial Index
No.8 $6.00 Chinchilla Burial Records Index
No.9 $6.00 Part A: Greenmount Burial Register Index
Part B: Beauaraba Burial Register Index
No.10 $6.50 Part A: Millaa Millaa Burial Register Index
Part B: Yungaburra Burial Register Index
Part C: Cardwell Burial Register Index
Part D: Tully Burial Register Index
No.11 $6.50 Moreton Shire Burial Records Index:
Femvale; Glamorganvale; Grandchester; Haigslea; Harissville; Marburg Luth; Marburg Angl; Marburg Semin; Mt Walker; Stone Quarry; Tallagalla; Walloon.
No.12 $14.50 Innisfail Cemetery (Geraldton)
No.13 $7.50 Hughenden Cemetery Burial Register Index
No.14 $12.00 Mareeba (Old) Cemetery Burial Register Index
Mareeba (New) Cemetery Burial Register Index
No.15 $6.50 Part A: Chillagoe Burial Register Index
Part B: Irvinebank Cemetery Burial Register Index
Part C: Kuranda Ccmaery Burial Rcgister Index
Part D: Dimbulah Cemetuy Bmial Reglstcr Index
Part E: Mohammedan Cemetery Burial Register Index
Part F: Mount Carbine Cemetery Burial Register Index
Part G: Mount Molloy Cemetery Burial Register
No.16 $6.50 Part A: Biloela Cemetery Burial Register Index
Part B: Biloela Lawn Cemetery Burial Register Index
No.17. $6.00 Part A: Jambin Cemetery Burial Register Index
Part B: Cracow Cemetery Burial Register Index
Part C: Baralaba Cemetery Burial Register Index
Part D: Wowan Cemetery Burial Register Index
Part E: Moura Cemetery Burial Register Index
Part F: Theodore Cemetery Burial Register Index
No.18 $4.00 Part A: Blackwater Cemetery Burial Register Index
Part B: Duaringa Cemetery Burial Register Index
No.19 $4.00 Additional Stone Quarry/Jeebropilly Area Cemetery Burial Records Index

Genealogical Society of Queensland Inc. (continued)

No.20 $6.50 Part A: Killarney Cemetery Burial Register Index
Part B: Pratten Cemetery Burial Register Index
Part C: Holy Cross Cemetery Burial Records Index
Part D: Swan Creek Cemetery Burial Records Index
Part E: Yangan Cemetery Burial Records Index

No.21. $14.50 Part A: Southport General Cemetery Burial Register Index
Part B: Southport Lawn Cemetery Burial Register Index

No.22. $6.50 Part A: Pentland Cemetery Burial Register Index
Part B: Cape River/Kennedy Cemetery Burial Register Index
Part C: Ravenswood Cemetery Burial Register Index

No.23 $5.00 Gayndah Cemetery Monumental Inscriptions Index

No.24 $8.50 Part A: Wondai Cemetery Burial Register Index
Part B: Proston Cemetery Burial Register Index
Part C: Tingoora Cemetery Burial Register Index
Part D: Wheatlands Cemetery Burial Register Index
Part E: Mondure Cemetery Burial Register Index

No.25 $8.50 Part A: Laidley Cemetery Burial Register Index
Part B: Ropely Lutheran Cemetery Burial Register Index

No.26. $13.50 Part A: Ingham (Old) Cemetery Burial Register Index
Part B: Ingham (New) Cemetery Burial Register Index
Part C: Halifax Cemetery Burial Register Index
Part D (Ingham) Columbarium Burial Register Index

No.27. $9.50 Part A: Yelarbon Cemetery Burial Register Index
Part B: Goondiwindi Cemetery Burial Register Index

No.28 $6.50 Part A: Nebo/Fort Cooper Cemetery Burial Records Index
Part B: Capella Cemetery Burial Register Index
Part C: Sarina Cemetery Burial Register Index

No.29 $13.50 Part A: Crows Nest Cemetery Burial Register Index
Part B: Crows Nest Lawn Cemetery Burial Register Index
Part C: Cabarlah Cemetery Burial Register Index
Part D: Djuan-Bergen Cemetery Burial Register Index
Part E: Geham Cemetery Burial Register Index
Part F: Douglas (Gomaren) Cemetery Burial Register Index
Part G: Jandowae Cemetery Burial Register Index

No.30 $7.50 Part A: Bollon Cemetery Burial Register
Part B: Dirranbandi Cemetery Burial Register Index
Part C: St George Cemetery Burial Register Index

No.31 $6.00 Part A: Manton Cemetery Burial Register Index
Part B: Index of Burials in the Shire of Carpentaria

No.32 $9.50 Part A: Milbong Cemetery Burial Register Index
Part B: Teviotville Cemetery Burial Register Index
Part C: Coulson Cemetery Burial Register Index
Part D: Kalbar Cemetery Burial Register Index
Part E: Boonah Cemetery Burial Register Index

Genealogical Society of Queensland Inc. (continued)

No.33 $14.00 Part A: Booie Cemetery Burial Register Index
Part B: Kumbia Cemetery Burial Register Index
Part C: Memerambi Cemetery Burial Register Index
Part D: Taabinga (War Graves) Cemetery Burial Register Index
Part E: Taabinga (Columbarium) Cemetery Burial Register Index
Part F: Taabinga (Stillbirths) Cemetery Burial Register Index
Part G: Taabinga Lawn Cemetery Burial Register Index
Part H: Taabinga Cemetery Burial Register Index
Part I: Kingaroy Cemetery Burial Register Index

No.34 $7.50 Part A: Avondale/Invicta Burial Register Index
Part B: Booyal Cemetery Monumental Inscriptions Index
Part C: Cordalba Cemetery Burial Register Index
Part D: Apple Tree Creek Cemetery Burial Register Index

No. 35 $6.00 Murgon Cemetery Burial Register Index

No.36 $8.50 Part A: Springsure Cemetery Burial Register Index
Part B: Emerald (old) Cemetery Burial Register Index
Part C: Emerald (new) Cemetery Burial Register Index

No.37 $9.50 Part A: Windorah Cemetery Burial Register Index
Part B: Stonehenge Cemetery Burial Register Index
Part C: Jundah Cemetery Burial Register Index
Part D: Isisford Cemetery Burial Register Index
Part E: Blackall Cemetery Burial Register Index

No.38 $7.50 Part A: Wandoan Cemetery Burial Register Index
Part B: Taroom Cemetery Burial Register Index

No.39 $8.50 Nanango Shire Cemeteries Burial Regisisters
No 40 $9.50 Belyando Shire Cemeteries Burial Register Index
No.41 $18.00 Burdekin Shire Cemeteries Burial Register Index
No.42 $8.50 Proserpine Cemetery Burial Register Index
Proserpine District Lone Graves Index

No.43 $6.50 Kilcoy Shire Cemeteries Burial Register Index
No.44 $12.00 Cloncurry General Cemetery Burial Register Index
Cloncurry Lawn Cemetery Burial Register Index
Cloncurry Memorials Burial Records Index
Burketown Cemetery Burial Register Index

No.45 $6.50 Cecil Plains Cemetery Burial Register Index
Kooroongarra (Old) Cemetery Burial Register Index
Millmerran (Old) Cemetery Burial Register Index
Millmerran (New) Cemetery Burial Register Index
Tummaville Cemetery Burial Register Index
Yandilla Cemetery Burial Register Index
Silverleigh Cemetery Burial Register Index
Yarraman Cemetery Burial Register Index

No.46 $20.00 Maroochy Shire Cemeteries Burial Register Index
No.47 $12.00 Bowen Cemetery Burial Register Index
No.48. $5.00 Part A: Alpha Cemetery Burial Register Index
Part B: Jericho Cemetery Burial Register Index

Genealogical Society of Queensland Inc. (continued)

No.49. $12.00 Gladstone Cemetery Burial Register Index
No.50. $14.50 Part A: Dalby Cemetery Burial Register Index
               Part B: Dalby Lawn Cemetery Burial Register Index
No.51 $6.50   Cooktown Cemetery Burial Register Index
No.52 $5.00   Part A: Calliope Cemetery Burial Register Index
               Part B: Mt Larcom Cemetery Burial Register Index
               Part C: Targinnie Cemetery Burial Register Index
               Part D: Builyan Cemetery Burial Register Index
No.54 $6.00   Part A: Goomeri Cemetery Burial Register Index
               Part B: Kilkivan Cemetery Burial Register Index
No.55 $6.50   Part A: Gunalda Cemetery Burial Register Index
               Part B: Gunalda Cemetery Monumental Inscriptions Index
               Part C: Tiaro Cemetery Burial Register Index
               Part D: Netherby/Debra Cemetery Monumental Inscriptions Index
               Part E: Miva Cemetery Burial Records Index
No.56 $ apply Maryborough Cemetery Burial Register Index
               (ABORIGINAL) - DORAN Annie
No.57 $15.00 Maryborough Cemetery Burial Register Index
               DORAN Charles - KRONING Anna
No.58 $15.00 Maryborough Cemetery Burial Register Index
               KRONING Bertha - ROBERTS Hugh
No.59 $15.00 Maryborough Cemetery Burial Register Index
               ROBERTS Ida ZWISTLER
No.60 $10.00 Charters Towers Cemetery Burial Register Index A - DOWNIE
No.61 $10.00 Charters Towers Cemetery Burial Register Index DOWNS - KOCK
No.62 $10.00 Charters Towers Cemetery Burial Register Index KOETER-RANIE
No.63 $10.00 ChartersTowers Cemetery Burial Register Index RANKIN- ZONED
No.64 $10.00 Part A: Charters Towers Pioneer Cemetery Burial Register Index
               Part B: Harry Birgan Lawn Cemetery Burial Register Index
               Part C: Charters Towers Columbarium Cemetery Burial Register Index

Rockhampton North Cemetery
No.65 $10.00 Burial Register Index A CULLOUGH
No.66 $10.00 Burial Register Index CULLUON - HERWIN
No.67 $10.00 Burial Register Index HESLIN - McGUIN
No.68 $10.00 Burial Register Index McGUIRE - RUNDLE
No.69 $10.00 Burial Register Index RUSSELL - ZURVAS

Rockhampton South Cemetery
No.70 $10.00 Burial Register Index A CROSKEY
No.71 $10.00 Burial Register Index CROSS HEROLD
No.72 $10.00 Burial Register Index HERON McKILLOP
No.73 $10.00 Burial Register Index McKIM - SABIN
No.74 $10.00 Burial Register Index SADDLER - ZULERT

Genealogical Society of Queensland Inc. (continued)

No.75 $12.00 Mount Isa Cemeteries Burial Register Index
    Part A: Baby Graves
    Part B: Columbarium
    Part C: Conventional
    Part D: Lawn
    Part E: Memorial Rose Garden
    Part F: Camooweal Cemetery

Alex Gow Funeral Directors' Records Index Books
No.76 $15.00 1-5 1913-1922
No.77 $15.00 6-10 1922-1930
No.78 $10.00 11-15 1930-1935
No.79 $10.00 16-20 1935-1940
No.80 $15.00 21-25 1940-1945
No.81 $15.00 26-30 1945-1950
No.82 $15.00 31-35 1950-1955
No.83 $15.00 36-40 1955-1960
No.84 $15.00 41-45 1960-1965
No.85 $15.00 46-49 1965-1969
No.86 $15.00 50-53 1969-1973
No.87 $10.00 54-56 1973-1975
No.88 $10.00 Beaudesert Shire Cemeteries Burial Records Index 1878-1996

Index to Canon and Cripps Funeral Directors Records
No.89 $15.00 Part 1 AAROE - BRIND
No.90 $15.00 Part 2 BRINDABLE - CRONK, Albert
No.91 $15.00 Part 3 CRONK, Albert FORTESCUE
No.92 $15.00 Part 4 FORTEY - HENKEY
No.93 $15.00 Part 5 HENLEIN LACHLAN
No.94 $15.00 Part 6 LACK - McPHIE
No.95 $15.00 Part 7 McQUADE - POTFIELD
No.96 $15.00 Part 8 POTGER - SHORNEY
No.97 $15.00 Part 9 SHORT - TROUSON
No.98 $15.00 Part 10 TROUT - ZWAR

Queensland Cemetery Holdings of the Genealogical Soc. of Queensland	$5.00
LeGrand (Beaudesert) Funeral Directors Records Index	$7.00
Lohrisch (Beenleigh) Funeral Directors Records Index.	$6.00

Mount Thompson Memorial Gardens Cremation Register Index.
10 September 1934 -17 November 1941 The First 5000: A-Z	$15.00.
17 November 1941-19 May 1948 The Next 10000: A -Lambert	$15.00.
17 November 1941-19 May 1948. The Next 10000: Lambert-Z	$15.00
15,000 -19,999 (1948 -1950)	$15.00
20,000- 24,999 (1950-1952)	$15.00.
25,000- 29,999 (1952-1954)	$15.00

Narrabri Shire (NSW) Cemeteries Burial Register Index $13.50

Genealogical Society of Queensland Inc. (continued)

Miscellaneous
The following Roman Catholic Parish Registers are also being produced in booklet form.
East Brisbane Baptisms 1863-1987;
East Brisbane Marriages 1967-1987;

East Brisbane Burials 1986-1987	$6.00
Gayndah Baptisms 1871-1995 (A - LAVERTY)	$6.00
Gayndah Baptisms 1871-1995 (LAW ZIPF)	$6.00
Above two vols bought together	$10.00
Gympie Marriages 1886 1963	$8.00
Kalinga Baptisms 1837-1986; Marriages 1937-1966	$6.00
Kangaroo Point Marriages 1930 1978; Burials 1963 1987	$8.00
Kangaroo Point Baptisms 1915 1994	$8.00
Laidley Marriages 1892-1994	$6.00
Laidley Baptisms 1891-1993	$8.00
Rosewood Baptisms 1915-1987; Marriages 1915-1962	$6.00
St. Marys Ipswich Baptisms 1849-1945 (A - COSGROVE)	$8.00
1849-1945 (COSTELLO - GILFOYLE)	$8.00
Baptisms 1849-1945 (GILL - KLUPP)	$8.00
Baptisms 1849-1945 (KNEHR MILES)	$8.00
Baptisms 1849-1945 (MILLAR - RICHARDS)	$8.00
1849-1945 (RICHARDSON ZULINSKI)	$8.00
(St Mary's Ipswich Baptisms 1849-1945 all six books.)	$40.00
Windsor Marriages 1928-1984	$6.00

Gold Coast & Albert Genealogical Society Inc

Post Office Box 2763 Southport QLD 4215, Australia

	Aus	O/S
Rootes Journal published quarterly	$3.50	$4.00
Gold Coast Bulletin Index Vol.1 20 Sept1997 to 31 Mar1998	$10.00	$16.00
Gold Coast & Albert Genealogical Society Inc. Members Interests	$4.50	$5.00
Index to the Lutherans of the Logan District of Queensland	$14.50	$17.50

Ipswich Genealogical Society Inc.

Ipswich Gen. Soc. Inc., P.O. Box 323, Ipswich, Queensland, 4305, Australia

Overseas purchasers please write for postage details.

	Cost/Aust.
1. Hayward/Webb Index (an Index (3 vols) of BMDs extracted from the Queensland Times Newspaper. 1866 1900	$10.00 + $2.00 p&p
2. Ipswich & District Pioneer Register pre 1914, Vol. 1	$25.00 + $10.00 p&p
3. Index to Oaths of Allegiance	$5.00 + $1.00 p&p

Maryborough District Family History Society Inc.

Upstairs, Heritage Centre, Wharf Street (P.O. Box 408) Maryborough Qld 4650 Australia

Maryborough Heritage Register Series:
Pioneer register 1848 1868.
   List of Pioneers of Maryborough and details of their lives $30.00
Postage: Surface - $13.85, Economy - $17.85, Airmail - $23.85

Whose House is That $10.00
House names of Maryborough & district and various owners
Postage: Surface - $4.35, Economy - $9.85, Airmail - $10.85

Early Land Sales in Maryborough from 1852 $17.00
List of purchases and description of land, section etc
Postage: Surface - $4.35, Economy - $9.85, Airmail - $10.85

Monumental Inscriptions
Maryborough Cemetery - Lutheran Section $10.00
Postage: Surface - $4.35, Economy - $9.85, Airmail - $10.85
Maryborough Cemetery -
Methodist, Baptist, Salvation Army, Independent Sections $15.00
Postage: Surface - $4.35, Economy - $9.85, Airmail - $10.85

Shipping
Immigration to Maryborough 1862 - 1869 (boats, voyages &
   passenger lists) $20.00
Immigration to Maryborough 1870-1874 Index of above) $30.00
Postage: Surface - $4.35, Economy - $9.85, Airmail - $10.85

"Mine Host of Maryborough and District $10.00
List of Licensed Publicans and Pubs to 1924
Postage: Surface - $4.35, Economy - $9.85, Airmail - $10.85

"Up the Creek and early History of Bidwell and Magnolia Districts $18.00
Includes many family histories of early and present settlers of the area
Postage: Surface - $4.35, Economy - $9.85, Airmail - $10.85

CANADA

ALBERTA

NB Prices in this section are in Canadian Dollars

Alberta Family Histories Societies

P.O. Box 30270, Station B, Calgary, Alberta, Canada T2M 4P1
Web Site: http://www.afhs.ab.ca

Monumental Inscriptions

		Cost
1.	Aldersyde: Mount View Mennonite Cemetery	$2.00
2.	Banff: Mountainview & Banff Cemeteries	$15.00
3.	Beiseker: St. Marys Catholic Cemetery	$3.00
4.	Black Diamond/Turner Valley: Foothills Cemetery	$5.00
5.	Blackie: Blackie Cemetery	$2.00
6.	Bottrel: Bottrel or Westbrook Cemetery	$10.00
8.	Carstairs: Carstairs Cemetery	$10.00
9.	Carstairs: West Zion Mennonite Cemetery	$3.00
10.	Cremona: Big Prairie Cemetery	$2.00
11.	Crossfield: Crossfield Cemetery	$7.00
12.	Dewinton: Pine Creek Cemetery	$2.00
13.	Didsbury: Didsbury Cemetery	$10.50
14.	Didsbury: Westcott United Church cemetery	$2.00
15.	Granum: Granum Cemetery	$5.50
16.	High River: Highwood Cemetery	$17.00
17.	Irricana: Irricana Town Cemetery/United Church Cemetery	$2.00
18.	Millarville: Christ Church Anglican Cemetery	$7.00
19.	Namaka: Namaka Mennonite Cemetery	$2.00
20.	Okotoks: Okotoks & Okotoks Union (R.C.) Cemeteries	$15.50
21.	Olds: Hainstock Cemetery (Fairview)	$3.50
22.	Olds: Olds Cemetery	$18.00
23.	Olds: Westerdale Cemetery	$2.00
24.	Olds: East Olds Baptsist Cemetery	$2.00
25.	Rosebud: Rosebud Cemetery	$2.00
26.	Springbank: Springbank Old Church & Springbank United Church	$2.00
27.	Stavely: I.O.O.F. & St. Vincents R.C. Cemeteries	$12.00
28.	Strathmore: Strathmore Cemeteries	$7.00
29.	Sundre: Bergen Cemetery	$2.00
30.	Sundre: Sundre & District Cemetery	$3.00
31.	Sundre: Eagle Valley Cemetery	$2.00
32.	Sundre: Lobley Cemetery	$1.50
33.	Births, Deaths & Marriages, 1883-1889, Calgary Newspapers	$7.50
34.	Births, Deaths & Marriages, 1890-1899, Calgary Newspapers	$20.00
36.	Irish Genealogy, Bibliographical Guide to sources in Calgary Libraries	$3.00

Alberta Family History Societies (continued)

38. Nominal Rolls, 50th Battalion CEF 1914-1915 by Wyn van der Schee	$6.00
39. Obit. Index - Turner Valley Oilfields Residents, Past & present By Florence Denning	$9.00
40. South Calgary High School 1915-21, 1928-29, Calgary Normal School 1929-30 Class Lists.	$6.00
42. The Barr Colonists 1903, Names, ages & occupations.	$5.00
43. The McDonald Family of Cochrane & Mount Royal Ranch:	$5.00
44. Cochrane: St. Andrews, St. Marys R.C. Cemeteries	$7.00
45. Canmore: Canmore, Exshaw Cemeteries	$7.00

Enquire of the Society for postal charges.

Alberta Genealogical Society

Web Site: http://www.telusplanet.net/public/turnbl/ags
Suite # 116, 10440 108 Ave, EDMONTON, ALBERTA, T5H 3Z9

Alberta Cemetery Index (October 1994): is an 18 page listing of all known Alberta Cemeteries by nearest town. An explanation at the front, by way of using bold or italics, indicates which of these cemeteries have been recorded, which have been published, and which have been entered on the "Index to Alberta Cemetery Records etc.
(a) $7.00 (b) $8.00 (c) $9.00.

Alberta Cities Towns and Villages (August 1993): is a 20 page booklet compiled by an AGS member from various Alberta maps and official Government sources. This is a list of 1580 names, many that are not on the latest Alberta Maps.
(a) $7.00 (b) $8.00 (c) $9.00.

Alberta Index to Registrations of Birth, Marriages and Deaths 1870 1905
is a 648 page book containing about 32,000 names compiled by members of the AGS from vital statistic files for those years before Alberta became a Province.
(a) $55.00 (b) $57.00 (c) $66.00.

Tracing Your Ancestors in Alberta: is a 180 page book compiled by Victoria Lemieux and David Leonard, of the Province of Alberta Archives. This lists what research material can be found at various areas of Alberta.
(a) $20.00 (b) $21.00 (c) $25.00

Alberta Genealogical Society (continued)

Occasional Papers are free standing publications of materials presented at Alberta Genealogical Societys annual convention or papers prepared by members of the Society. Papers available for purchase are:

Back Across the Water to Britain & Record Sources in the United States and the United Kingdom by Arlene Denney, 1988	$2.25
Births, Deaths and Marriages on the Carlstadt Circuit 1910-1920 by Medicine Hat Branch, 1984	$3.75
English Education Records in Genealogy by Margaret M. Russell, 1986	$4.50
European Migration to North American by Peter Goutbeck, 1986	$5.00
European Records by Gerald M Haslam. Ph.D., 1988	$2.25
Experiences and Challenges in Genealogy by Terrence M.Punch CG(C) 1989	$2.75
Fur Trade Genealogy by Dr. John Foster, 1986	$2.25
Genealogical Research in Ontario from notes by, Brian Gilchrist, 1988	$4.25
Genealogical Sources in Calgary by Jan Roseneder,1988	$2.25
Genealogy and History also Research in Ontario by Elizabeth Hancocks, 1984	$5.90
German Immigration to Nova Scotia in Mid-eighteenth Century by Ronald Romkey, 1983	$7.75
Germans from Russia by Vincent Folk, 1987	$2.75
Highland Clearances (Scottish) by Elaine Sanderson, 1987	$3.00
Huguenot Migrations Europe and North America by Michael Harrison, 1986	$5.00
I Was in Alberta Before It Was A Province by Susie Patterson, 1984	$2.25
Internal European Migrations by Joachim Nuthack, 1986	$2.25
Ireland: After Finding Your Ancestors Birthplace, What Then? by Elaine Sanderson, 1989	$3.00
Notes of E.J. Lawrence Trip (to Ft Vermillion in 1879) by (daughter) Dr. Susan Skinner,1984	$3.75
Ontario On The Prairies (The founders of Medicine Hat) by Dr. Roy Wilson, 1983	$4.40
Outline Re: Scandinavian Research by Dr. Ken Dormier, 1986	$2.25
Research in Atlantic Canada by Terrence M. Punch CG(C),1989	$4.00
Researching the Prairies by Laura Turnbull,1988	$3.75
Using English Ecclesiastical Court Records by Elaine Sanderson,1989	$3.00
Writing and Publishing Family Histories by Gordon Stobie, 1987	$3.50
What's in Relatvely Speaking (A comprehensive index to Volumes 1 to 10 by Jochim Nuthack, 1984)	$14.00

Prices for the Occasional Papers include mailing costs within Canada, write for price when mailing outside Canada.

Alberta Genealogical Society (continued)

Cemetery Publications

(O/seas postage, write for details)

#	Publication	Names Listed	Cost	Mailing Canada
2009	Alberta Beach 4 Cemeteries Lac Ste Anne Darwell	Area	440	$4.25 $1.25
442	Alix, Fairview (Stone) Cemetery	172	$2.00	$1.00
402	Ardrossan. Fairmount Cemetery	148	$2.00	$1.25
2004	Armena Area, 12 Cemeteries Haylakes, Armena, Kingman	1384	$11.00	$2.00
	Athabasca, Athabasca Cemetery	1819	$11.00	$2.00
2000	Athabasca Cty 20 Cems County Athabasca East Half	929	$8.75	$2.00
749	Barrhead Area, Belvedere All Saint Cemetery	117	$2.90	$1.00
795	Barrhead Area, Barrhead-Bloomsbury Pentecost Cemetery	82	$1.50	$1.00
702	Barrhead Area, Our Lady of Mt.Carmel Naples Cemetery	51	$1.50	$1.00
758	Barrhead Area, St Aidan's Glenreagh Cemetery	70	$2.00	$1.00
2019	Barrhead Area, 35 Cemeteries Barrhead and Area	4012	$27.00	$3.00
701	Barrhead Area, Manola Community Cemetery	236	$2.00	$1.00
289	Bassano, Bassano Cemetery	1110	$6.50	$2.00
2003	Bawlf Area, 9 Cemeteries Camrose, Bawlf, Roundhill	964	$8.25	$2.00
502	Beiseker Area, Zion United Church Cemetery	90	$1.50	$1.00
530	Beiseker Area, St Mary's Catholic Cemetery	313	$3.00	$1.25
713	Bellevue Area, Union Cemetery Bellevue	138	$2.50	$1.00
642	Bentley, Bentley Cemetery	1010	$7.50	$1.50
568	Blackfalds, Blackfalds Cemetery	245	$2.75	$1.00
486	Bon Accord, Bon Accord Cemetery	368	$4.00	$1.50
149	Bow Island, Bow Island Cemetery	512	$2.50	$1.25
303	Boyle, Boyle Cemetery	400	$4.50	$1.50
2005	Brooks Area, 13 Cemeteries County Newell, Bassano and Brooks Areas	735	$6.50	$2.00
209	Brooks, Brooks Cemetery	2021	$13.75	$2.00
225	Brooks Area, Scandia Cemetery	71	$1.50	$1.00
329	Bruderheim, Bruderheim Moravian Cemetery	352	$5.00	$1.50
585	Busby Area, Forest Hill Cemetery	296	$2.50	$1.00
1594	Calmar Area, St Margaret Mary's Cemetery	32	$1.50	$1.00
574	Calmar, Calmar Cemetery	286	$2.75	$1.00
324	Camrose, Camrose Municipal Cemetery	5902	$9.50	$2.50
466	Champion Area, Cleverville Cemetery	56	$2.00	$1.00
2010	Cherhill Area, Cemeteries Cherhill Area	608	$7.00	$2.00
2006	Clive Area, 7 Cemeteries County Lacombe	2116	$14.25	$2.50
2059	Consort Area, 16 Cem Altario, Consort, Veteran Ar.	1942	$7.00	$2.00
	Coronation Area,16 Cems Brownfield, Castor,Coronation	3640	$10.00	$2.50
619	Cowley Area, Livingstone Cemetery	262	$3.60	$1.25
253	Craigmyle, Craigmyle Cemetery	394	$3.50	$1.25
122	Czar Area, Sardis Lutheran Cemetery	22	$5.00	$1.25
622	DeWinton, Pine Creek Cemetery	163	$4.50	$0.00
275	Delia Area, St Marks Lutheran Cemetery	20	$1.50	$1.00

Alberta Genealogical Society (contined)

274	Delia, Delia Cemetery	796	$5.00	$2.00
252	Delia Area, Hand Hills Baptist Cemetery	203	$1.50	$1.00
313	Drumheller, Drumheller Cemetery	5822	$16.00	$3.00
2052	Drumheller Ar., 11 Cemeteries Hanna Morrin Area	2299	$9.00	$2.50
1634	Drumheller, Dalum Lutheran Cemetery	158	$2.00	$1.25
354	Drumheller Ar., Homeland (Tarbuck) Cemetery	7	$1.50	$1.00
725	Eckville Area, Gilby Kalmu Cemetery	317	$2.50	$1.25
58	Edgerton, Edgerton Cemetery	533	$5.00	$1.25
481	Edmonton, Little Mountain Cemetery	467	$4.00	$2.00
451	Edmonton East, Clover Bar Cemetery	781	$5.00	$1.50
1593	Egremont Area, St George's Uk Orth (St John) Cemetery	132	$3.00	$1.25
1696	Fenn Area, Lakeview-Fenn Cemetery	61	$1.50	$1.00
146	Foremost, Foremost Town & Catholic Cemetery	177	$2.50	$1.25
2030	Formost Area, 30 Cems Taber, Bow Island,	1900	$8.00	$2.00
1221	Gadsby, Omega Gadsby Cemetery	579	$5.75	$2.00
1687	Gem, Menn Gem Cemetery	61	$1.50	$1.00
452	Gibbons, Emanuel Anglican Cemetery	90	$2.00	$1.00
2119	Gibbons Area, 20 Cemeteries Gibbons, Redwater Ar.	2498	$8.50	$2.00
2001	Grande Prairie, 21 Cems County Grand Prairie and Ar.	1984	$10.50	$2.50
1002	Grande Prairie, Glen Leslie Presb. Cemetery	282	$6.50	$2.00
1774	Halkirk, Halkirk Cemetery	239	$2.75	$1.25
2047	Hanna Area, 26 Cemeteries Drumheller, Hanna Ar.	1290	$7.00	$2.00
	Note: does not include #213 Hanna or #313 Drumheller.			
213	Hanna, Hanna Cemetery	2144	$14.00	$2.50
2013	Hardisty, 4 Cemeteries Hardisty Alliance Area	1434	$8.00	$1.50
1270	Hay Lakes Area, St Peter and Paul, Armena Cemetery	44	$1.50	$1.00
2081	Hobbema Area, 6 Cemeteries Hobbema, Pigeon Lake Area	1319	$7.00	$2.00
777	Innisfail Area, Raven Union Cemetery	367	$3.50	$1.25
604	Innisfail, Innisfail Cemetery	4311	$8.75	$2.00
1172	Innisfree Area, St Albans Anglican, Chailey Cemetery	12	$1.50	$1.00
119	Irma, Irma Town Cemetery	721	$7.00	$2.00
60	Islay, Islay Cemetery	293	$2.00	$1.25
592	Jarvie, Jarvie Cemetery	254	$2.00	$1.25
593	Jarvie Area, Christ the King RC Cemetery	58	$2.00	$1.00
366	Josephburg, Josephburg Church of Christ Cemetery	220	$5.00	$1.25
328	Josephburg, Bethany Lutheran Cemetery	96	$2.00	$1.00
364	Josephburg, Good Hope Cemetery	72	$2.00	$1.25
293	Kelsey Area, Melville Cemetery	249	$4.60	$1.25
2024	Killam Area, 31 Cems Daysland, Forestburg,Hardisty	7963	$15.00	$3.00
2007	Kinsella Area, 3 Cemeteries Near Kinsella	374	$3.75	$1.25
2017	Kitscoty Area, 16 Cemeteries Kitscoty, Marwayne Area	2488	$18.00	$2.50
1136	Lac St Anne, Lac St Anne RC Mission Deaths	1044	$6.75	$2.00
2071	Lacombe Area, 10 Cems Bentley, Blackfalds, Eckville and Lacombe Area	3058	$9.00	$2.00
537	Lacombe, Lacombe Fairview Cemetery	3912	$25.75	$2.50
302	Lamont Area, Hackett Cemetery	275	$2.50	$1.25

Alberta Genealogical Society (continued)

301	Lamont, Lamont Town Cemetery	158	$2.00	$1.00
1482	Lamont, St John Bpt Uk Gr Cath Cemetery	54	$2.00	$1.00
1712	Leduc Leduc, Old and New Cemeteries	1219	$8.00	$2.00
347	Lethbridge, Mountain View Cemetery	18833	$18.00	$3.00
349	Lethbridge, St Patrick's Cemetery	1536	$11.00	$2.00
2103	Lloydminster, Lloydminster Cemetery	4792	$12.00	$3.00
382	Magrath, Magrath Cemetery	1360	$11.00	$2.00
2096	Manning Area, 19 Cems Grimshaw, Manning, Paddle Prairie	1460	$7.00	$2.00
	Maple Creek, Sk Maple Creek Saskatchewan Cemetery	3629	$20.00	$2.50
2012	Mayerthorpe, Mayerthorpe 6 Greencourt Cemeteries	1031	$7.50	$2.00
76	Medicine Hat, Medicine Hat Hillside Cemetery	18936	$21.00	$2.50
104	Medicine Hat, Ar.Whitlaw and Highland Cemeteries	42	$1.50	$1.00
77	Medicine Hat, Ar.Kin Coulee Cemetery	563	$5.00	$1.50
1341	Mirror, Mirror Cemetery	612	$5.00	$2.00
2118	Morinville Ar.,7 Cems Legal, Morinville, Villeneuve	3296	$10.00	$2.00
1285	Namao, Namao Community (Sturgeon) Cemetery	423	$3.25	$1.25
761	Neerlandia, Neerlandia Chr. Rfm Cemetery	166	$2.75	$1.00
1259	New Norway, Duhamel RC Birth, Marriage, and Deaths	1289	$4.50	$1.50
1277	New Sarepta, God's Acre Moravian Cemetery	102	$2.75	$1.25
461	Nobleford Ar., White Lake Cemetery	147	$1.50	$1.00
2008	Onoway Area, 10 Cemeteries Onoway District	1097	$8.00	$1.50
2022	Oyen Area, 16 Cems Oyen, Acadia Valley, Loverna SK	2596	$8.50	$2.00
941	Peace River, Peace River Mount Pleasant Cemetery	1736	$13.00	$2.00
544	Pibroch, Christ Church Ang. Cemetery	90	$1.50	$1.00
504	Pine Lake, Pine Lake Holy Trinity Anglican Cemetery	149	$3.00	$1.50
1401	Ponoka Area, Earlville Rutherford Cemetery	107	$1.50	$1.00
2082	Ponoka Area, 11 Cems Bashaw, Ferintosh, Ponoka Area	1092	$6.50	$2.00
506	Ponoka, Forest Home Cemetery	5135	$9.00	$2.50
102	Provost, Provost Cemetery	1393	$7.00	$2.00
	Provost Area, 10 Cemeteries Provost, Cadogan, Metiskow	1207	$9.50	$2.00
2016	Provost, 6 Cemeteries Czar, Huhenden, Amisk Area	1263	$9.50	$2.00
179	Ranfurly, Ranfurly Cemetery	266	$3.20	$1.25
1411	Raymond,Raymond Temple Hill Town Cemetery	2559	$8.00	$2.00
535	Red Deer Area, Mt Pleasant Springvale Cemetery	74	$1.55	$1.25
1664	Red Deer, Red Deer Advocate Obits 1992- 1993	894	$5.00	$1.50
	Red Deer Area, Hillsdown (St Paul's Ang.) Cemetery	54	$1.50	$1.00
	Burnt Lake Cemetery	100	$2.00	$1.00
	Redwater Area, Eldorena Ruth Greek Catholic Cemetery	98	$1.50	$1.00
1602	Redwater Area, St Mary's Anglican Cemetery	52	$1.50	$1.00
2080	Rimbey Area, 12 Cems Rimbey, Blufton, Ponoka Area	990	$7.00	$2.00
683	Rimbey, Rimbey Mt Auburn Cemetery	1849	$7.50	$2.00
353	Rosebud, Rosebud Cemetery	72	$1.50	$1.00
316	Rowley, Rowley Cemetery	159	$2.00	$1.25
355	Rumsey, Rumsey Cemetery	299	$2.50	$1.25
1342	Ryley, Ryley Cemetery	589	$14.50	$2.50
2011	Sangudo Area, 9 Cemeteries Sangudo, Rochfort Bridge	857	$8.00	$1.50

Alberta Genealogical Society (continued)

450	Sherwood Park, Colchester Cemetery	46	$1.50	$1.00
580	Spruce Grove, Spruce Grove Union Cemetery	250	$2.00	$1.00
582	Spruce Grove, Glory Hills Alliance Cemetery	55	$1.50	$1.00
1430	St Albert, St Albert Aboriginal Cemetery	97	$1.50	$1.00
513	St Albert, St Albert RC Cemetery	3589	$25.00	$2.50
1375	Stettler Area, Red Willow Cemetery	308	$1.50	$1.25
319	Stettler, Stettler-Lakeview Cemetery	3171	$22.00	$3.00
2067	Stettler Area, 18 Cems Donalda, Stettler, Byemoor Area	3240	$9.50	$2.00
1507	Stirling, Stirling, Village Cemetery	529	$4.00	$1.50
656	Stony Plain, Inga Community Cemetery	335	$3.50	$1.25
660	Stony Plain, Hope Chr Ref Ch Glory Hills Cemetery	223	$2.50	$1.00
1336	Taber, Taber Memorial Gardens Cemetery	3879	$24.50	$3.00
1468	Thorsby Area, Whitsuntide Greek Orth Cemetery	86	$1.50	$1.00
1684	Three Hills Ar., Mount Davis Cemetery	185	$2.00	$1.25
388	Three Hills Ar., Sarcee Butte Cemetery	138	$1.50	$1.00
2051	Three Hills Ar., 28 Cems Elnora, Trochu, Carbon,Acme	4104	$10.50	$3.00
1414	Three Hills, Three Hills Town Cemetery	1252	$7.00	$2.00
389	Three Hills Ar.,Ghost Pine Creek Ang. Cemetery	56	$1.50	$1.00
2002	Tofield Area, 7 Cems Tofield Ryley Area	2355	$14.50	$2.50
1504	Tofield Area, St. James Newton Logan Cemetery	56	$1.50	$1.00
958	Valley View, Valley View Cemetery	293	$3.00	$1.25
85	Vermilion Ar., Vermilion Town Cemetery	2235	$15.50	$2.00
2018	Vermilion Ar., 11 Cemeteries Vermilion,Clandonald Area	1358	$11.50	$2.50
178	Viking Area, Lornedale Cemetery	95	$1.50	$1.25
2014	Viking Area, 6 Cemeteries Viking, Bruce	1945	$13.50	$2.00
177	Viking Area, Mt Carmel RC (Old & New) Cemetery	61	$1.50	$1.00
59	Wainwright Ar., Rosedale UC Cemetery	65	$2.00	$1.00
2020	Warner Area, 10 Cems Stirling, Warner, Milk River	1837	$7.50	$2.00
589	Westlock Area, Hazel Bluff Cemetery	545	$3.00	$1.25
705	Westlock Area, St Mark's Linaria Cemetery	112	$1.50	$1.00
2092	Wetaskiwin, 15 Cems Millet, Wetaskiwin East Area	1830	$7.50	$2.00
2091	Wetaskiwin, Wetaskiwin City 4 Cemeteries	6666	$13.50	$3.00
2090	Wetaskiwin, 19 Cems Winfield, Westrose, Falun Area	1384	$7.50	$2.00

BRITISH COLUMBIA

British Columbia Genealogical Society

P.O. Box 88054, Lansdowne Mall, Richmond, B.C., Canada V6X 3T6

Shipping & Handling rates, minimum 75 cents, up to $50.00 20%, over $50.00 15%.

Title		
P-0	1881 Census of B.C., by Lorne Main (First Census taken in B.C.)	$11.75
P-02	Ontario Township & County Maps, by E. Hancocks, (Set of 7 county maps showing Township and County seats for early settled areas of Ontario). Indexed 9 pp	$5.25

British Columbia Genealogical Society (continued)

P-03	The Canadian Genealogical Handbook, by Eric Jonasson, (2nd.ed)., 1978, (An essential tool for genealogical research in Canada).	$16.35
P-06	Cemetery Recording Instruction Booklet, BCGS,1995 (3rd ed. revised) (Guide for recorders of monumental inscriptions). 30 pp	$5.00
P-08	Index of Newspapers,1904-1914, Delta, B.C	$18.50
P-11	Scottish Roots, by Alwin James, Loanhead, Midlothian,1981, A guide for overseas researchers & beginners in Scottish research. 184 pp	£11.00
P-16	A Lemieux Index, by J.R. Dahling, U.E. (1983), illus., maps. (The Canadian descendants of Pierre/Louis Lemieux of Rouen, Normandy, France, with English family names related through marriages).	$21.60
P-18	An Intermediate Guide to Salt Lake City Library English Research Sources, by Barbara Rogers, (BCGS 1984), illus. (Pre-1841 English research sources at the LDS Church Library)	$12.65
P-19	Heads of Household in British Columbia in 1874, Pat Vibert, ed., (BCGS 1984), (Compiled early directories. Lists names, addresses & occupations of approximately 15,000 men.	$13.50
P-20	Index to 1881 Census for Manitoba and East Rupert's Land, by Lorne Main, 1984, (First census of this region) 243 pp.	$16.50
P-21	Index to 1881 Canadian Census of Northwest Territories and Algoma, Ontario, by Lorne Main (1984), (First census of this region)	$13.75
P-22	British Columbia Vital Statistics from Newspapers 1858-1872 (including in an appendix vital statistics from diaries 1852-57). Brian J. Porter, ed., BCGS (1994), (This Index to births, marriage and death notices in early B.C. newspapers makes a good Companion to P-23 below) 172 pp	$22.00
P-23	Vancouver Voters,1886: A Biographical Dictionary, ed. Peter S.N. Claydon, Valerie Melanson et al, BCGS (1994), illus., map. (Family histories of pioneers on the first Vancouver City Voters list, and their descendants) see (2) Book report page for more info. 892 pp	$65.00
P-25	B.C. War Memorials, (6177 names of serving members of Canadian Armed Forces) 88 pp	$8.25
P-26	Pioneer Register, Pioneers in B.C. Before 1900, (2nd.ed)	$9.75
P-27	Advanced Guide to Salt Lake City Library English Research, ed. Barbara Rogers (BCGS 1992), third guide to the LDS library by B. Rogers	$6.25
P-28	B.C.G.S. Surnames Index Supplement 1994	$4.00
P-29	B.C.G.S. Surnames Index 1996, (Alphabetical list of surnames being researched worldwide by members of the B.C.G.S.) 172 pp	$12.50
P-30	B.C.G.S. Surnames Index Supplement 1998, 7 pp	$3.00
R-01	A General Introduction to Genealogical Research, (BCGS, Revised 1997). Updated chapters originally published as separate leaflets on using various research sources, e.g., libraries, wills, maps, newspapers, census & parish records, internet, computers, etc 140 pp.	$ 18.00

Memorial Inscriptions

C-01	Alexandria, Harrison Mills & Hemlock Rd., 1 pp	$0.70
C-02	Armstrong, Lansdowne Cemetery, 8 pp	$2.85
C-03	Armstrong, Armstrong-Spallumcheen Cemetery, 39 pp	$5.75

British Columbia Genealogical Society (continued)

C-04	Blind Bay, Blind Bay Cemetery, 2 pp	$1.00
C-05	Bridesville & Sidley, Bridesville Cemetery & Solitary Stone, 6 pp	$2.20
C-06	Gibsons, Seaview, Gibson's Family, Mt. Elphinstone & Cape Scott Cemeteries, 19 pp	$4.60
C-07	Coldstream, Municipal Cemetery, 6 pp	$2.20
C-11	Goldbridge, Bridge River Cemetery, 7 pP	$2.55
C-12	Golden, Golden Municipal Cemetery, 22 pp	$4.55
C-13	Golden, Legion Cemetery & Henderson Private Cemetery, 6 pp	$2.20
C-14	Camp McKinney & Haida Cemetery & Solitary Stone, 2 pp	$1.00
C-I 5	Midway, Municipal Cemetery, Cemetery on the Range & Bubar Family Cemetery, 7 pp	$2.00
C-16	Rock Mountain, Catholic Cemetery & list of known graves, 2 pp.	$1.00
C-17	Saanich, Holy Trinity Anglican Church Cemetery, 23 pp	$4.55
C-19	Pender Harbour, Forest View and Kleindale Cemeteries, 4 pp	$1.95
C-20	Spences Bridge, two plots on Highway #1, 1 pp	$0.70
C-21	Rock Creek, Rock Creek Cemetery, 10 pp	$3.15
C-22	Edgewater, Edgewater Cemetery, 6 pp	$2.20
C-23	Donald, Donald Cemetery, 2 pp	$1.00
C-24	Hills, Hills Community Cemetery, 2pp	$1.00
C-25	Fort Langley, 65 pp	$14.05
C-26	Vananda, Woodland Cemetery, 4 pp	$1.95
C-27	Zeballos, Municipal Cemetery 1pp	$0.70
C-28	Chase, Chase Cemetery with Plot plan, Cenotaph, Malley Family Cemetery, 24pp	$4.55
C-29	Soda Creek, Soda Creek Cemetery, 2 pp	$1.00
C-30	Lone Bute, Lone Butte Cemetery, 1 pp	$0.70
C-31	Stanley, Stanley Cemetery, 1pp	$0.70
C-32	Langley, St. Andrew's Anglican Church (Ashes); Fort Langley, St. George Anglican, 2 pp	$0.70
C-33	Surrey, St. Oswald's Anglican Church Cemetery, 3 pp	$1.60
C-34	Abbotsford, Abbotsford, Municipal (Musselwhite) Cemetery, 26 pp.	$4.73
C-35	Lac La Hache, Lac La Hache Cemetery, 3 pp	$1.60
C-36	Lac La Hance, Felker Family Cemetery, 1 pp	$0.70
C-37	Granite Creek, Granite Creek Cemetery, 2 pp	$1.00
C-38	Tulameen Public Cemetery & Rabbitt Family Cemetery, 2 pp	$1.00
C-39	Greenwood, Greenwood Cemetery including Knights of Pythias section, Boundary Falls (1 stone), 20 pp	$4.85
C-40	Surrey, St. Helen's Anglican Church cemetery, 6 pp	$2.20
C-41	Armstrong, Pelly Family Cemetery, 1 pp	$0.70
C-42	Burnaby, St. Stephen's Churchyard, 1 pp	$0.70
C-43	Gulf Islands, includes Gabriola, Galiano, Mayne, Pender, Saltspring, Saturna & Thetis Islands, approx. 100 pp	$8.80
C-44	Barkerville, Pioneer Cemetery, 12 pp	$3.20
C-45	Nanaimo, Nanaimo Pioneer Cemetery, 4 pp	$1.95
C-46	Victoria, St. Luke's Anglican Church Cemetery, Cedar Hill Cross Road, 28 pp	$4.95

British Columbia Genealogical Society (continued)

C-47	Victoria and Lower Mainland, Jewish Cemeteries, 289 pp.	$25.00
C-48	Victoria, Pioneer Square Cemetery, 21 pp	$4.50
C-49	Quesnel, Pioneer Cemetery, 23 pp	$4.55
C-50	North Delta, Trinity Lutheran, 10 pp	$3.15
C-51	Clinton, Clinton Cemetery, 15 pp	$4.35
C-52	Celista Cemetery, Sorrento, St. Mary's Cemetery, Notch Hill Cemetery & Eagle Bay Cemetery, 27 pp	$5.10
C-53	Alberni, River Bend Cemetery,17 pp	$4.40
C-54	Forest Grove, Forest Grove Cemetery, 3 pp	$1.60
C-55	New Westminster, Fraser Cemetery (Vol.1 A-K, Vol. 2 L-Z), 485 pp	
	Per volume	$25.00
	Per set	$50.0
C-56	West Vancouver, Capilano View Cemetery, 377 pp	$25.00
C-57	Hatzic, Hatzic Cemetery, 177 pp	$12.65
C-58	New Westminster, St. Peters Catholic Cemetery (some Fraser incl.) 243pp	$25.00
C-59	Delta, Boundary Bay Cemetery, 109 pp	$10.75
C-60	South Abbotsford, Mennonite Church Cemetery, 21 pp	$4.50
C-61	Nanaimo, Municipal Cemetery 1927-1951, 27 pp	$12.50
C-63	Surrey, Sunnyside Lawn Cemetery, M.I. & Graves without stones, 130 pp	$14.50
C-64	Surrey, Hazelmere Cemetery, M.I. & Graves without stones, 30 pp.	$7,70
C-65	Mission, Mission Municipal & Westminster Abbey,120 pp	$20.30
C-66	Revelstoke, Revelstoke Municipal Cemetery (aka) Mountain View Cemetery, 65 pp	$13.20
C-67	Nanaimo, Nanaimo Municipal Cemetery Index 1952-1976, 56pp	$12.50
C-68	Burnaby, Masonic Cemetery, (Vol.1 A-K, Vol. 2 L-Z), 486 pp	
	Per volume	$25.00
	Per set	$50.00
C-69	Surrey Centre, 152 pp	$21.50
C-70	Keremeos, 39 pp	$9.85
C-72	Lakeview, Roe Lake, 6 pp	$2.20
C-73	St. Matthews, Oakridge, Vancouver, 3 pp	$1.60
C-74	Old Agassiz,15 pp	$4.35

NEWFOUNDLAND
Newfoundland & Labrador Genealogical Society

Colonial Building, Military Rd., St. Johns NF, A1C 2C9

Parish Registers
St. Pauls Anglican Church, Trinity, Newfoundland
    Index of Names, Baptisms, Marriages & Burials

Vol.1   1753-1867 $28.00 (incl.post)
Vol.2   1867- Early 1900s $25.00 (incl.post)

Newfoundland & Labrador Genealogical Society (continued)

Miscellaneous

Annual Research Index 1994	$4.00
Annual Research Index 1996	$4.00
Handbook for recording Inscriptions in Cemeteries	$4.00
Researching Your Family History in Newfoundland	$17.00

(postage for the above 4 books is $1.50 per publication, if ordering from the United States please forward payment in US dollars.) Rest of the world please apply for postage charges.

ONTARIO

La Societe De L'Histoire Des Familles Du Quebec Quebec Family History Society

Web Site: http://www.cam.org/~qfhs/index.html

Book Sales & Publications

P.O.Box 1026, Postal Station Pointe Claire, Pointe Claire, Quebec H9S 4H9

Quebec Parish Register Transcriptions		Price	Local Post p&p
007	Christ Church Montreal Marriage Index 1766 1850	$15.00	$4.00
016	Sutton Township BMD Prot. 1850 1899 (SIMMONS)	$36.00	$4.00

1851 Quebec Census Index Transcriptions			
008	Hemmingford Twp, Hemmingford Cnty	$15.00	$3.00
009	Parish of Sherrington, Napierville County	$8.00	$3.00
010	Huntingdon Village, Huntingdon County	$6.00	$3.00
018	Shipton & Windsor, Richmond County	$18.00	$4.00

Province of Quebec Land Grants 1736 1890			
014	Surname Index A Z (Full set, unbound)	$100.00	$20.00
014A	Surname Index A	$3.00	$1.00
014B	Surname Index B	$10.00	$3.00
014C	Surname Index C	$9.00	$3.00
014D	Surname Index D	$7.00	$2.00
014E	Surname Index E	$2.00	$1.00
014F	Surname Index F	$4.00	$1.00
014G	Surname Index G	$7.00	$2.00
014H	Surname Index H	$5.00	$2.00
014I	Surname Index I/J	$2.00	$1.00
014K	Surname Index K	$2.00	$1.00
014L	Surname Index L	$9.00	$3.00
014M	Surname Index M	$10.00	$3.00
014N	Surname Index N	$2.00	$1.00

La Societe De L'Histoire Des Familles Du Quebec
Quebec Family History Society (continued)

		Price	Local Post
014O	Surname Index O	$2.00	$1.00
014P	Surname Index P	$6.00	$2.00
014Q	Surname Index Q	$2.00	$1.00
014R	Surname Index R	$5.00	$2.00
014S	Surname Index S	$6.00	$2.00
014T	Surname Index T	$3.00	$1.00
014U	Surname Index U	$2.00	$1.00
014W	Surname Index W	$3.00	$2.00
014Y	Surname Index Y/Z	$2.00	$1.00

Monumental Inscriptions

		Price	Local Post
006C	A Directory of Monumental Inscription Lists. In & Near the Province of Quebec.	$5.00	$2.00
004	Hawthorn-Dale Cemetery Montreal Que	$20.00	$3.00
005	Lachute Protestant Cemetery. Argenteuil County	$20.00	$5.00
019	Rawdon Area (Six) Cemeteries Montcalm County	$18.00	$4.00
144	Index to Richford VT Cemeteries (SIMMONS) (Vermont indexes include many Quebec references)	$26.00	$4.00
174	Sorel Anglican Cemetery. Richelieu County	$6.00	$2.00
175	Philipsburg Protestant Cemetery. Mississsquoi County	$10.00	$3.00
190	Sutton, Quebec Area Cemeteries. Brome County (SIMMONS)	$30.00	$5.00
192	Cote St. Charles Hudson (Wesleyan) Vaudreuil County	$10.00	$2.00

Miscellaneous

017	Index to Richford VT Gazette (1880-1957)(SIMMONS)	$26.00	$4.00
141	Guide to Quebecs Parishes & Civil Registration 1621-1992	$40.00	$5.00
145	Family Histories Index (FORTIN)	$30.00	$5.00
211	Quebec City Gazette Marriage Notices 1846-1855 (Transcript by Ernest Smith)	$15.00	$5.00
212	Quebec City Gazette Death Notices 1846-1855 (Transcript by Ernest Smith)	$15.00	$5.00

SASKATCHEWAN

Saskatchewan Genealogical Society Inc.

PO Box 1894 Regina, Saskatchewan, S4P 3E1, Canada
For postage add: SK $3.00 for first book and 50 for each additional book.
Out-of-province add: $4.00 for first book and 50 for each additional book.
United States and overseas: we will bill for postage amount.
Discount available for bulk orders, send for details
Make cheque or money order payable to Saskatchewan Genealogical Society Inc.
Foreign and US orders payable in US funds.

Births, Deaths, Marriages from Regina Newspapers 1883-1889	$15.00
Births, Deaths, Marriages from Regina Newspapers 1890-1899	$23.00
Births, Deaths, Marriages from Regina Newspapers 1900-1905	$18.00
Births, Deaths, Marriages from Regina Newspapers 1906-1910	$18.00

Purchase all 4 volumes of Births, Deaths and Marriages from Regina Leader/Newspapers at one time for $65.00 plus postage.

RCMP Obituary Index 1933-1989	$20.00
A Subject Index to the Saskatchewan Genealogical Society BULLETIN, Volume 1, 1970 to Volume 22, 1991	$7.00
Frautz and the Fratautzers: The Rise and Fall of a German Village Community in Bukovina.	$27.00

*On United States orders add $5.00 U.S. funds for postage and handling.

Fürstenthal: A German Bohemian Community in Bukovina $25.00
*On United States orders add $5.00 U.S. funds for postage and handling.

Change of Name - The Saskatchewan Gazette 1917 to 1950 $15.00

NETHERLANDS

Centraal Bureau Voor Genealogie

Web Site: http://www.cbg.nl
Postal Address P.O.Box 11755, NL-2502 AT The Hague
Visiting Address Prins Willem-Alexanderhof 22, The Hague, The Netherlands

Foundation for Genealogy, Heraldry and related sciences. The Foundation has vast collections of books and manuscripts, etc. The collection of the 'Koninklijk Nederlandsch Genootschap voor Geslacht-en Wapenkunde and of the state are in custody. It gives service to the public in reading rooms and in doing research in the collections (at a charge). It issues a quarterly, a yearbook and many other publications.

ONE NAME SOCIETIES

The Guild of One Name Studies

Email: sales@one-name.org

Web Site: www.one-name.org

Ron Duckett, Outwoods Hills Farm, Lower Outwoods Rd., Burton on Trent, DE13 0QX

	(b)	(c)	(d)
Register of One Name Studies	£4.10	£4.35	£5.70
Organising a One-Name Gathering	£2.05	£2.25	£2.90
Sources for One-Name Studies	£2.50	£2.90	£3.60
Atlas of British Surnames	£8.60	(sole distributers for the U.K.)	
One-Name Journals & Newsletters from the Desktop by Roy Stockdill.	£2.95	£3.50	£3.90

The Courtenay Society

The Hon. Archivist, The Courtenay Society, Powderham Castle, Exeter, Devon, EX6 8JQ
(All payments in sterling please and cheques made out to The Courtenay Society).

Courtenay The French Line C1126-C1750   £15.00 + p&p
A Genealogical survey of the French Courtenay family from Pierre I of France who married Elizabeth Courtenay C1150, through 14 generations. Compiled by the Societies Honorary Consultant Genealogist. Edited by A.B.Rowland. 20 pages including index and heraldic information. Thermally bound A4. U.K. post & packing £1.50.

The Powderham Genealogical Database
This book contains information recorded in the genealogical database of the Courtenay Archives at Powderham Castle on the 30th June 1996. Illustrated by line drawings and contains historical as well as genealogical information. Published in 4 parts of approx 40-50 pages with a separate index of surnames in the four parts. Thermally bound A4.

If the volumes are purchased separately:
Index of Surnames (free to purchasers of all four parts)   £15.00 + p&p
    Vol.1 Generations 1-16   £25.00 + p&p
    Vol.II. Generations 17-21   £25.00 + p&p
    Vol.III Generations 22-25   £25.00 + p&p
    Vol.IV Generations 26-30   £25.00 + p&p

Postage & Packing: Write for details of current charges.

The Holdich Family History Society

Mr. R.J.Holdich, Wheelwrights Cottage, 21 Great Hales Street, Market Drayton, Shropshire TF9 1JW

	(a)	(b)	(c)
Martlet Monograph no.1: The Wadenhoe Manor Survey of 1543	£1.30	£1.75	£2.25
Martlet Monograph no. 2: The Wadenhoe Manor Court of 1545	£1.30	£1.75	£2.25

The Family History Society of Martin

Mr. A.J.Martin, BA (Hons), FRGS, 5 Otlinge Close, Orpington, Kent, BR5 3SH

A Review of The Early Generations or 'The Baronial Martins'	£5.00
Notes on The Parochial & Family History of the Deanery of Trigg Minor in the County of Cornwall by Sir John Maclean F.S.A. Compiled by J.R. & E.G. Gilbert	£4.00
A Collection of Martins: Martins found during research by Anthony J. Martin.BA (Hons) F.R.G.S.	£2.50

The publications above are post free.

The Morgan Society (England & Wales)
Clan Morgan, Clan MacFie

Morgan Publications, 11 Arden Drive, Dorridge, Solihull, West Midlands B93 8LP

Please send sterling cheques with order for 'Remittance Total' payable to 'Morgan Publications'. Overseas purchasers paying by cheque in their own currency should add the equivalent of $8.00 US to cover exchange costs.

Postage & Packing Charges

Total Value of Order	UK & Ireland	Overseas (Airmail)
One Item	£1.00	£3.00
Up to £10.00	£2.00	£4.00
£11.00 to £30.00	£3.50	£6.00
£31.00 upwards	£7.00	£12.00

	Cost
Extensive MacFIE Bibliography	£5.00
Extensive Morgan Bibliography	£5.00

Morgan Emigration

The First British Empire	£4.00

The Morgan Society (England & Wales)
Clan Morgan, Clan Mac Fie MacFie (continued)

Morgan Genealogy

Parish Register - Origins	£2.00
Early Morgans from Welsh Parish Registers in chronological order	£3.00
Early Morgans from English Parish Registers in chronological order	£3.00
Early Morgans in the West Midlands	£3.00
Earliest Shropshire Parish Registers	£5.00
Staffordshire - Earlybirds	£3.00
Warwickshire - Earlybears	£3.00
Worcestershire - Earliest of all ?	£3.00
Herefordshire - Welsh Speakers	£3.00
Isle of Man - Comeovers	£2.00
Ireland - Pre 1700 chronological order	£5.00
Gloucestershire - Across the Severn	£3.00
Somerset - Morgan Wanderers	£3.00
Wiltshire - More Morgans	£3.00
Anglesey - Island refuge	£3.00
Montgomeryshire - Norman & Morgans	£3.00
BIG R 1997- Morgans Transcribed	£10.00
BIG M 1997- Morgan Interests	£10.00

Morgan History

Glamorgan Morgans from the earliest days	£2.00
Morgan Origins including variant names and some Biographies	£5.00
Early Morgan History with Biographies	£5.00
Scotland Morgans including origins with possible line from Dal Riada	£5.00
Irish Morgans and links	£4.00
Scotland - From Morgund to MacBeth	£6.00
USA - Early History	£2.00
West Midlands - Industrial arrivals	£4.00
Placenames with Morgan connections	£3.00

MacFie Genealogy

The Earliest Births, Christenings and Marriages of Cathies; McCaithies; Duffies; MacDuffies; Fees; Guffies; McGuffies; Haffies; McHaffies; Mcveighs and MacFies all variants) from the combined Parish Registers of Ireland; Isle of Man and Scotland in chronological order.

Lists of each name	£10.00
Early Fees; McFees; Duffy; McDuffies and variants from Irish sources.	£5.00
Gaelic Phonebook Analysis - Ireland; Isle of Man and Scotland	£3.00
Early marriages of MacDuffies and MacFies in Ireland; Isle of Man & Scotland	£5.00
Lancashire - Parish Registers	£3.00
Isle of Man - Celtic Invasion	£3.00
Isle of Man - McFee marriages	£2.00

The Morgan Society (England & Wales)
Clan Morgan, Clan MacFie (continued)

MacFie History

The Clan Chief - An effort to clarify the whereabouts of any of Malcolm, the last Clan Chief	£5.00
Church Links with Clan MacFie	£4.00
Colla Uais- Is there a link ?	£2.00
Names from Duffy to McFie	£2.00
Duffy Origins	£5.00
Have the MacFies got it wrong ?	£5.00
Dunkeld - An analysis	£4.00
MacDuffies in Ulster	£2.00
Fee - Irish original ?	£2.00
Conn-Colla Uais-Colum Cille	£4.00
Irish Plantations	£2.00
Irish Septs	£4.00
Islay and the MacFies	£3.00
The Kingdom of Man and the Isles	£3.00
An Irish Line ?	£2.00
The first Lords of the Isles	£5.00
The Magnificent MacDuffies	£5.00
Scottish Highland Clans	£4.00
MacFie Derivation and recent story	£5.00
MacFies in Ireland	£5.00
The Isle of Man Story	£3.00
The First Reformation	£5.00
The Clan Alpin Confederation	£3.00
Oronsay Priory	£2.00
Christianity in Colonsay & Oronsay	£3.00
Early MacDuffie sightings	£4.00
Clan MacFie Nomenclature	£2.00
Return of the MacDuffies	£4.00
Clan Abbots - An analysis of Dunkeld	£5.00
Iona and the MacDuffies	£5.00
Placenames	£3.00
Bute - A fishing enigma	£3.00
Lords of the Isles to 1493	£5.00
Lords of the Isles - Finality	£5.00
Later MacDuffie sightings	£4.00
The Scots in Northern Ireland.	£5.00

The Palgrave Society

Derek A. Palgrave, MA FRHistS, FSG
Crossfield House, Dale Road, Stanton, Bury St. Edmunds, Suffolk IP31 2DY

	Cost
The Palgraves of Rollesby: a brief history 1773-1973	£0.75
North Barningham: the Church, the Hall & the Palgrave Family	£0.75
The Archives of Flegg relating to the Palgraves	£0.75
Heraldry in North Barningham Church	£0.75
The Palgraves of Ludham	£0.75
St. Peter, North Barningham:a Guide to the Church	£0.75
The Palgraves & John Murray: a selection of letters	£3.00
Palgrave: selected poems by Francis Turner Palgrave	£3.50
The History & Lineage of the Palgraves	£15.00

Please contact the above address for postage charges.

Swinnerton Society

Mr. Keith Livesey, Beechfield, 8 Park Rd., Hale, Altrincham, Cheshire WA15 9NJ
Email: livestree@aol.com

Swinnerton Family Trees, Volume 1.
Swynnerton & the Swinnertons by the Rev. Brian Swinnerton (being revised)
Two Early Staffordshire Charters by the Rev. Charles Swynnerton
Two Ancient Petitions from the PRO by the Rev. Charles Swynnerton
Introduction to 'A History of the Family of Swynnerton by the Rev. Charles Swynnerton
Each of the above: U.K. £1.00; U.S.A. $3; Canada $4; Australia $3.

A History of the Family of Swynnerton: Facsimile reprint of the original history of the family published in 1880 complete with family trees & index. 208 pages.
U.K. £12.00; U.S.A. $20; Canada $30; Australia $27.

Daughter of the Raj by Margery Thomas.
Our Presidents personal story. Born Margery Swynnerton, in Simla in 1894, she tells of her childhood in India in the days of the Raj: of nursing on the Eastern front in the Great War as a VAD: of England after the war completing her training at Barts Hospital and then to Africa with her husband in the Colonial Service.
U.K. £5.00; U.S.A. $12; Canada $15; Australia $15.

All prices include postage & packing. Would overseas members please send dollar notes.

The Boer War Diary of Edward Swinnerton.
A vivid personal account of a soldier during the campaign fought in South Africa. Edited by his nephew Joe Swinnerton.
U.K. £4.50 incl. postage. (write for o/seas prices)

Swinnerton Society (continued)

A History of the Village of Swynnerton & the Swinnertons of Warwickshire.
A general synopsis of the history of the village and the original family who lived there. Plus the history of some of their descendants the Warwickshire branch of the family. Also an article on the Heraldry of the Family by our archivist. Researched and produced by a former chairman of the Society, Joe Swinnerton.
U.K.£7.00 incl. postage. (write for o/seas prices)

Fire & Fury Over England. The Second World War 10 lost months.
The diary of a former chairman of the Swinnerton Society, Joe Swinnerton, telling of his service in the army in World War II. 120 pages with many illustrations.
U.K. £7.00 incl. postage (write for o/seas prices).

The above three books obtainable from J.E. Swinnerton, 2 Greaves Avenue, Walsall WS5 3QE

OTHER SOCIETIES

British Record Society

Mrs. C. Busfield, Hon. Treasurer, Stone Barn Farm, Sutherland Rd., Longsdon, Stoke-on-Trent, ST9 9QD

89	Archdeaconry Court of London Probate Records Vol.I 1363-1649	£32.00
90	Archdeaconry Court of Suffolk Probate Records at Ipswich (Sfk) Vol.I 1444-1700 names A-K	£12.50
91	Archdeaconry Court of Suffolk Probate Records at Ipswich (Sfk) Vol.II 1444-1700 names L-Z	£14.50
92	Northamptonshire Administrations, from 1710	£11.50
93	Probate Records of Bishop and Archdeacon of Oxford Vol.I 1516-1732 names A-K	£17.00
94	Probate Records of Bishop and Archdeacon of Oxford Vol.II 1516-1732 names L-Z	£17.00
95	Probate Records of the Court of the Archdeacon of Sudbury (Sfk) Vol.I 1354-1700 names A-K	£16.00
96	Probate Records of the Court of the Archdeacon of Sudbury (Sfk) Vol.II 1354-1700 names L-Z	£16.00
97	Testamentary Records in the Commissary Court of London Vol.III 1571-1625	£32.00
98	Testamentary Records in the Archdeaconry Court of London Vol. II 1661-1700 & Deanery of Arches, 1620-1845	£25.00
99	Pre 1650 Surrey Wills.	£39.00
100	Prerogative Court of Canterbury Administrations, Vol VI, 1631-1648	£36.00
101	Lincoln Consistory Court Wills & Inventories 1660-1700	£32.00

British Record Society (continued)

102	Testamentary Records in the Commissary Court of London Vol.IV 1626-1649 & 1661-1700 names A-G	£39.00
103	Consistory Court of Ely Probate Records, 1449-1858 Part I, names A-E	£36.00
104	Bedfordshire Probate Records 1484-1858 Part I, names A-Kimnot	£32.50
105	Bedfordshire Probate Records, 1484-1858, Part II, names Kimpton-Z	£35.00
106	Consistory Court of Ely Probate Records, 1449-1858 Part II, names F-P	£36.00
107	Consistory Court of Ely Probate Records, 1449-1858 Part III, names Q-Z	£36.00
108	Testamentary Records in the Commissary Court of London 1626-1649 & 1661-1700 Vol IV, Part II names H-S	£36.00
109	Oxfordshire Probate Records, 1733-1857, and Peculiars 1547-1856	£19.00
110	Consistory Court of Carlisle 1661-1750	apply
111	Testamentary Records in the Commissary Court of London 1626-1649 & 1661-1700 Vol.IV Part III names T-Z	apply

Post & packing, British purchasers add £4.00 for 1 book and £1.25 for each additional book in the same package.

Surface Mail O/s add the currency equivalent of £4.25 for one book & £2.50 for each additional book in the same package. Unless they pay by sterling cheque, they should also add the equivalent of £2.00 to cover bank charges.

Discounts: Individual subscribers to the British Record Society are eligible for a discount of 35% on original volumes & 10% on reprints. Enquiries about other volumes in print or on microfiche please write to the address at the top of this entry.

SPECIALIST INDEXES

The Romany and Traveller Family History Society

Romany & Traveller FHS, 6 St James Walk, South Chailey, East Sussex BN8 4BU

Romany Routes: Index to Volumes 1 & 2. Price including p&p: UK £1.90; Europe £2.20; Elsewhere Surface £2.20; Airmail £2.75.

Register Of Traveller Research - Supplement No 1 1997 Price including p&p: UK £1.25; Europe £1.55; Elsewhere - Surface £1.55, Airmail £2.10.

The Winchester Confessions Transcribed and annotated by Alan McGowan. Price including p&p: UK £2.90; Europe £3.20; Elsewhere - Surface £3.20, Airmail £3.75.

The Romany and Traveller Family History Society (continued)

Our Vardo - A record of the history and restoration of a Romany waggon (A5, 12 pages). Peter Shallcross. Price including p&p: UK £1.00; Europe £1.30; Elsewhere - Surface £1.30, Airmail £1.85.

Index Of Buckland And Buckley Names From The JGLS (AS, 48 pages). Extracted by Leonard Ing. Price including p&p: UK £3.40; Europe £3.70; Elsewhere - Surface £3.70, Airmail £4.25.

Memories of The Marsh - A Traveller Life in Kent. Betsy Stanley. Price including p&p: UK £3.90: Europe £4.20: Elsewhere - Surface £4.20, Airmail £4.75.

On The Gypsy Trail - Sources for the Family History of Gypsies (AS, 32pp). Alan McGowan. Price including p&p: UK £2.90; Europe £3.20; Elsewhere - Surface £3.20, Airmail £3.75.

The Sussex Gypsy Diaries 1898-1926. Journals kept by police. Records: site of encampment, numbers encamped with names of adults, whether van dwellers or Gypsies, date of arrival & where last encamped, date of departure & destination. Price including p&p: UK £4.50; Europe £5.40; Elsewhere Surface £5.40; Airmail £5.90.

NOTES

NOTES

NOTES

NOTES